Fiction, Film, and Faulkner

Fiction, Film, and Faulkner

THE ART OF ADAPTATION

Gene D. Phillips

THE UNIVERSITY OF TENNESSEE PRESS

KNOXVILLE

Publication of this book has been aided by a grant
from Research Services, Loyola University of Chicago.

Frontispiece: William Faulkner, director Clarence Brown, and
Dan White (Will Legate) on the set of *Intruder in the Dust*.
(University of Tennessee Library/Clarence Brown Collection)

The paper in this book meets the minimum requirements of the
American National Standard for Permanence of Paper for Printed
Library Materials. ∞   The binding materials have been chosen
for strength and durability.

Library of Congress Cataloging in Publication Data

Phillips, Gene D.
    Fiction, film, and Faulkner.

    Bibliography: p.
    Includes index.
    I. Faulkner, William, 1897–1962 – Film and video
adaptations. 2. Film adaptations. I. Title.
PS3511.A86Z94618   1988   813'.52   87–27201
ISBN 0–87049–564–x (alk. paper)

To Ken Russell

There is no point in hating Hollywood;
that would be like hating the Sphinx. It's
just there, and it will go on being there,
whether we like it or not.

Ken Russell, to the author

Contents

    and *Barn Burning* (1980)   164

    Epilogue   181
    Notes   189
    Bibliography   199
    Filmography   205
    Index   211

Illustrations

Foreword:
Fiction versus Film

Jerry Wald *

Ramses II is said to have put to death his scribes and amanuenses after they had committed his thoughts to papyrus and clay tablet. It may have been the pharaoh's way of protecting the copyright, or of insuring for himself full credit for the published material.

Although his method was a trifle extreme, it parallels in a way the fate of many Hollywood screenwriters. Oblivion, anonymity, lack of recognition – these are the lot of many Hollywood writers, especially those who live in the shadow, as it were, of a celebrated play or novel through their adaptation of it. Hollywood knows no greater resignation than that of the writing craftsman called upon to adapt Shakespeare, Sheridan, or Shaw.

The screenwriter who adapts a well-known play or novel lives in a special kind of purgatory, for he can never entirely please the original author; and *everyone* who has read the original work has positive and definite ideas and illusions about plot, characterization, background, and motivation which a mere screenwriter, and a mere producer, and a few mere stars, and a couple of mere million dollars, can never equal.

It is a fact that all who have ever seen a play or read a book consider themselves experts in regard to it. There are even readers who will claim they understand the original better than its creator. As a result, a screenwriter is often between the Scylla of the author and the Charybdis of the public, and heaven help him if he is not lucky enough to steer a middle course past both of them.

*Producer of *The Long Hot Summer* and *The Sound and the Fury*.

Somerset Maugham was asked his feelings about the way Hollywood had handled some of his works—*The Painted Veil, The Letter, Razor's Edge, Of Human Bondage,* and others. "If your characters are well conceived," he reportedly stated, "they can withstand anything . . . even Hollywood."

When I first heard this well-put if acerbic remark, I sucked in my breath rather sharply, for I was then committing Maugham's own "Rain" (one of his short stories in *The Trembling of a Leaf*) to motion picture production. Not that the problems of screen adaptation were new to me. I feel a share of responsibility for how they are handled, and while I naturally hope audiences will like our adaptations, I am also eager that they should *listen*—and thus discover how we serve the original authors and playwrights *within the framework of the screenplay.*

The screen adapter must perform the thankless task of "tampering with," "altering," "scissoring," and "rewriting" recognized classics, and the odds are against him before he begins. Yet, if he be a skillful and conscientious craftsman, he performs a service to the motion picture, and to literature itself. There have been novelists and playwrights, including the greatest curmudgeon of them all, G.B. Shaw, who have expressed deep appreciation of, and respect for, the way their works have been transferred to the screen.

The time has come, I believe, for critics and literateurs to admit that the screen is an art form, and that Hollywood has many screenwriters who have mastered film writing technique with the same degree of skill and assurance as that with which Thomas Mann and Somerset Maugham mastered theirs. . . .

The two key problems in adaptation are length and changes. Screenwriters *must* select, picking out the main thread, the most important characters, the central theme, and the best excerpts of dialogue in order to make a story of "suitable" length, generally not more than 110 to 120 minutes. Theatre audiences may accept a *Strange Interlude* which begins in the afternoon, breaks for dinner, and resumes until midnight, but movie audiences will not. I think it ought to be an axiom that a story which cannot be told in at least ten reels isn't worth telling on the screen.

The second key problem of adaptation, *what* to cut, is far more complex than the problem of length, and, in its way, more important. It is not just a question of scissoring—taste, tact, and judgment are involved. Only the most gifted of screenwriters can *keep the intent, the flavor, the theme, and the spirit of the original.* . . .

Producer Jerry Wald with Paul Newman on the set of *The Long Hot Summer* (1958). Wald produced this Faulkner film and another, *The Sound and the Fury* (1959). Faulkner himself worked for Wald as a screenwriter during his years at Warner Brothers. (Movie Star News)

When the screen adapter thinks he has solved the two key questions—cutting to motion picture length and devising essential character and plot changes—his work begins.

Motion picture critics who gnash their teeth because a favorite novel or stage play did not come to the screen in the way they imagined it should, do not always know all the ramifications of what is involved. A good mechanic will tell you your automobile engine is powerful enough to drive a plane. Why aren't there more backyard plane builders when there are so many automobile engines available in the junk yards? The answer is it takes a knowledge of aerodynamics to construct a plane that will fly. And it takes a lot of other specialized knowledge too.

Screen adapting involves translating ideas from one *medium* to another. The novelist can spend a chapter or more to describe what is going on in the mind of his hero. He can spend paragraphs to create mood, or merely to tell his reader that the hero is making up his mind. (Thomas Mann's *Magic Mountain* has been characterized as a novel based on one reflection.) The playwright can banter dialogue back and forth for a scene, or an act, to depict character, establish mood, or expostulate on an idea. The screenwriter enjoys no such luxuries. He has to move to the next point of action even as he arrives at the previous one. He cannot dwell on a single thought too long: he cannot pause to reflect; he should rarely if ever use dialogue to tell part of his story as a narrative. The watchword of all screenwriters is "economy" – in dramatic interpretation and in cost. The novelist can have an army of elephants move through the Alps into Italy for a dramatic chapter dealing with Hannibal's invasion of the peninsula. The screenwriter must devise ways of suggesting the same incident economically. . . .

Above all the responsibility of a screenwriter is the one to the original author – to keep the faith. The screen adapter may have to delete a favorite passage or character; but he does not do so in ignorance, nor through lack of judgment, and certainly not from lack of respect for the original. He does it for creative economy. . . .

Not all novelists and playwrights think the adapters of their works are literary misfits and servile hacks. William Faulkner, in accepting the Nobel Prize, said the films of his works were outstanding pictures, faithful to the originals. Pulitzer Prize winner Robert Penn Warren said the film of his *All the King's Men* revealed to him greater aspects and possibilities than he had realized in his novel. There have been many other such expressions of satisfaction and appreciation of what Hollywood and its writers have done with classics and bestsellers.

Philip Dunne (*The Robe*) has best expressed what the sincere adapter feels:

> The price we pay for the explicitness of our medium is that what we gain in realism, we lose in the free play of the imagination. It is precisely here that the screenwriter can best demonstrate his artistry, or, if you prefer, his craftsmanship. If he can, in a radically different medium, express the intent of the novelist; if he can capture the spirit and the inner essence, the style of the original, then

he has done his work well. Then he will hear the audience say, even if no scene, no dialogue remains intact from the book: "They didn't change a thing. That's exactly the way I remember it." Once or twice I have had this happen, and to hear it is sufficient reward for all effort.

During the course of his trial on charges of fraud, the Dutch painter Vandermeer, who had forged Dutch masters, was highly indignant when some of his work was referred to as inferior to the original. He insisted that he had actually improved on the technique of the ancient masters. Hollywood screenwriters cannot afford the luxury of such boasts. But sometimes the public does this boasting for them.

Acknowledgments

First of all, I am most grateful to four people. Louise Faulkner Meadow, William Faulkner's sister-in-law, accompanied me around Oxford, Mississippi, on a tour of the sites associated with Faulkner's fiction. James M. Faulkner, both in Oxford and on the occasion of his giving an illustrated lecture on William Faulkner at Loyola University of Chicago, kindly recounted his memories of his uncle. W. McNeill Reed shared his recollections of Faulkner, who was his life-long friend. Film director Howard Hawks, who was acquainted with Faulkner throughout his Hollywood years, was also most helpful.

I would like to single out the following people from among all those who assisted me:

Charles Silver of the Museum of Modern Art Film Study Center in New York, Adam Reilly of the Denver Center of the Performing Arts, and Bruce Kawin of the University of Colorado, for providing me with valuable research materials.

Loyola University of Chicago, for granting me an academic leave in order to complete this project.

Jerry Wald's essay on Hollywood and the screenwriter, which appears as the foreword to this book, is reprinted with the kind permission of the National Board of Review of Motion Pictures from *Films in Review* 5, no. 1 (1954), 62–67. It is copyrighted © 1954 by *Films in Review*.

Some material in this book appeared in a different form in the following publications and is used by permission: *Literature/Film Quarterly* 1, no. 3 (1973), 263–73, copyright © 1973 by Salisbury State College; *Hemingway and Film* (New York: Ungar, 1980), pp. 48–59, copyright © 1980 by Frederick Ungar Publishing Co., Inc.

Fiction, Film, and Faulkner

Prologue

It is in terms of bringing something strong and
vital to the screen that the complex work of William
Faulkner particularly appeals to the film maker.

Jerry Wald, producer

William Faulkner was very much aware of the intrinsic differences between fiction and film as two separate modes of artistic expression. "You
can't say the same thing with a moving picture as you can with a book," he
once told an interviewer, "any more than you can express with paint what
you can with plaster. The mediums are different." Because the natures of
fiction and film are disparate, a novel "resists" translation to the screen, to
use critic George Bluestone's expression; and Faulkner's fiction has resisted
such adaptation as much as any writer's. Admittedly one winces when recalling the lesser motion pictures based on his work; but some of the film
versions—notably the movies of *Intruder in the Dust* and *The Reivers*—
departing in various ways from Faulkner's original story, nonetheless do
capture on their own terms the flavor of their respective literary sources.

This book on Faulkner and the movies is a companion volume to the
author's previous studies of the film adaptations of the fiction of other great
writers, and especially to the book on the films of F. Scott Fitzgerald.[1] As
subjects, Fitzgerald and Faulkner obviously have a lot in common. Both
had several of their works committed to celluloid. And both preferred writing fiction to composing screenplays, though both were willing to serve
time in Hollywood in order to subsidize their careers as novelists.

It is deeply ironic that, despite the years Faulkner worked for movie
studios, only one screen adaptation that he made of his own work ever
found its way onto film. Hence the primary purpose of this study is to deter-

mine to what degree the films of Faulkner's fiction—nearly all of which were scripted by others—are worthy renditions of the stories from which they were derived.

Certain elements in Faulkner's novels would immediately recommend them for screen adaptation. His episodic plots are easily modified; his boldly drawn central characters are generally caught in an emotional crisis with which filmgoers can readily identify; and his stories are more often than not melodramatic enough to grip a movie audience's attention. But, as Regina Fadiman cogently argues in her excellent analysis of Clarence Brown's film of *Intruder in the Dust*, a movie can never be a replica of the literary source on which it is based. And therein lies the problem in bringing Faulkner's fiction to the screen. For Faulkner, like Fitzgerald, was by nature a storyteller accustomed to constructing scenes on the printed page which could not always easily be transferred to the screen. For example, he created passages that detail a character's subjective reflections on his experiences in subtly nuanced interior monologues. But, as critic Edward Murray has written, it is nearly impossible for filmmakers "to find adequate technical means for duplicating or even approximating Faulkner's complex interior monologues."[2] Murray's challenging remarks about the critical problems associated with filming Faulkner indicate the rich lode to be mined in an examination of these films.

Although a work of fiction must undergo many superficial alterations in dialogue, characterization, and plot when it is transformed into a movie, these changes must not depart in any significant fashion from the fundamental conception and intent of the original author. The faithful screen adaptation is one that remains essentially true to the original author's personal vision, that is, the latter's basic view of the human condition, as expressed in the work that is to be filmed. As producer Jerry Wald states in the foreword to this book, the screenwriter must be at pains to "keep the intent, the flavor, the theme, and the spirit of the original."

Faulkner's thematic vision centers on the Judeo-Christian concept that one achieves redemption by sacrifice and suffering. Faulkner thought that God was, as he put it, in the "wholesale," not the "retail," business; by which he meant that God as a rule does not intervene directly in individual lives.[3] As one of his characters expresses it, with the stark simplicity of Bible-Belt Christianity, God "don't tell you not to sin. He just asks you not to. And He don't tell you to suffer," in order to be saved. "But He gives you the chance."[4]

Despite the fact that Faulkner never pretended to present a coherent religious philosophy in his work, Cleanth Brooks, one of the foremost Faulkner scholars, is nevertheless right in calling him a "profoundly religious writer" whose characters operate in a Judeo-Christian environment and, regardless of their personal shortcomings, represent a spiritual concern with "discipline, sacrifice, and redemption."[5] There are some indications of this theme in Faulkner's own screen work, which is taken up in Part 1 of this book; but his personal vision is most apparent in the film adaptations of his fiction, which are analyzed in Part 2, the heart of the book.

The faithful film adaptation, then, is designed to capture on film the thematic meaning—that is, the essential spirit—of the source story. It follows that a filmmaker must respect the spirit or theme of the material being filmed, to the extent of consciously tailoring his or her personal directorial style to the demands and specifications of the tale being brought to the screen.

In her thought-provoking book on the film of *Intruder in the Dust*, Regina Fadiman contends that fidelity to the original work on which a film is based is not necessarily an appropriate norm by which to evaluate the movie in question. A motion picture, she insists, must ultimately be judged on its own merits. It is true that the relationship of a film to the work of literature on which it is based is not the sole criterion by which a movie can be appraised; one can use other criteria as well, such as its place in the total canon of the movies made by its director—especially if he is an eminent moviemaker like Howard Hawks or Clarence Brown. Nonetheless, studying the film in terms of the fictional work which inspired it remains a fruitful critical pursuit.

For example, one cannot adequately comprehend the way in which episodes from two Faulkner novels, *Sanctuary* and its sequel, *Requiem for a Nun,* were effectively integrated into a single, continuous story in the 1961 film entitled *Sanctuary,* unless one carefully examines the individual plots of the two separate books on which the movie was based. Furthermore, there is little doubt that films based on the work of a major novelist such as Faulkner gain interest precisely because they are associated with the canon of a great writer. And even when a particular movie fails to do justice to its literary source, it can sometimes tell us as much about the relationship of the two media as one which is artistically more successful.

One previous scholarly study of Faulkner and the movies merits special mention. In *Faulkner and Film* Bruce Kawin, whose research on Faulkner and film I much admire, examined both the screen versions of Faulkner's fiction and Faulkner's own scenarios. Kawin's book concentrates primarily on Faulkner's screen work and allocates less space to the film versions of Faulkner's fiction composed by other screenwriters. The present volume takes a different approach, reversing the emphasis of Kawin's earlier study in order to provide a more detailed analysis of the screen adaptations of Faulkner's fiction in addition to treating Faulkner's own screen work.

Before discussing the films of Faulkner's fiction, we will examine Faulkner's work as a screenwriter, to ascertain how successful he was in constructing the scenarios on which he worked, most of which were derived from the writings of other authors. Faulkner once said that he never became a good screenwriter because "it ain't my racket"; there are those who might disagree.[6]

PART ONE

Faulkner as Screenwriter

CHAPTER I

Golden Land:
The MGM and Twentieth
Century–Fox Screenplays

> Movies and I don't agree chronologically.
> In Oxford there is one show at seven o'clock,
> and the town goes to bed at nine-thirty. It's
> not that I don't like the movies, but my life
> just isn't regulated that way.
>
> *William Faulkner*

"Hollywood is a surreal place," British filmmaker John Schlesinger once remarked to me. "The first time I saw a crane planting a full-grown tree in a garden, I realized that Hollywood is not organic; nothing grows or develops naturally there." Schlesinger's observation recalls how in "Golden Land," Faulkner's short story set in Hollywood, the author describes a solid mat of flowers blooming against a canyon wall, looking as if they were not growing there naturally, but rather had been temporarily leaned against the wall by someone who would eventually return to take them away. He too thought Hollywood was a surreal place.

"Golden Land" is the only Faulkner story based entirely on Faulkner's sojourns in the film colony; and, as Joseph Blotner points out in his definitive 1974 biography of Faulkner, this 1935 tale is permeated with the distaste felt by Faulkner, a small-town southerner to the end of his days, at having to live, for the purpose of gainful employment, anywhere but home.[1] The story relates the uniformly depressing tale of Ira Ewing, a greedy Beverly Hills real estate agent whose domestic life has gone sour; his wife is a selfish shrew, his son is an embittered homosexual, and his daughter, a studio extra, is embroiled in a front-page Hollywood sex scandal. Although Ira does not seem to realize it, the empty life of luxury which he has provided for his family in the sun-drenched "golden land" of California has helped to ruin them all; for, as one critic noted, the family members lack any values that would lend meaning or purpose to their lives.

Faulkner's abiding dislike of "Tinsel Town" has led some commentators on his life and work to surmise that he carried out his studio assignments hastily and carelessly, just to "take the money and run." Yet there is a great deal of evidence that Faulkner did conscientiously try to give the studios that hired him an honest week's work in return for his weekly wages. In fact, the sheer number and variety of the more than forty scenarios to which he applied his creative energies over the years attest to the seriousness with which he viewed his obligations to his employers. Samuel Marx, chief of the Story Department at MGM while Faulkner worked there, vouched for that seriousness in more than one interview in later years.

Faulkner at MGM

Metro-Goldwyn-Mayer was the first studio to invite Faulkner to Hollywood, and his professional association with that company lasted off and on for a year, from May 1932 to May 1933. Faulkner had been brought to Marx's attention by Leland Hayward, the head of the talent agency for which Ben Wasson, Faulkner's literary agent at the time, worked. Marx had been encouraged to hire accomplished writers by Irving Thalberg, production chief at Metro, whom Marx remembered as "an ardent reader and a great respecter of good writing."[2] (Thalberg had earlier invited F. Scott Fitzgerald to collaborate on a screenplay at Metro.) Accordingly, Marx did not hesitate to follow Hayward's recommendation and solicit Faulkner's services as a screenwriter at MGM. For his part, Faulkner welcomed the opportunity to increase his income, since the sales of his fiction were woefully insufficient to support a family, especially in Depression-ridden America. Faulkner signed a six-week contract with Metro, with the understanding that his tenure at the studio could be extended for a longer period, as it eventually was.

Faulkner first appeared in Marx's office on the MGM lot on 7 May 1932. Short of stature, soft-spoken, and shy, Faulkner seemed somewhat apprehensive about the prospect of embarking on a kind of work in which he had absolutely no previous experience. He tried to mask his insecurity with little pleasantries such as volunteering to write, not feature films, but short subjects such as newsreels and Mickey Mouse cartoons – the two types of movies he claimed to be most familiar with.

Marx, however, tactfully brushed aside these curious remarks and advised Faulkner that his first assignment was to create a scenario for Wallace Beery's next vehicle, a picture called *Flesh*, about wrestling. With that, Marx sent the novelist off to a nearby projection room to view a recent Beery film. As Faulkner later commented, he was so frighted by the idea that he would not measure up to the high expectations the studio had for him, that he became increasingly nervous as he watched the opening reel of the picture. Finally, in a panic, he retreated to the nearest exist and did not reappear at the studio for more than a week.

When Faulkner showed up once more at Marx's door, he explained that he had spent some of the intervening days roaming around Death Valley. Although some scholars are willing to accept Faulkner's rather extravagant explanation of his whereabouts during his absence, it seems hardly likely that Faulkner, who did not at the time possess a car, somehow traveled 150 miles to wander alone for several days in the desert. Surely it is wiser to assume, as Marx did, that this was simply Faulkner's laconic way of saying that he had needed the time in which he had played truant to shore up his courage to try his hand at a new line of work, one for which he was not at all sure he was qualified.

Faulkner in all probability spent at least part of the time that he was incommunicado on a drinking spree, something he often did when he was confronted with a situation he was afraid he could not handle. Indeed, Marx told Bruce Kawin that Faulkner, during their first interview, had showed signs of having recently been on a binge. Faulkner had arrived on that earlier occasion with an open cut on his face which Marx had reason to suspect was the result of a drunken fall. But knowledge of Faulkner's drinking problem did not deter Marx from retaining him on the writers' roster at Metro. There were other known drinkers on the Story Department payroll, Marx explained, "and as long as they didn't get drunk around my office, that was up to them."

Faulkner's daughter, Jill Faulkner Summers, noted in a television documentary on her father's life and work that, although he could go for months without touching a drop, once he started on a bender, "he drank until he was ready to quit"; then, when he saw fit "to sober up, he would."[3] (Faulkner's wife Estelle was no help in dealing with his drinking episodes because she had her own difficulties with alcohol.)

In any event, when Faulkner returned to the studio on May 16 after his "French leave," he was ready to get down to work. By now another writer had taken over the screenplay for *Flesh*, so Marx allowed Faulkner to experiment with devising some original scenarios of his own, one or another of which might prove screenworthy. Faulkner holed up in his office in the Writers' Building and began turning out preliminary sketches for movie scenarios, called treatments, which he duly submitted to Marx in the hope that the studio would permit him to develop one or more of them into full-length screenplays.

Manservant

The first of these treatments was entitled *Manservant* and was derived from an early unpublished Faulkner short story called "Love," written in 1921. Reduced to its simplest terms, the plot of *Manservant* concerns Maj. Nigel Blynt, a British officer who has fallen in love with an Englishwoman named Judy, whom he knew when he was serving in India. The manservant of the title is a Malayan named Das, who is devoted to Blynt for saving his life during World War I. While Blynt is staying with friends in England, their Italian maid conceives a passion for him, but he spurns her and remains true to Judy. The maid seeks revenge by lacing Blynt's bedtime drink with poison. By way of a series of creaky plot machinations, Blynt's dedicated manservant is forced into a situation in which he knowingly drinks the poisoned draft and gallantly dies in Blynt's stead; the major is reunited once and for all with Judy in the contrived happy ending.

The turgid, implausible storyline, reminiscent of gaslight melodrama, was reason enough for the studio to turn the treatment down. Still, strictly in filmic terms, Faulkner's scenario for *Manservant* and other early scenarios already give evidence of a developing awareness on his part of cinematic techniques, an awareness that must have begun to germinate in his youth, when he went regularly to the movies. (More than one screenwriter has reported learning to write for the movies mostly by going to the movies.) Although, as Faulkner suggests in the epigraph at the beginning of this chapter, he may have ceased to be a habitual moviegoer in later life, his brother Murry has testified that when he and his brothers, William included, were growing up, they went to the movies every chance they got, just like everybody else in town "who could walk and possessed a nickel."[4]

Since Faulkner had started going to the pictures long before they learned to talk, it is far from surprising that even his very first scenarios contain at least some scenes which emphasize the visual over the verbal. Indeed, it is quite clear at times in *Manservant* that Faulkner is building a particular scene with the camera in mind. Thus, in the opening sequence, set in India, atop Blynt's bureau there is a photograph of Judy, whom he plans to meet shortly at the train station for a rendezvous. When she appears in the subsequent scene, therefore, there is no need to employ dialogue to identify her for the audience, since Faulkner has already established her identity visually in the previous scene.

Another scene is probably the best example of visual storytelling in the whole scenario. In it the jealous maidservant peeks through a window at Blynt, who is in the company of another young woman. When the maid looks at Blynt, her expression is one of smouldering passion; but when she peers at his female companion, her face becomes contorted with anguish and hatred. Hence, in a single image and without a word of dialogue, Faulkner has telegraphed her lust for Blynt and her hostility toward any other woman who ventures near him.

This is not to say that Faulkner did not sometimes plot very talky scenes in his scenarios. In his treatment for *Manservant*, for example, he devised a sequence in which the background of the principals is elaborated in a conversation among three British officers who know the past histories of all the characters in question. Such a longwinded scene, topheavy with expository dialogue, would surely have made moviegoers restless, had it reached the screen as Faulkner planned it. All in all, though, *Manservant* was a creditable job for a beginning scenarist, and Marx accordingly allowed Faulkner to try some more original scenarios.

In an early sketch of his Nobel Prize acceptance speech, Faulkner said, "A few years ago I was taken on as a script writer at a Hollywood studio. At once I began to hear the men in charge talking of 'angles,' 'story angles,' and then I realized that they were not even interested in truth, the old universal truths of love and honor and pride and pity and compassion and sacrifice." Kawin aptly notes in his definitive edition of Faulkner's MGM scripts that they frequently deal "with just those old universal truths," beginning with the manservant's noble, self-sacrificing demise in Faulkner's first scenario. One might add that these same truths can also be discerned in his best work at Fox and Warner later on.[5]

The College Widow

Faulkner's second scenario, *The College Widow*, had its origins not in one of his short stories, as *Manservant* did, but in a conversation he had had with Tallulah Bankhead, who had gone to school with his wife Estelle. He had met the actress during a visit to New York City six months before he went to Hollywood. When Bankhead told Faulkner how much she admired his work and asked him to write a film especially for her, he replied, "Well now, I'd like to help a southern girl who's climbing to the top."[6] Journalist Robert Coughlin implies in his short book, *The Private World of William Faulkner*, that Faulkner never got around to doing any preliminary writing on the Bankhead project during his stay in New York, but Faulkner's correspondence with his wife at the time clearly indicates that he wrote an outline for the proposed screenplay even before he left New York for home, although nothing came of it at the time. (This is one of several careless oversights that mar Coughlin's otherwise informative monograph.)

It seems reasonable to assume, as Blotner does, that the three-page plot synopsis entitled *Night Bird*, which Faulkner made the basis of his more detailed treatment for *College Widow*, is the very same story outline he had sketched out with Bankhead in mind while he was in New York. Never one to waste any piece of writing on which he had expended some of his time and talent, Faulkner presumably brought the plot outline along with him to Hollywood and had it ready when it came time to develop a second scenario for the studio—just as he had already resurrected his unpublished short story "Love" to serve as the basis for *Manservant*.

Despite the fact that Faulkner made several adjustments in the plot of *Night Bird* when he elaborated it into the treatment for *College Widow*, both versions of the story tell essentially the same tragic tale of the transformation of Mary Lee Blair from a college widow—that is, a young woman who is not a student but dates college men—to a night bird, a tawdry prostitute who flits from male to male. The principal reason for Blair's moral decline is the corrupting influence of a mysterious male stranger, with whom she carries on a sordid affair that inevitably causes a scandal in the small college town. In the end she elects to leave the town where she has spent most of her life in order to spare her family further disgrace. Once again the scenario contains some deft visual touches, as when Blair, returning from a tryst with her mysterious lover, takes a cleansing shower, as if to wash away the taint of moral corruption with which he has sullied her. But, Faulkner implies, this superficial purification is a futile gesture on Blair's part, since she will eventually drift permanently into a life of promiscuity.

College Widow generated no enthusiasm in the front office at Metro, apparently because the plot was thought to be far too lurid to receive the approval of the industry censor. Certainly that was the stance taken some two years later by Anne Cunningham, a reader in the MGM Story Department, when she was asked to reevaluate the scenario. Cunningham submitted a resoundingly unfavorable report on *College Widow*, dismissing it as totally unsuitable for filming in the face of prevailing censorship restrictions. The studio's initial decision to shelve the project was upheld once more when *College Widow* came up for reconsideration yet again in 1945.

Scenarios Focusing on Aviation

By the end of May 1932, Faulkner had completed his third scenario, *Absolution*, the first of five consecutive scenarios dealing in one way or another with flying. It was a subject he had already explored in his fiction and one very close to his heart, as he was an aviator himself. Pervading this quintet of scenarios, as Kawin perceptively points out, is a preoccupation with male comradeship. In *Absolution* Faulkner handles this theme somewhat simplistically, making this first scenario of the series seem little more than a trial run for better ones to come.

There is no hint of homosexuality in these scenarios' recurring motif of male friendship; to suggest otherwise would be to misconstrue the value Faulkner placed on male companionship in his writings. This theme of companionship surfaces in fictional works such as his short story "Turn About," on which his screenplay for *Today We Live* was based, as well as in his screen work. For Faulkner a solid male friendship was founded on a wholesome mutual esteem between two men, even though such a relationship admittedly may sometimes turn sour and lead to conflict, as it does in *Absolution*.

In Faulkner's treatment for that work, as a reader in the Story Department succinctly summarized it, "a worthless girl destroys a beautiful friend-

Ronnie (Franchot Tone) and Diana (Joan Crawford) in *Today We Live* (1933), coscripted by Faulkner from his short story "Turn About." This is the only screen version of his fiction that Faulkner himself coauthored. (Museum of Modern Art/Film Stills Archive)

ship between two boys."[7] Specifically, the jealous rivalry between the two young men, John and Corwin, over the manipulative Evelyn – whose name suggests her kinship with Eve, the archetypal temptress – erupts finally and fatefully when the men meet in France as members of the same flying squadron during World War I. One day while their squadron is flying a mission, Corwin spitefully attacks John in a deadly earnest effort to shoot him down; and John, the more experienced pilot of the pair, is forced to blast his erstwhile friend out of the sky. When he remorsefully breaks the bitter news of the circumstances of Corwin's death to Evelyn at their next meeting, he is shocked to discover that she had never really cared for either of them, even though they had all known each other since childhood.

In his deepening anguish over killing his friend over a woman who never deserved their love in the first place, John later seeks out Corwin's grave in a war cemetery. There he hopes to obtain absolution from his dead comrade for what he has done, by finishing his own life in the same way he ended Corwin's, with a bullet. In scenarios to come, Faulkner would adroitly show that women could be integrated into the masculine world of his heroes as something more than a mere bone of contention between two males, but that was really Evelyn's sole role in *Absolution*.

Like the two scenarios before it, Faulkner's preliminary treatment for *Absolution* was not deemed promising screen material by MGM's front office, and the project was dropped. At the beginning of June Faulkner was assigned for the first time to develop a scenario around a plot not derived from a story line of his own invention. His task was to revise *Flying the Mail*, a treatment that by turns had already passed through the hands of no less than four other writers. The film was to be a starring vehicle for Wallace Beery, for whom Faulkner had been scheduled to write *Flesh* before he went AWOL from the studio on his first day there.

The scenario for *Flying the Mail* was inspired by a series of magazine articles by air mail pilot Bogart Rogers. The articles paid tribute to the courage of Rogers' fellow fliers, men who, in the primitive days of air mail service after World War I, were prepared to risk personal peril of any kind to get the mail through. In the fictionalized movie version of the pilots' exploits, Beery was to play Wally, a veteran aviator of long standing, who decides to accept the challenge of flying the mail. In Faulkner's treatment, Wally's foster son Bob, who joins him in this hazardous endeavor, becomes in some ways as much a "sidekick" as a son to the older man.

Wally and Bob do have disagreements from time to time, but because of the difference in their ages, their comradeship is never threatened by their falling in love with the same woman, as happened to the two buddies in *Absolution*. Wally has a mistress of long standing named Min, while Bob becomes enamored of a young woman who turns out to be Wally's daughter. Wally, it seems, had deserted the daughter and her now deceased mother several years back. The relationship between Wally and Bob is significantly strengthened when Wally's surrogate son marries his daughter; in addition, at the end Bob manages to persuade Wally to marry Min, so that his children will have a pair of legitimate grandparents.

Kawin has demonstrated quite convincingly that Faulkner succeeded in putting together a coherent scenario that was much more interesting than any of the previous versions of *Flying the Mail*. Despite this, the studio was still not satisfied that the story would make a successful motion picture, and for the fourth time in a row, a property on which Faulkner had worked was scrapped. Because nothing he had written during his tenure at Metro so far was slated for production, it seemed that Faulkner's days at the studio were numbered. And so they would have been, had it not been for the timely intervention of film director Howard Hawks, whom Faulkner had not yet met even though they were both working at MGM.

Today We Live

Howard Hawks had been impressed by Faulkner's fiction long before his brother William Hawks, a Hollywood agent, brought to his attention Faulkner's World War I short story "Turn About," which had appeared in the *Saturday Evening Post* in spring 1932. The director agreed with his brother that "Turn About" could provide the basis for a good action movie; he therefore purchased the screen rights to the story and invited Faulkner to adapt the tale for the screen.

When Hawks met Faulkner for the first time in July 1932 to discuss the projected film, the novelist promised to supply him with a script in five days. After the formal part of their meeting was over, Hawks decided that he would get to know his new associate better by offering him a drink. One drink led to another, and they woke up the following morning in a motel somewhere in the vicinity of the studio. Hawks later remembered that, upon awakening, he found Faulkner "fishing cigarette stubs out of a mint julep." Hawks, like Faulkner, had a fondness for alcohol, although he was not the problem drinker Faulkner was. Hawks also shared Faulkner's predilections for fishing, hunting, and flying. "He's a broken-down aviator, like me," Faulkner once remarked of Hawks.[8]

Faulkner made good his promise to deliver the first draft of the screenplay for "Turn About" in five days, and Hawks was pleased enough with it to show it immediately to Irving Thalberg, who approved it for production without qualification. Later on, Joan Crawford became available to appear in the film, and the production chief, who was confident that her participation in the picture would markedly increase its box office potential, directed Faulkner to write a part for her into his script, which until then had had an all-male cast of characters. Faulkner at this point was willing to make every effort to see something he had written for MGM at last reach the screen, so he complied with this unexpected directive with little noticeable complaint, beyond muttering stoically that he did not remember any "girl" in the original story. After some consultation between director and writer about the revised screenplay, Hawks allowed Faulkner to return to Oxford in August to complete the second draft of the script there, and he duly sent it on to Hawks later that month. Faulkner went back to Hollywood in October at Hawks's behest to revise the screenplay further with the aid of screenwriter Dwight Taylor. This third draft, dated 25 October 1932, was the last one on which Faulkner worked and was the basis for all further revisions of the script. Additional alterations were made in the screenplay by screenwriter Edith Fitzgerald; and the final draft was ready by the end of November, though both Taylor and Fitzgerald made a few more minor modifications in the screenplay before it went into production under a new title, *Today We Live.*

Faulkner's original short story, a fairly straightforward action yarn, had its genesis in a discussion he and some mutual friends had with Robert Levett, a veteran World War I flier. Levett recounted the exploits of the mosquito fleet of British torpedo boats whose death-defying mission was to sneak into mine-infested enemy waters and blow up German ships. Faulkner was so moved by the heroism of these young seamen that he felt compelled to write a short story about them. "Turn About" begins with Captain Bogard (Gary Cooper), an American fighter pilot modeled on Levett, taking Claude Hope, a young British naval pilot, on one of his bombing missions. Since "turn about is fair play," Claude invites Bogard aboard his torpedo boat to observe him and Ronnie Boyce Smith, his fellow crewman, making a raid on an enemy vessel. When Claude and Ronnie are subsequently killed on one of their expeditions, Bogard on his own initiative executes an especially daring daylight aerial raid as a last tribute to the young Englishmen he had come to admire so much.

Hawks told Kawin that Faulkner's first draft of the script followed the short story fairly closely, with the notable addition that Claude is blinded by an exploding shell during a torpedo run, a plot twist Hawks himself suggested during their preliminary discussions.

Faulkner must be commended for working a female character into the screen version of "Turn About," since there was obviously no place for a heroine in his original conception of the story. He did so by introducing into the script a sister for Ronnie named Diana (Joan Crawford), who has been close to both her brother (Franchot Tone) and to Claude (Robert Young). Claude, a ward of their family, has been like a brother to both Diana and Ronnie since they were all children together. It is easy to concur with Kawin's contention that Faulkner created this situation in the script by recalling a similar one in *Absolution,* in which the relationship of John, Corwin, and Evelyn likewise started in childhood—although in the earlier scenario Evelyn was not the sister of either young man. Perhaps Faulkner also had in mind *Flying the Mail,* where the "brother-sister" bond of Wally's daughter and his foster son Bob blossoms into love; Faulkner likewise has Claude fall in love with his surrogate sister Diana. Diana is further integrated into the screenplay when she becomes the object of Bogard's affection as well.

When Claude is blinded during a sea patrol, Diana chooses her childhood sweetheart over Bogard. But Claude realizes that it is sympathy more than love that has inspired her choice, and he does not want to accept her on those terms. This dramatic situation reaches a climax when Claude and Ronnie learn that Bogard has been selected for his most perilous mission yet, the bombing of a strongly fortified enemy battleship. They mutually agree to volunteer secretly to take on this daredevil assignment in his stead and torpedo the target from their small craft. Bogard learns of their heroic decision to risk their lives on his behalf too late to stop them; and, as in the short story, Claude and Ronnie lose their lives in a deadly sea skirmish. In the film's bittersweet finale, Diana and Bogard mourn the loss of the courageous young men, whose fate brings into vivid relief the meaning of the film's title: we must live for today, for tomorrow we may die.

One major difference between Faulkner's version of the screenplay (encompassing the first three drafts) and the final shooting script was the deletion of all of the scenes depicting Ronnie, Claude, and Diana going through childhood and adolescence together, although there are still references in the final screenplay to the life-long relationship of the trio. Hawks reportedly gave as his motive for eliminating this material that the young actors who were to play Ronnie, Claude, and Diana as children were having trouble mastering a British accent. This explanation does not seem very compelling, since presumably the child actors could have been replaced. (Metro was able to find several youngsters who could speak with a British accent for its production of *David Copperfield* only a couple of years later.) Perhaps Hawks was afraid that the screenplay was going to be too long. Several scenes had been added at various stages of the revision process, mostly occasioned by the introduction of Diana into the story; it stands to reason that there would have to be some deletions in the final shooting script if it was to be kept to a manageable length.

Hawks's concern that the screenplay was overlong was clearly manifested when he scuttled some scenes that had been contributed by Edith Fitzgerald to beef up Diana's part. But Faulkner's scenes depicting Claude, Ronnie, and Diana's youthful years were virtually the first scenes to go, and that is a great pity. For, as Kawin remarks, the emphasis in the screenplay as Faulkner originally wrote it "is on the deep bonds and shared experience" which united the three of them in childhood and continued to endure as they grow into adult life.[9] It was primarily because of the longstanding relationship among them that Claude and Ronnie, to insure that their beloved Diana can be united with the man she really wants to marry, decide to take over Bogard's dangerous mission at the end of the movie. Obviously, it is not as evident in the finished movie as it was in Faulkner's version of the screenplay that the abiding bonds among the three provide the chief motivation for Claude and Ronnie's heroic self-sacrifice. In the final shooting script, the childhood relationships of the trio are only referred to in the dialogue and are not depicted graphically on the screen as Faulkner had envisioned.

Hawks had been right to worry at the script stage that the completed movie might be too long, since *Today We Live* previewed at 135 minutes, and was cut to 113 minutes before release in April 1933; even then, *Variety* was not alone in complaining that the picture might well have been trimmed a bit more. Yet movie critics across the land praised the film for the air and sea battles that punctuate the story. For the record, the aerial combat sequences were largely lifted from Howard Hughes's production of *Hell's Angels* (1930). Since Hughes had used forty World War I aircraft, seventy-eight pilots, and thirty cameramen to shoot the flying sequences for *Hell's Angels*, Hawks wisely figured that this aerial photography could not be bettered at the time, and made very effective use of it in *Today We Live*.

Faulkner had not fared badly at all in his initial creative collaboration with Hawks. With *Today We Live* Faulkner earned his first official screen credit as a scriptwriter. Now that he had been involved with a movie script that actually had been produced, he was granted the opportunity by Metro to write another screenplay without a collaborator.

War Birds

Faulkner had returned to Oxford after he completed work on *Today We Live* and was allowed to remain there while he proceeded with nearly all of his subsequent MGM assignments. His next project, in which Hawks was initially much interested, was to adapt for the screen *Diary of an Unknown Aviator,* which had been published as a book in 1926 and serialized in *Liberty* magazine the same year under the title *War Birds*. The book had been derived by Eliot White Springs from the diary of John McGavock Grider, a pilot killed in France during the First World War.

In fictionalizing the deceased flier's diary for the screen, Faulkner decided to draw on his own fictional work. Faulkner had already made use of his fiction in *Manservant* and *Today We Live;* but the interplay between his fiction and his screenwriting in the case of *War Birds* (the title of the proposed film) is more complicated. Here Faulkner contrived to combine material from the Springs book with elements from no less than three of his fictional works. Faulkner borrowed from his 1929 novel *Flags in the Dust* a dramatic situation centering on two of the book's key characters, the Sartoris twins John and Bayard, who, like the real Grider, saw action as aviators in France during World War I.[10] He also drew material from two 1931 short stories closely related to the novel, "All the Dead Pilots" and "Ad Astra." John Sartoris figures in the first story and Bayard in the second.

In the novel Bayard Sartoris returns home from the war burdened with guilt he feels for having failed to prevent his brother John's death in an air battle in which they both took part. The desperately unhappy Bayard is unable to adjust to civilian life and systematically courts death until he is finally killed while recklessly piloting a plane he knows is unsafe.

"All the Dead Pilots" is mostly a humorous account of John's raucous competition with another member of his squadron for the attentions of a very attractive young French woman. In referring to John's eventual death in combat, however, the narrator of the story makes the serious point that the war has left the airmen who have survived bitterly disillusioned, and, as the title of the tale implies, emotionally and spiritually dead. "Ad Astra," which reverberates with the same conviction, is set shortly after the armistice and portrays a drunken conversation among Bayard and some other fliers, including a German prisoner of war, about the futility and meaninglessness of the war just ended. The story's title, a reference to the Latin proverb "Ad astra per aspera" ("To reach the stars, one must pay the price"), implicitly reinforces this theme. The phrase suggests that while the spirits of the aviators may have soared as they flew missions during the war, their spirits have plummeted back to earth with the stark realization that their victories in aerial combat were all too often purchased with the lives of their fellow pilots. Accordingly they try to submerge in drunken revelry the resulting disenchantment they feel at what Cleanth Brooks terms "the terrible waste of youth's reckless bravery."[11] For Bayard, this tragic loss of young lives is epitomized in the death of his brother John.

The screenplay for *War Birds* does include some individual episodes from its three fictional sources, but Faulkner modified this material considerably as he worked it into the script. *War Birds* begins in the early 1930s, with Bayard Sartoris still very much alive and not at all the victim of the despair that characterized his morbid behavior in "Ad Astra" and *Flags in the Dust*. Bayard at this point presides over a household made up of John's widow Caroline (who was married to Bayard, not to John, in *Flags*); John's fourteen-year-old son Johnny; Lothar Dorn, a German veteran; and a French woman named Antoinette. We soon learn that Antoinette is the young lady (from "All the Dead Pilots") whom John pursued in France, while Dorn is identified as the German flying ace (from "Ad Astra") who shot down John's plane.

Inevitably young Johnny guesses the truth about both Antoinette and Lothar, and frantically demands to know from his mother why these two unspeakable foreigners, both of whom the family has strong reason to resent, are living in their home. Caroline responds by relating, with the help of her late husband's diary, the whole story of John's experiences overseas, which are dramatized in flashback. By establishing John Sartoris's diary as the source of the flashback sequences in the story, Faulkner makes use of the diary format of Spring's book, and that allows him to weave into the fabric of the script some passages drawn right from the book. For example, when John Sartoris is making his first entry in his diary, the words he records mirror some of John Grider's thoughts about going off to war.

During one of the flashback sequences, Bayard accidentally meets Lothar just after the cessation of hostilities. When Bayard discovers that Lothar killed his brother, Bayard's first inclination is to shoot the German on the spot. But in the wake of the armistice, Bayard decides that the killing must now stop once and for all; and his confrontation with Dorn ends with Bayard finally throwing his gun away for good. Bayard's epiphany even extends later to asking Lothar, and Antoinette as well, to come back to the

United States with him. He does so because he is convinced that human relationships can survive in spite of "wars and all the other disasters that men can invent" to upset them, and that furthermore, in sharing their mutual memories of John, he will continue to live on among those who have survived him. "In us," says Bayard, "he is not dead."[12]

Naturally John's widow is at first completely distraught when Bayard brings home both her husband's mistress and his killer. As time goes on, however, the group becomes more and more reconciled to each other and adapt to living together as a family. This arrangement is temporarily threatened by Johnny's traumatic discovery of the real identities of Antoinette and Lothar. But in the end, as film historian Todd McCarthy succinctly puts it, Johnny "maturely accepts what his mother has already forgiven."[13]

In the script of *War Birds*, then, Faulkner came up with an alternate ending for *Flags in the Dust*, one in which Bayard gradually builds a new life for himself and others, something he was quite incapable of doing in *Flags*. The final image in the screenplay, that of the ghost of John Sartoris in his phantom airship, gazing down with a beatific smile on the "family" which Bayard has brought together in his memory, implies that John too has at last found peace, as Bayard has, by reconciling himself to the past.

The Last MGM Scenarios

For whatever reason, *War Birds* never found a place on Hawks' production schedule. Meanwhile, Faulkner went on to other things. By spring 1933 he was busy composing an original screenplay which had the awkward working title of *Mythical Latin-American Kingdom Story*. As Faulkner had reached back to his earlier MGM scenarios for creative ideas that would aid him in fashioning the script of *Today We Live*, so he now turned to his unfilmed scenarios for material that would help him flesh out the plot of *Kingdom*, an adventure drama set against the background of a revolution in a Third World republic.

As Kawin observes, the character of Otto Birdsong, an aircraft mechanic who has abandoned his wife and daughter, resembles the Wallace Beery character in *Flying the Mail*. Marion, Birdsong's daughter, is just as bent on tracking down her long-lost father as was Wally's daughter in *Mail*. Birdsong is portrayed as devoted to Bowden, an American pilot who saved his life during World War I, just as Das, the manservant in the *Manservant* scenario, maintained a blind devotion to Blynt out of a similar motive.

This last of Faulkner's five Metro scenarios about flying did not get off the ground, perhaps because Faulkner himself gave up on it. An examination of the screenplay reveals his diminishing enthusiasm for the project. To put it bluntly, the script as Faulkner left it does not really come to an end; it simply runs down, leaving important characters such as Marion to disappear from the action, remaining unaccounted for at the conclusion. Although the *Kingdom* screenplay is the only one of Faulkner's Metro scenarios that seems carelessly handled, since Faulkner never got around to revising it, it probably deserved the oblivion to which the studio consigned it. A rather devastating report from a reader in the Story Department accurately described the script as containing "one or two characters that might have been very interesting if the author had taken the trouble to develop them."[14]

Faulkner probably lost interest in developing *Kingdom* to its full dramatic potential because he was growing tired of doing screen work and was anxious to get back to writing fiction fulltime. As a matter of fact, he said that if he were to devote any more time to reworking *Kingdom,* he would prefer to turn the story into a novel rather than revise it further as a movie script; but in the end he did neither.

It was around this time that an incident occurred which has since become a Hollywood legend. Faulkner had received permission from the studio to compose the screenplays he worked on after *Today We Live* while remaining at home in Mississippi. Sam Marx and Howard Hawks were both parties to this agreement, but not everyone in the MGM power structure was aware of it. Consequently, one of the studio administrators, in the course of checking up on Faulkner's work, was amazed when he discovered that for some weeks Faulkner had been receiving a regular paycheck from Metro without ever setting foot on the studio lot, and that this unconventional arrangement had apparently been in effect for some time.

Although those are the facts of what happened, this oft-repeated story was recast in the telling into a humorous anecdote. Faulkner is said to have asked one of the studio brass if he could work at home. Assuming that Faulkner meant the place he was staying in Hollywood, the official agreed. Later on, when he checked on Faulkner's whereabouts, Faulkner was nowhere to be found. It was then that the executive realized that to Faulkner home meant Oxford, Mississippi. Even though in later years Faulkner himself enjoyed telling this latter rendition, this amusing version of the episode gives the false impression that Faulkner had failed to obtain proper authorization from anyone at Metro to work away from Hollywood and had misled the front office into thinking that he had not left town. At the time this version of the facts unfortunately helped to perpetuate among some of his superiors at Metro the notion, dating back to the "Death Valley" episode recounted above, that he was fundamentally unreliable.

Given that Faulkner's reputation in some quarters at MGM was not very high, his relationship with the studio administration was not helped by the additional consideration that the projects he had recently worked on while remaining in Oxford had little hope of going before the cameras. It was not surprising, therefore, that his privilege of staying on the studio payroll while living in Mississippi was finally abrogated. Hence, his last assignment before being dropped altogether from Metro's roster of writers was to proceed from Oxford directly to New Orleans, where he was to work on the dialogue for a picture called *Louisiana Lou,* which was being shot on location in and around that area. "I could have got on a train in Oxford and been in New Orleans eight hours later," Faulkner recalled afterward, "but I obeyed the studio and went to Memphis, where an airplane occasionally did leave for New Orleans." After three days, one finally did.[15]

Faulkner arrived in the city on 26 April 1933 and reported immediately to the director of the movie, Tod Browning, known for making the first and best sound version of *Dracula* (1931). Faulkner and Browning got on well personally, and the director sent word back to the studio that he wanted Faulkner to return to Hollywood with the film unit to continue working on the script there. This Faulkner refused to do because, among other reasons, his wife was about to have a baby, and he felt he should go back to Oxford and finish working on *Louisiana Lou* there. Once back in Oxford, Faulkner in due course received a wire from Marx which regretfully informed him that, because he insisted on continuing to work at home, his relationship with the studio would have to be terminated. "Studio feels this method of working is not feasible," Mark explained. "Consequently we will be most happy to continue you on staff here at any time you will come to California."

Storyteller that he was, Faulkner embellished this incident every time he related it in later years. According to him, a telegram arrived from MGM while he was still in New Orleans which read, "Faulkner is fired." Browning assured him that he would see to it that Faulkner was reinstated immediately. But the next communique from Metro, which came right after the first, stated, "Browning is fired."[16]

Metro's treatment of Faulkner, as evidenced by Marx's thoughtful wire to him, was much more considerate than Faulkner's apocryphal version of the episode would lead one to believe. Still, he was right in maintaining that Browning did not want the studio to fire him and that the director was himself taken off the picture, though not until a few months after Faulkner. (The movie was finally released the following year as *Lazy River*, but nothing that Faulkner had contributed to the screenplay survived in the finished picture.)

Faulkner took his dismissal by Metro, which went into effect on 13 May 1933, with equanimity, since he had, for the time being at least, lost interest in screenwriting. "They want to can me, and I am ready to quit," he had advised Browning by letter after the latter had gone back to Hollywood without him. "Don't say anything more to the studio about keeping me on. Just let it go."[17]

Faulkner at Fox

Faulkner returned to Hollywood briefly in the summer of 1934 at the behest of Howard Hawks to prepare a treatment for *Sutter's Gold,* a western Hawks was tinkering with at Universal. When Hawks eventually opted against proceeding with the project, he later invited Faulkner to collaborate on the screenplay for a World War I epic he was planning to make for Twentieth Century–Fox. And so, in December 1935, Faulkner became a contract writer at Fox, where he was to remain intermittently employed on various properties until late summer 1937.

The Road to Glory

The war picture Hawks had asked Faulkner to collaborate on was *The Road to Glory* (1936), which was to be based on a 1932 French film directed by Raymond Bernard, *Les Croix de Bois* (*Wooden Crosses*). Because the cast of *Croix de Bois* was composed of French war veterans, the largescale battle sequences that had been shot on location for the original movie conveyed a documentary-like authenticity that, as film historian William K. Everson avers, could hardly be duplicated on the back lot at Fox. Consequently Hawks went along with the studio's suggestion that he interpolate these mass-action sequences into his film, much as he had insinuated footage from *Hell's Angels* into *Today We Live*. The battle scenes in *Croix de Bois* were not, however, actual combat footage, as Blotner mistakenly asserts in both editions of his Faulkner biography.

Faulkner and his cowriter, Joel Sayre, created a screenplay that meshed elements of the original film's plot with some reminiscences Hawks had heard in Paris from a veteran who had fought at Verdun. Together the writing team came up with a serviceable script for *Wooden Crosses*, as the film was being called at that point, by the end of December; and that draft of the screenplay became the basis for all subsequent revisions. The script was worked on further by Sayre and screenwriter Nunnally Johnson, who was also associate producer of the film; and it was put into final form by Faulkner and Hawks before the movie, now titled *The Road to Glory*, went into production. In due course the front office notified Faulkner that he, along with Joel Sayre, was to be listed in the screen credits as cowriter of the picture. *Road to Glory* thus became the second film on which Faulkner had labored for which he would receive an official writer's credit, as none of the movie work he had done since *Today We Live* had reached the screen.

The Road to Glory may be viewed as a companion piece to *Today We Live*, in that it treats the way in which war alters the relationships of comrades and loved ones. In *The Road to Glory*, Capt. Paul Laroche (Warner Baxter) is obsessed by his grave sense of responsibility for sending men to their deaths in battle. His position is made even more intolerable when his own father (Lionel Barrymore) becomes a soldier in his company.

Death eventually claims Paul himself, and the film ends with his companion-in-arms, Lt. Michel Denet (Fredric March) repeating to the new recruits virtually the same speech Paul had given earlier in the picture. The cycle of death goes on, but each soldier's unflinching dedication to duty and to his comrades keeps him going stoically onward. That dual dedication is dramatized most particularly in this film, as it is in *Today We Live*, when Paul, accompanied by his father, undertakes a military mission which means almost certain death, so that Michel can go on living and ultimately marry the girl they both love—an act strikingly similar to what Claude, with Ronnie's help, does in the earlier film. Paul, like Claude, is spurred to make this generous act of self-sacrifice because he has been blinded in a previous battle and prefers to have the girl he loves marry the man she really wants, rather than wed him out of pity.

In his penetrating article on the relationship of *Road to Glory* and *Croix de Bois*, William Everson indicates how imaginatively incidents that are rather lightly sketched in the French film are elaborated in depth by Faulkner and Sayre. For example, a relatively minor episode in *Croix*, in which the sound of digging makes the French troops aware that enemy sappers are planting dynamite beneath their trenches, is expanded into a major sequence in *Road*. In the latter version, says Everson, this same incident "is given the full showmanship treatment" by the American writing team, who build it into a suspenseful episode in which Paul and Michel are just barely able to evacuate their men from the trenches before the explosives are discharged. Rarely has the strain of trench warfare been so strikingly depicted on film.

Both the screenplay and the direction of the movie were lauded by reviewers when the film was released. Hawks, it was said, had done a masterful job of matching the battle footage he shot on the Fox lot with the graphic material he took from *Croix*. Each frame of the French film was like "a dark mezzotint," remembers Hawks's script supervisor, Meta Carpenter Wilde; "Hawks would reshoot endlessly to achieve the photographic quality of the French movie."[18]

Thus, screenwriter George Garrett seems right on target when he contends that the screenplay for *Road to Glory* proves that Faulkner could tackle "a job on order and for hire" and do it well, thereby vindicating the confidence that Hawks had placed in him from the start of their professional relationship.[19] *The Road to Glory* can still be seen on late night television, and it remains one of Hawks's—and Faulkner's—finest films.

Faulkner seemed to work better with Hawks than with any other director in Hollywood. Indeed during his entire career in Hollywood Faulkner earned screen credits for making substantial creative contributions to the screenplays of six motion pictures; five of those six pictures were directed by Howard Hawks.

Slave Ship

The only screen writing credit which Faulkner ever received for a non-Hawks film was *Slave Ship* (1937), a potboiler on which he toiled at Fox while his contract still had some time to run and Hawks had moved to another studio. The film once again starred Warner Baxter and Wallace Beery. Asked about his part in shaping the script of *Slave Ship*, Faulkner replied that he had acted as "a motion picture doctor" on the film, by which he meant that he

Capt. Paul Laroche (Warner Baxter) and Lt. Michel Denet (Fredric March) in *The Road to Glory* (1936), coscripted by Faulkner. Rarely has the strain of trench warfare been captured so strikingly on film. (Museum of Modern Art/Film Stills Archive)

"reworked sections in this picture" already written by other hands.[20] More precisely, Faulkner, along with writer-associate producer Nunnally Johnson, worked over an earlier draft of the script which had been written by another team of writers. Since some of his proposed revisions were not incorporated into the final shooting script, Faulkner did not see himself as being quite as responsible for the screenplay of *Slave Ship* as he had been for the scripts of *Today We Live* and *Road to Glory*.

Nevertheless, when novelist-screenwriter Graham Greene reviewed *Slave Ship* for the British Journal *Night and Day,* he evidently assumed Faulkner had had more of a hand in the shaping of the completed picture than was actually the case. Greene began his notice by calling this adventure tale of mutiny on the high seas good escapist entertainment: "It has excellent moments — seamen flinging knives from topgallants, and Wallace Beery as the soapy and mutinous mate, less soft-hearted than he has been for years. . . . " Still, he added, the presence of Faulkner's name and that of director Tay Garnett (*China Seas*) in the film's credits had led him to assume that the movie's course was "set for distinction; but it remains a hot-weather picture."[21] If he ever saw this review, Faulkner at least would have been pleased that Greene, who was his colleague both as fiction and film writer, esteemed him as a distinguished author who deserved to be associated with a better grade of movie.

The Last Fox Scenarios

Of the other films Faulkner collaborated on before he finished at Fox in August 1937, *Submarine Patrol* and *Drums Along the Mohawk* were both slated to be directed by John Ford. But as things turned out, hardly any of the material he wrote for either picture found its way into the final shooting script. After a year at Fox, Faulkner was becoming as discouraged and apathetic about screen work as he had been after a year at Metro. His growing restlessness was betrayed by a remark at the end of his otherwise carefully constructed treatment for *Drums Along the Mohawk*, a costume drama. He lackadaisically summarizes the closing conversation between Lana, a married woman, and Mary, a new bride, in this manner: "Lana tells Mary whatever sappy stuff we need here about love conquers all things, etc."

Faulkner was understandably disappointed that much of what he had written at Fox and at Metro had never reached the screen. Yet he was not really morose about the way he had been treated by the film industry. In Hollywood, Pauline Kael has said, it is easy for the writer to see himself as "an underling whose work is trashed; at best, he is a respected collaborator without final control over how his work is used." The screenwriter therefore can become very bitter about the movie moguls "who he feels have no right to make decisions about his work" but do so just the same.[22]

Although Faulkner would have been the first to concede that movie work could frequently seem frustrating and unrewarding, he personally had reached the conclusion that if a writer was to survive in the movie colony, he must realize that "a moving picture is by its nature a collaboration, and any collaboration is compromise because that is what the word means —

to give and take." Faulkner had already demonstrated his willingness to compromise during his first ventures in Hollywood, most particularly when he dutifully manufactured a role out of whole cloth for Joan Crawford in *Today We Live*. Howard Hawks was not exaggerating, therefore, when he once said of Faulkner that he was an obliging collaborator, "a master of his work who does it without a fuss."[23]

In summary, Faulkner had tried his best to adjust to the demands of living and working in the movie capital. And he was prepared to go back to Hollywood in the years to come whenever his ailing finances required it. Faulkner was far from finished with Hollywood.

CHAPTER 2

Exiled in Paradise:
The Warner Screenplays

I'll be glad when I get back home. . . .
There's nobody here with any roots. Even
the houses are built out of mud and
chicken wire.

William Faulkner

This is a nice town full of very rich
middle-class people who have not yet
discovered the cerebrum, or at best the soul.
Beautiful, damned monotonous weather, and I am
getting quite tired of it, will be glad
to farm again.

William Faulkner

One might well wonder why Faulkner found it necessary to continue writing for the movies throughout the 1930s and into the 1940s, even after he began to acquire a reputation as an important novelist. The answer is not far to seek. Joel Sayre recalled that Faulkner, who had become family head after his father died in 1932, had numerous dependents to take care of in that period: his wife, her two children by a previous marriage, their own daughter, his mother, and the widow and small child of his brother Dean. Sayre explained that "it was impossible for him to support all these people from his book and magazine earnings," which were never large. Hence Faulkner continued to seek employment in Hollywood.

As an indication of how hard up Faulkner was in these days, Sayre recounted that someone in Hollywood once sent a box of Faulkner novels to him in Oxford, with the request that he autograph them. The package came back by return mail unopened. "I'd have been glad to autograph them for you," Faulkner later explained when he met the sender in Hollywood, "but we couldn't afford the return postage."[1]

Faulkner at Warner Brothers

Faulkner's last prolonged period of exile in the film colony was when he worked intermittently at Warner Brothers between summer 1942 and fall 1945. Though he would occasionally get away for a breather, the bulk of his time during those years was spent in Warner's employ. During his tenure at Warner's, Faulkner was sometimes given the job of revising a troublesome script on which other writers before him had worked. Albert I. Bezzerides, a colleague of Faulkner's at Warner's, always wondered why Jack L. Warner, the studio head, would allow a distinguished author like Faulkner to be assigned to do donkey work of this sort. "I guess Warner thought that if he gave these dog assignments to wonderful writers, somehow they'd turn a dog into a silk purse; and it never worked."[2] Still, an ailing script often was the better for Faulkner's ministrations, as Bezzerides would be the first to agree.

Among the screenplays which Faulkner helped to revise were *Background to Danger* and *The Adventures of Don Juan*. Both pictures were produced by Jerry Wald, who would later make movies of two of Faulkner's novels in the 1950s. Wald once explained that he liked to have Faulkner revise a screenplay because "he had a particularly excellent sense of story construction." For example, when a preliminary assembly of the footage of *Background to Danger* (1943), a formula spy thriller starring George Raft, was put together, Wald was dissatisfied with the results but could not figure out exactly why. He screened the rough cut of the movie for Faulkner, who commented afterward, "I know what's the matter: too much running around." Faulkner then spent two weeks writing some new scenes for the movie which, said Wald, "straightened out the story and made the picture 'work.'"[3]

Faulkner was less adept at creating screen dialogue, according to Wald, than at making adjustments in narrative continuity, because writing dialogue for a novel is quite different from writing dialogue for a movie. It seems that, although Faulkner wrote good literary dialogue, his film dialogue tended to be too cerebral and verbose for screen purposes. In this regard Wald remembered that actor Sydney Greenstreet phoned him from the set where one of the additional scenes Faulkner had written for *Danger* was being shot and informed him most emphatically that he simply could not deliver a particularly long and complicated speech as Faulkner had originally written it; the lines were duly modified. Screenwriter Leigh Brackett, who collaborated with Faulkner at one point, agreed with both the positive and negative aspects of Wald's assessment of Faulkner's skills as a script writer: "He was a master at story construction, but his dialogue did not fit comfortably in the mouths of the actors, and was often changed on the set."[4]

Faulkner was only one of the many scenarists brought in to retouch the script for *The Adventures of Don Juan*, an Errol Flynn swashbuckler that did not reach the screen until 1948. Given Faulkner's proclivity for writing literary dialogue for the scripts he worked on, it is not surprising that when he submitted his version of the screenplay of *Don Juan* to Wald, the producer passed it on to yet another writer, who was given the task "of going through the script page by page and polishing the dialogue" which Faulkner had written.[5]

Besides working on the properties assigned to him by the studio, Faulkner also sought to launch a few projects of his own, which he hoped to persuade Warner or some other studio to produce. One possibility he considered was dramatizing a short story entitled "The Curious Case of Benjamin Button" by F. Scott Fitzgerald, who had died a couple of years before. In spring 1943 Faulkner asked his literary agent, Harold Ober, who had also been Fitzgerald's agent, for advice about obtaining permission from Fitzgerald's widow Zelda to turn the tale into a play, with a view to subsequently adapting the stage version for the screen.

"Benjamin Button" was a rather unlikely choice for Faulkner to latch onto as a promising vehicle for both a play and a film. It is a curious fantasy centering on someone who is born old and then grows progressively younger as the years go by, until he finally dies as a baby. In a prenote to the story in the original edition of *Tales of the Jazz Age*, Fitzgerald explained that the plot of "Benjamin Button" had been inspired by Mark Twain's statement that "it was a pity that the best part of life came at the beginning and the worst part at the end." Fitzgerald added that "by trying the experiment upon only one man in a perfectly normal world, I have scarcely given his idea a fair trial."[6] How Faulkner might have transformed this odd tale into either a play or a film script we shall never know, since, fortunately or unfortunately, he eventually gave up the idea.

Another independent project that Faulkner wanted to develop while he was employed at Warner's began as the result of a discussion with director Henry Hathaway (*Wing and a Prayer*) and producer William A. Bacher (*Leave Her to Heaven*). Hathaway for some time had been mulling over the idea of doing a film about the Unknown Soldier, and had interested Bacher in it too. One writer with whom they initially discussed their concept for the movie, Leslie Rivers, commented, "The only thing that would satisfy you would be if your Unknown Soldier was Jesus Christ."[7] Rivers himself did not wish to pursue the project, but Hathaway and Bacher picked up on his remark and worked it into their proposal for the movie; then they took the project to Faulkner. He was entranced by the idea of Christ's returning to earth right in the middle of World War I in the guise of an ordinary corporal, in order to bring his message of peace to a war-torn world and inspire the human race never to make war again. Then, after once again being rejected and put to death by recalcitrant humanity, Christ would be buried in the tomb of the Unknown Soldier. Faulkner was particularly impressed with the identification of Christ with the Unknown Soldier. "Suppose that had been Christ . . . under that big cenotaph with the eternal flame burning on it," he said later in describing how the idea for the proposed scenario fired his imagination. He added elsewhere that the project also appealed to him because the death and resurrection of Christ are, after all, part of the background of any Christian, "especially the background of . . . a southern country boy" such as he had been. In writing a story thematically centered on the Passion of Christ, he would be able to draw on his own religious upbringing.[8]

Faulkner entered into an agreement with Hathaway and Bacher, in which he committed himself to write a preliminary scenario for the film. He would not, however, be able to develop this plot synthesis into a fullscale screenplay so long as he was still under contract to Warner Brothers, since he was not permitted during the period of his employment to undertake to write a screenplay not specifically assigned to him by the studio. Thus he decided to compose a fairly detailed treatment while the plot was still fresh in his mind, a treatment that would stand him in good stead later when he was able to expand it into a full-length screenplay.

Faulkner's scenario, tentatively titled *Who?*, which he wrote in fall 1943, became so elaborate, however, that he finally realized that he was no longer preparing a treatment for a screenplay at all, but was developing a complex storyline far better suited to the dimensions of a novel. He accordingly worked on the novel, eventually entitled *A Fable*, off and on for more than a decade. When the book was finally published in 1954, it won both the Pulitzer Prize and the National Book Award; but it was not made into a film either by his partners in the original project or by anyone else. When Hathaway, who started it all, read Faulkner's dense, lengthy novel, he was frankly bewildered by it. "I couldn't find my story," he said. "I didn't recognize anything."[9]

The De Gaulle Story

Because Faulkner was employed by Warner during the war years, he worked on a number of scripts about World War II. One of his more noteworthy efforts was *The De Gaulle Story;* but though he labored very assiduously on the script, the picture was never made. The original impetus for the production seems to have come ultimately from President Franklin Roosevelt, who personally encouraged Jack Warner, during a conversation at the White House, to make some movies that would help the war effort. It was further decided, with Roosevelt's concurrence, that Gen. Charles De Gaulle would be the ideal subject for one such film, since a movie about the gallant French leader would make him more familiar to the American people. Faulkner was assigned to the project by producer Robert Buckner (*Mission to Moscow*), who was aware of Faulkner's work on a previously successful war picture, *The Road to Glory.*

Working alone, Faulkner wrote an original treatment that integrated the factual account of De Gaulle's rallying the French people to fight for the liberation of Occupied France from Nazi domination with a fictional tale of two brothers, Georges and Jean Mornet. Among several sources of friction between the feuding Mornet brothers, the most crucial is Jean's support of the pro-Nazi Vichy government. His stance contrasts starkly with George's loyalty to the anti-Nazi Free French movement championed by De Gaulle. With the help of both his brother and his sweetheart Emilie, Jean gradually comes to see the tragic blunder he has made in collaborating with the Nazis, and in the end he aligns himself with the cause of the Free French.

Faulkner at one point described his work-in-progress as the story of "the collapse of France and the hopes and struggles for rejuvenation," seen in terms of a rural French village.[10] But Faulkner's storyline, though it vigorously endorsed the Free French cause, nevertheless was severely criticized by two of the Gaullists representing the general in America, Adrien Taxier and Henri Diamant-Berger, both of whom were consulted at different times about Faulkner's scenario.

Taxier, who examined Faulkner's preliminary treatment, faulted it for not emphasizing sufficiently the activities of the Free French Resistance movement against the Nazi occupation forces, and for presenting a German soldier in a favorable light by having him aid a Frenchman in escaping from a Nazi jail. After Faulkner revised the treatment to mollify Taxier, he proceeded with the first draft of the screenplay, which in time was passed on to Berger for his perusal.

Berger, who was harder to pacify than his compatriot, had several basic complaints about the script. He criticized the characterizations of the two brothers as unconvincing. In particular he thought that Jean, who temporarily sides with the pro-Nazi Vichyites, "is really shown as too stupid for words." Berger's principal objection, however, was that during the course of the screenplay De Gaulle is allowed to slip gradually from the foreground of the story into the background, as the clash between Georges and Jean over their conflicting loyalties more and more takes center stage. "De Gaulle does not insist on having his 'part' increased," wrote Berger, "but he thinks that he can lend his name and personality [only] to a picture which shows the accomplishment done by his movement being at least spiritually inspired by his activities."[11]

Once again Faulkner attempted to modify his work in the light of Gaullist criticism. But the more he tried to highlight De Gaulle's role in the action, the more he came to believe that it was a serious mistake to attempt to portray a contemporary world figure like De Gaulle in a movie scenario. "If we use him as a living character, we must accept the supervision of his representatives," Faulkner explained in a memo to Buckner. "They want to see a piece of Free French propaganda, not a moving picture in which those who see it will recognize their own human passions and griefs and desires." He was consequently convinced that making the movie under Gaullist supervision meant that "we must either please them and nobody else, or probably nobody at all." Faulkner said that he had reached the conclusion that De Gaulle should not be depicted in the film at all. His counterproposal was that the film should instead reflect the spirit of De Gaulle, "in terms of some little human people, with their human relationships which an audience can understand, whose lives and destinies were affected . . . by the same beliefs that made him De Gaulle."

There is little doubt that Faulkner was correct in contending that it was hopeless to continue trying to pacify the Gaullist advisors on the film. Indeed, Louis Daniel Brodsky and Robert Hamblin, the editors of the published screenplay, maintain that the tense situation which Taxier and Berger had created by their "recalcitrant objections" to Faulkner's script contributed in no small way to the shelving of the project. As Jack Warner later remarked in his autobiography, "there are some subjects that are so explosive and so open to misinterpretation" by well-meaning supporters of a cause that "you're a dead pigeon," no matter what you do.[12]

Among other reasons advanced by Faulkner scholars for the cancellation of *The De Gaulle Story,* one of the most compelling seems to be that Roosevelt himself changed his mind about the advisability of a movie about De Gaulle, primarily because De Gaulle was already proving an arrogant and abrasive ally. As a matter of fact, when Churchill informed Roosevelt of an especially unpleasant confrontation he had had with De Gaulle, Roosevelt's enthusiasm for a movie glorifying the troublesome general cooled considerably; he communicated his feelings to Jack Warner, who forthwith closed down the production.

Read today, Faulkner's screenplay for *The De Gaulle Story* seems of uneven quality, although this may well be because, once the picture was dropped from the production schedule, he did not have an opportunity to revise the script further, but had to move on to other assignments. Still, even as it stands, the script possesses no little merit, containing some memorable sequences.

In one very moving scene Emilie attempts to convert Jean to the cause of the Free French by recounting to him how she was raped by some Nazi soldiers. She goes on to tell about a passage that someone read to her afterward from a book by Ernest Hemingway: "It told about a young girl to whom that had happened also, and about an older woman who was very wise about people anyway, who said how, if you refused to accept something, it could not happen to you. And I was comforted. . . . "[13] Little did Faulkner know, when paying this touching tribute to Ernest Hemingway in his *De Gaulle* script, that in the not-too-distant future he would be adapting a Hemingway novel to the screen for their mutual friend, Howard Hawks.

In the meantime, Faulkner worked on some other properties for Hawks, now at Warner Brothers too. In fact, while Faulkner was still engaged in working on *De Gaulle*, Hawks had asked him to provide a couple of new scenes that the director needed for his current production, *Air Force* (1943), which had already been scripted by another writer; and Faulkner obliged. In discussing his association with Faulkner, Hawks told me, "Bill worked with me on several pictures," not just the handful for which he got a screen credit. "I could call on him any time and ask him for a scene, and he always gave it to me."

Air Force was a case in point. The picture, which centers on the crew of a bomber named "the Mary Ann," like *Today We Live* and *Road to Glory*, was a study of a group of fighting men under stress. In *Air Force*, the plane becomes the concrete embodiment of the mutual loyalty that unifies its crew; this group solidarity is compellingly dramatized in a scene Faulkner wrote overnight for the movie which portrays the death of the plane's captain. Quincannon, the delirious skipper, believes that the Mary Ann is taking off on a mission. As he goes over his takeoff checklist, each member of the crew standing around his hospital bed helps to sustain the illusion by enacting his customary role aboard the plane. When the navigator says that the course is due east, the captain murmurs, "That's right into the sunrise," and expires. Faulkner was justly proud of both the scenes he contributed to the film. "See *Air Force*," he noted in a letter to a relative. "I wrote Quincannon's death scene, and the scene where the men in the aeroplane heard Roosevelt's speech after Pearl Harbor" and were deeply moved by it.

Film scholar Tom Dardis is wrong in stating that Faulkner wrote a substantial number of scenes for the movie; errors of this kind mar his book on screenwriters, *Some Time in the Sun*. But he is right in affirming that word of Faulkner's contribution to the movie reached the front office and paved the way for his being allowed to do further work for Hawks.

Shortly after his brief stint on *Air Force*, Faulkner tried his hand at writing a scenario of his own, also centering on the courageous crew of a war plane, *The Life and Death of a Bomber*. He worked on the treatment in late 1942 and early 1943, but Warner's canceled the project in favor of a more ambitious war movie that Hawks was preparing, entitled *Battle Cry*. Faulkner was accordingly transferred to the Hawks picture. Dardis comments that the scenario of *Bomber* "reads very badly," but, again, Faulkner had no opportunity to polish his work once production was abandoned.[14]

Battle Cry

Nearly all of the major screen work that Faulkner accomplished during his time at Warner's was for Howard Hawks. Not all of the screenplays Faulkner prepared for Hawks were filmed, but even those that were not are nonetheless worthy of attention, since Faulkner invested a good deal of creative effort in all of them.

One of the unproduced scripts was *Battle Cry*—not to be confused with the 1954 Warner's movie of the same name. It was a project to which Faulkner was committed from April to August 1943.

Battle Cry was conceived as a colossal saga about World War II. It was intended to dramatize the heroic defense of liberty throughout the world by presenting a series of vignettes set in various countries involved in the conflict, including Russia, China, England, Greece, and France. An additional episode, called "the American sequence," was designed as one of the principal means of tying all of the other segments together. This sequence, to which the narrative periodically returns throughout the course of the screenplay, focuses on a platoon of beleaguered American soldiers stranded in the North African desert, desperately hoping for reinforcements that will probably never arrive. As they wait through the night for the Nazi onslaught that is surely to come the next morning, they bolster each other's spirits by trading stories about acts of heroism that have occurred on other fronts. These inspiring accounts, presented in flashback, make up the bulk of the screenplay. By the time the last tale is told, it is dawn; and the valiant band of fighting men prepare to face the enemy attack, which is just beginning as the screenplay draws to a close.

After a series of story conferences with Hawks, Faulkner wrote most of the first draft of the script himself, based on material drawn from a variety of sources, including magazine fiction. In addition to Faulkner, a couple of other writers, especially William Bacher, Hawks's chief assistant on the film, contributed to the development of the screenplay at this point. As we know, Bacher had been involved with Faulkner earlier in planning a film about the Unknown Soldier. Later on, screenwriter Steve Fisher (*Destination Tokyo*) assisted Faulkner in revising the script. Nevertheless Faulkner remained the chief architect of the script since, as Brodsky and Hamblin, the editors of the published screenplay, have shown, the studio files testify that the revised version of the screenplay of *Battle Cry,* dated 5 August 1943, was predominantly Faulkner's work.

As it happened, none of Fisher's contributions to the script was ultimately used; but Bacher made some minor but significant additions to the
revised screenplay. In fact, it was not Faulkner, as Todd McCarthy and
others have mistakenly assumed, but Bacher who composed the brief prologue at the beginning of the screenplay, as Bacher's memo of 18 June 1943
to Hawks makes clear. In this opening statement, which was to be spoken,
voice-over on the sound track, by a narrator, a battle cry is said to arise
from the throats of every free man the world over "when those things are
threatened which he has lived by and held above price, and which have
made his life worth the having and the holding." Nonetheless, as the editors of the published script comment, this prologue is surprisingly Faulk-
nerian in both substance and tone and hence fits into the fabric of the
screenplay very well. Indeed, the sentiments expressed in the prologue
about the implicit solidarity of the free peoples of the earth are very much
in harmony with a passage later in the screenplay, in which Faulkner has
an American G.I. reflect that the spirit of liberty which Americans have
always cherished is a dream that was shared "for three thousand years before there was any America, by men whose nationality was only the human
race: in Greece, in Italy, China, Russia. . . . "[15]

Bacher much admired the craftsmanship evident in Faulkner's work on
the screenplay of *Battle Cry*; in a memo dated 18 June 1943, he told Hawks
as much. Faulkner's own typically laconic judgment of the merits of the
script, expressed in a letter to his wife later that summer, was that he thought
he had written a good picture—which is about as close to self-praise as
he ever came. Nonetheless, Warner Brothers decided that the mammoth
production would be too costly and canceled the picture. This was doubly
unfortunate, since the screenplay gives every indication that, had the front
office allowed the production to proceed, *Battle Cry* might well have turned
out to be not just another routine war saga but an impressive motion picture of breathtaking scope. One can understand Faulkner's acute disap-
pointment that a movie to which he had devoted the better part of five
months was not going to be made. Fisher later remembered that when
Faulkner heard the depressing news, he dejectedly headed for the nearest bar.

Dreadful Hollow

Besides *Battle Cry*, the other unfilmed screenplay that Faulkner worked on
for Hawks during this period was for a horror film titled *Dreadful Hollow*.

It was not an original screenplay by Faulkner, as Faulkner commentators for a long time thought it was; rather, as Bruce Kawin has discovered, *Dreadful Hollow* was Faulkner's screen adaptation of a 1942 novel of the same title by Irina Karlova, a pseudonym for H.M.E. Clamp. Todd McCarthy adds that "Hawks bought Irina Karlova's novel in November 1944" and put Faulkner to work on the project soon afterward. Faulkner came up with a fascinating but somewhat overlong screenplay of 159 pages, which Hawks could not interest Warner in. McCarthy states that in 1951 Hawks was still actively trying to obtain financing for *Dreadful Hollow*, this time at Fox. But production chief Darryl Zanuck, Faulkner's former boss, rejected the screenplay on the grounds that it followed what he termed "familiar patterns like *Dragonwyck* and *Hound of the Baskervilles.*" McCarthy comments that Faulkner's script has less in common with the earlier Fox horror films to which Zanuck compared it than with "Faulkner's own tales of twisted . . . families" like the Compsons of *The Sound and the Fury*; "the difference is that *these* characters have roots in Transylvania," Dracula's place of origin.[16]

The title *Dreadful Hollow* is drawn from Tennyson's poem "Maud," which contains a line that aptly sets the somber tone of the tale: "I hate the dreadful hollow behind the wood." The story opens with Jillian Dare's coming to Rotherham Hall, a remote, forbidding English mansion where she has been engaged to look after the aging Countess Vera Czerner. Upon Dare's arrival, Larry Clyde, the local doctor, warns her more than once against staying on with the countess and her strange household; but the spunky young lady, true to her family name, is determined to cope with whatever she encounters at Rotherham Hall.

Some time afterward, a local youngster disappears; and in the wake of this mysterious happening Countess Czerner's niece, also named Vera, comes to visit her aunt. Meanwhile Clyde's investigations of the Czerner family history lead him to the startling discovery that young Vera is really old Vera, rejuvenated by the blood of the missing lad. The shocking revelation that the countess is really a vampire—something Clyde has long suspected—shortly is followed by the equally dreadful disclosure that the boy's corpse has been sewn up inside the torso of a stuffed wolf on display in the mansion. This gruesome fact is brought to light when the wolf suddenly crashes to the floor and splits open—and the bloody shoe of a child drops out.

In the chilling climax to the tale, Clyde arrives with the police, just in time to save Dare from a fate similar to that of the dead youngster; and the screenplay concludes with Dare and Clyde's engagement to be married. As Kawin points out in *Faulkner and Film*, in his thoughtful commentary on *Dreadful Hollow*, Faulkner is not guilty of undercutting the horror of his harrowing story by appending a conventional happy ending to it. Because of the courage and resourcefulness both parties have displayed in the course of the story, they have earned the right to this felicitous outcome of their common ordeal. Perhaps McCarthy crystalizes Faulkner's achievement in this screenplay best when he writes that, by artfully sidestepping the clichés of a hoary genre, Faulkner has managed skillfully to fashion a fresh and convincing retelling of the old vampire legends which has all the earmarks of a topnotch horror movie. Indeed, one can only fervently hope that it may yet be filmed.

To Have and Have Not

The first of the two Hawks films on which Faulkner collaborated during this period which actually made it to the screen was *To Have and Have Not* (1944), based on the 1937 novel by Ernest Hemingway. Whether or not Hawks was aware of it, in asking Faulkner to work on the film, he was giving him the opportunity to be involved in bringing to the screen a novel by his only serious rival as the foremost American novelist of their generation. In fact, the film of *To Have and Have Not* represents the only time in film history that two Nobel Prize-winners, Faulkner and Hemingway, were associated with the same motion picture.

Hemingway's novel, the only one which he set in his homeland, began its artistic life as a short story, "One Trip Across," about a smuggling expedition of a rum runner called Harry Morgan (named for the famous buccaneer), off the coast of Key West. This story was followed by a companion piece called "The Tradesman's Return." Hemingway then decided to lump the two stories together as the first two sections of a novel about Morgan, to which he added a third and longer segment to round out the account of Harry's life. The novelist failed to unify the narrative, however, and the book remains a patchwork of three clearly definable episodes which do not add up to a coherent, artistic whole.

In his last section, Hemingway introduced several minor characters who represent the "haves," the idle rich who are pictured lounging on their yachts in leisure and luxury. They were meant to contrast with the strug-

Harry Morgan (Humphrey Bogart), Marie (Lauren Bacall), and Frenchy (Marcel
Dalio) in *To Have and Have Not* (1944), derived from the Hemingway novel.
Faulkner coauthored the screenplay, making this film the only one in the history
of motion pictures to be the creative product of two Nobel Prize winners,
Hemingway and Faulkner. (Museum of Modern Art/Film Stills Archive)

gling "have-nots" represented by Harry Morgan, who is forced to employ his fishing launch for smuggling contraband cargo in order to make a living during the Depression.

Social comment of this kind was never Hemingway's strong suit, and the book's real theme is a much broader one, articulated by Harry as he lies near death in the wake of a shootout with some Cuban revolutionaries: "a man alone ain't got no bloody fucking chance."[17] Too late Harry has realized that he has needed others, just as they have needed him. This theme appealed to Faulkner as much as it did to Hemingway; comradeship, as we have seen, is an important element in Faulkner's fiction and in his film scenarios, including the screenplays he had already worked on for Hawks. Hawks recounted the genesis of the film version of *To Have and Have Not* this way:

> I tried to get Ernest Hemingway to write for pictures as Bill Faulkner had done for me on several occasions, but Hemingway said that he was going to stick to the kind of writing that he knew best. Once, on a hunting trip, I told him that if he would give me the worst story that he had ever written, we would make a good movie out of it. He asked me what I thought was his worst novel; and I said *To Have and Have Not*, which I thought was a bunch of junk. He said that he had written it when he needed money and that he didn't want me to make a movie out of it. But finally he gave in.

While they continued their hunting expedition, Hawks and Hemingway discussed the project, and Hawks convinced Hemingway that the most screenworthy part of the book was the first section, which consisted essentially of the short story, "One Trip Across," in which Harry Morgan becomes enmeshed in smuggling some aliens out of Cuba during the revolution of the 1930s. To fill out the plot, the script would draw on later portions of the novel as well; but Hawks told Hemingway that he also wanted the screenplay to include some events that would have taken place before the beginning of the novel, such as Harry's meeting and falling in love with Marie, to whom he has already been married for several years at the point when the novel begins.

Jules Furthman did an initial draft of the screenplay, along the lines of the scenario Hawks had discussed with Hemingway. Furthman then went on to another project; and in February 1944 Faulkner began on the film. By this time Hawks had decided to update the setting of the film to wartime Martinique, a French island under the control of the Vichy government. According to Kawin, who edited the published script of *To Have and Have*

Not, it was Faulkner who came up with the idea that the story could be altered so that Harry Morgan would become involved in smuggling anti-Vichy Free French adherents of De Gaulle, instead of fugitives from revolution-torn Cuba. Because of the months Faulkner had spent writing *The De Gaulle Story,* he was already intimately familiar with the milieu of this revised storyline of *To Have and Have Not.* Hawks therefore gave Faulkner permission to rework Furthman's screenplay.

The switch in the story's setting enabled Hawks to have Faulkner model the role of Harry Morgan, to be played by Humphrey Bogart, after the part of Rick, which Bogart had played in Warner's recent success, *Casablanca*; in the later film the Bogart character would once again be aiding members of the Free French Resistance movement to escape the Nazis. Hawks obviously hoped that his film would repeat the success of its predecessor.

With all these substantial changes in the plot, the screenplay was getting farther and farther away from Furthman's first draft of the script. While the sets were being rebuilt to fit the movie's new locale, Faulkner had to work against time to get as much of the revised script as possible written before the start of principal photography. Once shooting had actually begun at the beginning of March, he found himself working out a scene only a couple of days before it was scheduled to go before the cameras. Faulkner wrote to Harold Ober in April that ever since Hawks had started shooting, "I have been trying to keep ahead of him with a day's script."[18]

At times Hawks would revise snatches of dialogue with the aid of the actors on the set; at other times Faulkner himself would take the freshly mimeographed pages of a scene that he was not satisfied with right to the sound stage and put the finishing touches on the dialogue in tandem with director and cast. Faulkner seems to have enjoyed these give-and-take sessions very much, for he later said that "the moving picture work which seemed best to me was done by the actors and the writer throwing the script away and inventing the scene in actual rehearsal just before the camera turned."[19]

While it is clear from examination of the final shooting script that Faulkner and the others hardly "threw the script away," it is also true that this kind of improvising yielded some memorable bits of dialogue. Some of the nifty lines that one hears spoken on the screen are not in the final shooting script of *To Have and Have Not* and therefore must have been invented on the set. For example, right after Morgan insists to his new girlfriend Marie (Lauren Bacall) that there are no strings attached to him since he does not make personal or political commitments of any sort, he hears that his sidekick Eddy (Walter Brennan) is in the hands of the Gestapo-like Vichy police. As he runs from Marie's hotel room to go to Eddy's aid, she calls after him, "Look out for those strings. . . . You're liable to trip and break your neck." This dandy payoff line does not appear in the final shooting script and is, incidentally, as close as the movie version of *To Have and Have Not* comes to expressing explicitly the conviction of Harry Morgan at the end of the novel that a man alone has no chance.

Another sample of the teamwork that characterized the working out of the screenplay of this movie involved the scene in which Bacall made movie history in this, her very first film, by telling Bogart that if he wanted anything, all he had to do was whistle: "You know how to whistle, don't you . . . ? You just put your lips together and blow." About this scene Hawks recalled: "I wrote that line as part of her screen test; and it went over so well that Jack Warner insisted that we find a place to put it into the picture. Faulkner decided to put it in while Bacall was standing at the doorway of Bogart's hotel room with no-one else around, so that the audience wouldn't miss the implication."

Although Faulkner sometimes wrote acceptable screen dialogue, as mentioned before, he occasionally got carried away and wrote a lengthy scene which would have been fine for a novel, but was much too "talky" for a film. Once he showed up on the set of *To Have and Have Not* with a six-page patriotic speech for Bogart to learn. The actor took one look at the material and ruefully inquired, "I'm supposed to say all that?" Hawks remembered that he intervened and assured Faulkner that the scene could be cut down to size without doing violence to its meaning.

Faulkner was the first to admit that Jules Furthman had a way of telegraphing a great deal to the audience with little or no dialogue at all. In Furthman's original draft of the screenplay which served as the basis for Faulkner's rewrite, he suggested the kind of woman that Marie was, and how Harry would react to her, by this silent interchange: Marie looks at Harry, asking him to light her cigarette. Harry "looks at her for a minute, sizes her up, then tosses her the matches to light her own cigarette."[20]

One of the most compelling aspects of the Faulkner screenplay for *To Have and Have Not* is the convincing manner in which it shows Harry's growing kinship with the members of De Gaulle's Free French Resistance movement whom he encounters in the course of the film. Despite the fact that in the past Harry has consistently refused to dedicate himself to any

Humphrey Bogart and Lauren Bacall confer with Howard Hawks on the set of *To Have and Have Not*, one of the five films directed by Hawks for which Faulkner received a screen credit as script coauthor. (Museum of Modern Art/Film Stills Archive)

cause, he eventually decides to help the Free French despite grave personal peril. He does so because his own stubborn sense of independence is outraged by the cruel tactics employed by the agents of the Vichy government in their ruthless pursuit of French Resistance fighters. When Frenchy (Marcel Dalio), one of the Resistance workers, asks Harry why he has finally agreed to help them, Harry answers laconically, "Because I like you and I don't like them." This neat bit of dialogue implies that, beneath Harry's tough exterior, there is some humanity that can be touched. Film historian Robin Wood goes so far as to say that, in its depiction of Harry's ultimate commitment to the Free French cause, *To Have and Have Not* "embodies one of the most basic anti-Fascist statements the cinema has given us."[21] One might add that had Faulkner's screenplay for *The De Gaulle Story* been filmed, it would have made a still stronger indictment of Fascism than his script for *To Have and Have Not*.

To Have and Have Not (1944) proved to be an engrossing, entertaining movie, whose screenplay deftly distilled the best elements of Hemingway's diffuse novel. Moreover, along with *The Big Sleep*, it represents the peak of Faulkner and Hawks's collaborative efforts.

The Big Sleep

Hawks made a young woman named Leigh Brackett Faulkner's partner on the script of *The Big Sleep* (1946), which also was to star Bogart and Bacall. He told Faulkner and Brackett to revise Raymond Chandler's tough detective story wherever necessary in order to provide the picture with plenty of action. "It won't be a great work of art," he told his writing team; "just keep it moving."[22] And so they did.

"It was basically an entertaining film, even though I could never figure out who killed who," Hawks recalled. "When I was asked who killed the man whose car is fished out of the river, I said, 'I don't know. I'll ask Faulkner.' But Faulkner didn't know either. So I asked Chandler."

The novelist, jokingly invoking the old cliché from stage melodrama, replied, "The butler did it."

"And I said, 'Like hell he did; he was down at the beach house at the time!' The picture was a success, so I never worried much about logic again. But I've always been concerned about the overall structure of a film, since the audience has to be able to follow that, whether or not some of the details get lost along the way."

Chandler himself once said about writing crime fiction, "When you are in doubt about what to do next, you open a door on a man with a gun in his hand."[23] Faulkner and Brackett relied on that solution to the plot complications of *The Big Sleep* more than once. They completed their first draft of the screenplay at the end of summer 1944 in a little over a week. Then they revised and expanded their work into a second draft, dated 26 October 1944, which was further revised by Faulkner and later on by Jules Furthman.

The script's violent action is balanced at times by a sardonic type of humorous dialogue which the editors of the published edition of the screenplay have praised for approximating "the clipped, understated, often ironic quality" of Chandler's own dialogue.[24] One of the conversations between the hero, detective Philip Marlowe (Bogart), and the heroine, Vivian Sternwood Rutledge (Bacall), is typical of this brand of repartee. In the course of a discussion ostensibly about horseracing, Marlowe quips that Mrs. Rutledge looks like a slow starter, and she responds in kind that it all depends on who is in the saddle. By this point in the conversation it is abundantly clear that they are no longer talking about horses or racing—if they ever were.

Although Faulkner was responsible for some of the film's witty dialogue, these lines, along with other bits of comic relief, were probably added after Faulkner had departed from the picture. (Pauline Kael reports that this particular dialogue was "inspired" by a similar interchange between Richard Arlen and Ethel Merman in a 1938 horseracing farce, *Straight, Place, and Show.*)

Faulkner's last contribution to *The Big Sleep* consisted of revisions he made in the final shooting script in mid-December, on his way back to Oxford by train for a break from film writing. In forwarding these additional pages to Warner's Story Department, he attached a humorous note, wryly thanking the studio for arranging for him to have a seat in the day coach rather than a berth in the sleeping car, because otherwise he might have wasted some time during the journey "in dull and profitless rest and sleep" and would not, therefore, have used the time to make the revisions in the screenplay which he was now sending on to the studio.[25]

At this point Hawks brought in Jules Furthman, primarily to streamline some of the later scenes in order to keep the finished film from being overlong. Since the industry censor had turned down the Faulkner-Brackett ending, Furthman also had to provide a different conclusion for the movie. In the original screenplay, Marlowe had knowingly allowed the villainess, Mrs. Rutledge's sister Carmen Sternwood (Martha Vickers)—a murderess, nymphomaniac, and drug addict—to walk into a trap and stop a bullet that was meant for him. The censor would not sanction the movie hero's taking the law into his own hands in this fashion, even to save his own life. In the Furthman conclusion, Carmen is taken to a sanitarium instead of going to her death, the "big sleep" of the title; and Marlowe still manages to survive and end up with Mrs. Rutledge, who is unattached.

It has been said that tough-minded crime novelists such as Raymond Chandler helped to popularize the thriller by taking murder out of the rose garden and dropping it into the alley. So Chandler was pleased that the film version of *The Big Sleep* preserved the cynical, hard-boiled flavor of his fiction. Chandler's sole regret about the movie was that the original ending of the script, about which he had been consulted, had not been used in the picture. "I don't know what happened to this scene," he said in a letter to his English publisher. "Perhaps the boys wouldn't write it or couldn't. Perhaps Mr. Bogart wouldn't play it. You never know in Hollywood. All I know is, it would have been a hairraising thing if well done. I think I'll try it myself some time." Interestingly enough, Chandler mentioned in the same letter that he was especially happy with the first half of the film—the portion that Hawks had Furthman leave pretty much as Faulkner and Brackett had written it.

The Big Sleep has often been lauded as the sort of expert crime melodrama that makes other conventional detective movies seem little more than "private eye-wash." But perhaps the greatest compliment ever paid the film came with the release of the 1978 remake. When the later version is measured against the 1946 film, said *Variety,* the earlier film takes on even greater stature than before. It is said that when Alfred Hitchcock was asked for his opinion of a remake of one of his films, he would respond with another question: "What remake? I only know one."[26] Hawks justifiably could have said the same thing about *The Big Sleep.*

The Southerner

The only other important film to which Faulkner made a noteworthy contribution during his term at Warner Brothers in the 1940s was not a Warner film at all, but a United Artists production, *The Southerner* (1945). Sometime in mid-1944, Faulkner agreed to help out on the script for the movie because of his esteem for the film's director, the distinguished French filmmaker Jean Renoir (*Grand Illusion*). Renoir was working in Hollywood for the duration of the war. Murry Falkner once wrote to Howard Hawks that there were only "two men in Hollywood of whom I heard my brother speak in frank and voluntary admiration." One was Hawks, and the other by all accounts was Renoir.

Renoir had initially collaborated on the screenplay with Nunnally Johnson, with whom Faulkner had worked at Fox. When Johnson had gone on to another film, Renoir invited Faulkner to write some additional scenes required for the script. The plot of *The Southerner* turns on the attempts of Sam Tucker, a young farmer (Zachary Scott), and his family stubbornly to survive on their small farm, in the face of crop failure and other tragic reversals. The film is narrated by Sam's good-humored, sympathetic friend

Tim (Charles Kemper). Such a story could have been drawn from Faulkner's own novels about the South, and he understandably was pleased to have the opportunity to deal with material so close to his heart.

One scene which Zachary Scott definitely remembers Faulkner writing into the script is the one in which Sam catches the legendary catfish Lead Pencil, a fish so large its whiskers looked as big as lead pencils. Minor triumphs like landing Lead Pencil, Faulkner implies, help to raise Sam's spirits and keep him going, despite the multiple adversities with which he must cope. Another scene, which Faulkner said he worked on, was the one in which Sam and his family gather around the fireplace in their wretched shack for the ritual of lighting the fire in the hearth. This sequence, in which the Tuckers implicitly reaffirm their sense of community, is central to the entire film, writes film scholar Hart Wegner. For it is while the group is assembled in the light and warmth of the glowing blaze that they truly "become a family, and the ramshackle, swaybacked shed a home."[27]

John Brady, in his book on screenwriters, expresses wonder that Faulkner received no recognition in the film's screen credits for writing these and other scenes for the film; after all, the French director could barely speak English and certainly needed all the help with the script that Faulkner could give him. Yet the reason Renoir did not officially acknowledge the service Faulkner rendered on the film is easily understood. Technically Faulkner was under contract to Warner Brothers at the time and hence could not receive a screen credit for contributing to a movie produced by another studio.

Faulkner later told Malcolm Cowley that *The Southerner*, which went on to win the Grand Prize at the 1946 Venice Film Festival, represented the best work he ever did on a movie script. Given his congeniality with the subject matter, he may have been right.

The Brooch (Television)

Faulkner wrote very little for television, but during the early 1950s he did adapt a bit of his short fiction, "The Brooch," for that medium. Telecast as a half-hour segment of *The Lux Video Theater* on 2 April 1953, the teledrama was coscripted by Faulkner, Ed Rice, and Richard McDonagh. Like the great majority of the more than five thousand live television productions of the period, *The Brooch* is not accessible for viewing, analysis, and comment. But, to judge by the critical reaction to the program at the time, the production was less than notable.

In Faulkner's short story, a young man allows his mother to dominate both himself and his new wife, who inevitably leaves him. Afterwards he realizes how dreadfully dependent he is on his domineering mother and in despair takes his own life. In *Watching TV,* television historians Harry Castleman and Walter J. Podrazik describe the teleplay. The hero was presented "as a nice kid who married the sweet young thing from next door. The mother tried to interfere in their lives, but the husband stood up to her; the mother gave in, and they all lived happily ever after."

In defending the limp ending of the teleplay, the show's producers explained that the television code then in force prohibited the presentation of suicide as the solution of a drama. But, according to Castleman and Podrazik, in truth an upbeat ending was grafted onto Faulkner's tragic short story to mollify the program's sponsor, who insisted that every teleplay in the series have the broadest possible popular appeal, in practice meaning that "depressing" subject matter was not welcome on the show.

In criticizing the teledrama, *New York Times* television critic Jack Gould singled out for attack not the show's sponsor but Faulkner and the producers of the series. Gould excoriated Faulkner and the producers for "what amounts to literary sleight-of-hand. The advance fanfare over *The Brooch* obviously was an attempt to capitalize on Mr. Faulkner's justly earned fame; yet what the audience saw was substitute merchandise not of the quality advertised," so bowdlerized was the original story in the course of its transfer to the tube.[28]

Faulkner's own attitude toward the television versions of his fiction was simple enough. "I may be obtuse," he wrote to his literary editor at Random House around this time, "but I doubt if what a TV screen shows is going to hurt what Random House prints in books, anymore than what movie screens have shown" had harmed the fiction he had written. Putting it another way, Faulkner's fellow novelist James M. Cain (*Mildred Pierce*) once said, "People tell me, don't you *care* what they've done to your book? I tell them, they haven't done anything to my book. It's right there on the shelf. They paid me and that's the end of it."[29]

In his column on *The Brooch,* Gould quotes Faulkner as saying that he would probably feel more at home in the television medium when he got to know more about it. But that remark sounds like a statement consciously tailored for a network press release. Actually Faulkner would never feel any more at home writing for television than he did writing for the movies; indeed, it would not be long before he relinquished active involvement in both media.

The Graduation Dress was the last television production on which his name appeared as a screenwriter. An original teleplay coscripted by Faulkner and Joan Williams in summer 1952, it was belatedly acquired by the producers of *The General Electric Theater* for presentation on that half-hour series in fall 1960. Faulkner regarded the teleplay, dashed off in a single afternoon, as a routine effort and declined to help the network publicize the broadcast. His final piece of writing for television was an unproduced scenario composed in spring 1953, an adaptation of the material entitled "Old Man" in his 1939 novel *The Wild Palms*. A television version of "Old Man" was in fact broadcast in 1958, but it was not derived from his scenario.

Land of the Pharaohs

The last theatrical feature for which Faulkner received a screen credit was Howard Hawks's film *Land of the Pharaohs* (1955), another Warner release. By the time Hawks asked Faulkner to work on the script for the picture in winter 1953–54, he had ceased going to Hollywood on a regular basis. He had at last achieved not only fame but fortune, and no longer had to take such employment. Nonetheless, he decided to answer Hawks's call; and when a friend inquired why, Faulkner is said to have replied, "Mr. Hawks has carried me in pictures. . . . Whenever I needed money, he was always good to me; and if he needs me now, I'm going." Faulkner was not surprised that Hawks had opted to do a movie about ancient Egypt, though the director had never made a historical epic of this sort before. *Land of the Pharaohs,* said Faulkner, "was the same picture Howard has been making for thirty-five years." Essentially it was no different from a Hawks western like *Red River* (1948): "The Pharaoh is the cattle baron, his jewels are the cattle, and the Nile is the Red River. But the thing about Howard is, he knows it's the same movie; and he knows how to make it."[30]

Hawks decided to invite Faulkner and his fellow screenwriter Harry Kurnitz to work on the screenplay in Europe before moving on to Egypt for location shooting. When Faulkner arrived in Paris to meet him, Hawks remembered, it was clear the former had had "a few drinks too many" en route. "He somehow fell down and got a little bloody. I woke up, and two great big gendarmes were bringing him into my hotel room," Hawks continued. The policemen personally delivered Faulkner to Hawks's hotel because he happened to be wearing in his lapel the emblem of the French Legion of Honor, which their government had conferred on him a few years before. "They dropped him and got the chair kind of bloody. I had to get someone to take care of him for a week or two; and then he came out of it and started to work. We had a lot of fun, and we had a good premise for the story" – to wit, the building of the Pyramids.

During a preliminary story conference, Faulkner conceded that he had no idea how a Pharaoh talked and asked Hawks, "Is it alright if I write him like a Kentucky colonel?"

Then Kurnitz said, "I can't do it like a Kentucky colonel; but I'm a student of Shakespeare. I think I could do it as though it were *King Lear.*"

Hawks replied to both of them, "You fellows go ahead, and I'll rewrite your stuff" if need be.

Faulkner liked working with Kurnitz, who was much more knowledgeable about the technical side of filmmaking than he was. For his part, Faulkner observed, "I just try to figure out what a character would be likely to do in a given situation." He saw himself as an artisan rather than a true artist in the business of screenwriting, which, he added, "bears about the same relation to my books as letter writing."[31]

Land of the Pharaohs ultimately emerged as one of the better sword-and-sandal sagas to come out of Hollywood, but it was not in a class with the previous Hawks films which Faulkner had collaborated on. Faulkner was sometimes asked if lending his talents to commercial subjects of this sort did not undermine his ability to write serious fiction. David Niven, in his memoirs about Hollywood, recalls how Faulkner would reply to such a question: "Nothing can injure a man's writing if he's a first-class writer. If he's not a first-class writer, there's not anything can help it much." According to Niven, Faulkner had no sympathy for the kind of writer who insists that he would do great work if he were free of Hollywood. "It's not the pictures that are at fault," Faulkner contended. "The writer is not accustomed to money. It goes to his head and destroys him – not pictures. Pictures are trying to pay for what they get."[32]

In Faulkner's case, his employers usually got what they paid for. All six of the films for which he was officially credited as coscriptwriter were successful movies. The same can be said for films like *Air Force* and *The*

Southerner, to which he made a smaller but still vital contribution. Albert Bezzerides, his friend and colleague at Warner Brothers, explained how, when Faulkner was called in to do some "script doctoring," the "Faulkner touch" could make a good screenplay better. Faulkner, Bezzerides said, could take a crucial scene that needed improvement and build it into a meaningful moment in the film which would continue to resonate in later scenes, thereby raising the level of the entire picture. In this manner, "a whole picture can be made in a few scenes."[33] One need only think of the captain's death scene in *Air Force* and the kindling of the hearth fire in *The Southerner* to see what he means.

Even though Faulkner personally thought his capacities as a screen-writer were somewhat limited, as a rule he diligently applied himself to the assignments he was given and did the best he could. "I believe I am doing good work for these people now," he wrote to Ober in late summer 1945, not too long before leaving for Oxford once more. Even when he had trouble making a script work, he went on, it was usually because he was saddled with a project, such as *The Adventures of Don Juan,* "at which several before me failed.[34]"

Looking back on Faulkner's Hollywood years, one finds that two of the films on which his name appears, *To Have and Have Not* and *The Big Sleep,* deserve to rank as screen classics; while two more, *Today We Live* and *The Road to Glory* are not far behind. Not a bad record for a writer who, some months after he had finished coscripting *Land of the Pharaohs,* refused Jerry Wald's offer to adapt for the screen two of his own novels, *The Hamlet* and *The Sound and the Fury,* with these words: "I have never learned how to write movies."[35] A decade before, Wald had found a notepad Faulkner had left behind in his desk at the studio after departing for Mississippi. On it were written, over and over again, phrases like, "Boy meets girl, boy loses girl, boy wins girl." This was obviously Faulkner's way of reiterating that, more often than not, he had found screenwriting a chore and probably always would. His response to Wald about adapting *The Hamlet* and *The Sound and the Fury* for film expressed the same feeling.

As he grew older, Faulkner became increasingly convinced that in the years left to him, he should devote himself to the writing of fiction, as that was what he did best. His fellow novelist and screenwriter, F. Scott Fitzgerald, once said about himself, "Never any luck with movies. . . . Stick to your last, boy."[36] Faulkner would have identified with those words.

Some Faulkner commentators have speculated that his years as a screenwriter directly affected his writing of fiction, pointing out that his narrative style seemed to reflect the influence of cutting and dissolving from scene to scene, something he learned as a film writer. On the contrary, Kawin has demonstrated fairly conclusively that Faulkner's fiction was no more cinematic in style and construction after he went to Hollywood than before. Not even *A Fable* manifests any special signs of being intentionally based on film techniques, in spite of the fact that this novel was initially conceived as a film scenario and was not finished until after Faulkner had completed his three principal sojourns in Hollywood. Long before Faulkner began writing for the movies, his narratives were crisply cut, like cinema montage; this was because, as Kawin puts it, he simply "was doing something that cinema also did."[37] There seems to be no cogent evidence that Faulkner deliberately thought in cinematic terms when he wrote fiction.

Since Faulkner's scriptwriting was largely concerned with adapting other writers' work for the movies, there was not much room for him to reflect his own personal vision in his screen work, except when he was working on material of his own invention, as in some of his early MGM scenarios. When adapting another author's work for film, however, Faulkner endeavored to be true to the thematic intent of his source, as when in the screenplay for *The Big Sleep,* he and his coscripter stuck as close to Raymond Chandler's grim, gritty tale of madness and murder as the censor would allow. In turning to the film versions of Faulkner's own fiction, we shall see to what extent movie writers and all the other artists involved in transferring one of his works onto film have created motion pictures worthy of his fiction.

PART TWO

The Films of Faulkner's Fiction

CHAPTER 3

Through a Glass Darkly:
The Story of Temple Drake (1933)
and *Sanctuary* (1961)

> The past is never dead. It's not even past.
> *William Faulkner*

> *For me, the past is forever.*
> *F. Scott Fitzgerald*

Faulkner's fellow Mississippian Tennessee Williams used to say that a writer's life is his work and his work is his life. Although this book does not purport to be a biography of William Faulkner, before going on to analyze his fiction and the films made from it, it is appropriate to take a brief look at the private world in which he grew up, in order to survey the experiences that helped to shape the outlook of the budding young artist.

Portrait of the Artist as a Young Man

William Cuthbert Faulkner was born on 25 September 1897, in New Albany, Mississippi, the oldest son of Murry Cuthbert Falkner and Maud Butler Falkner, and the great-grandson of Col. William Clark Falkner. It was Colonel Falkner, according to the novelist's brother Murry, who removed the "u" from the family name, "saying that, as often as a man had to sign his own name, it was folly to keep an extra letter in it that changed neither the look nor the pronunciation."[1] Besides, great-grandfather Falkner wanted to distinguish his clan from some disreputable people named Faulkner who lived nearby. But young William eventually put the "u" back in the family name; among his younger brothers, John and Dean followed his lead, but Murry "Jack" Falkner never did.

Colonel Falkner, who was legendary in the family annals for his valiant leadership of a volunteer cavalry regiment during the Civil War, embodied for his great-grandson William the chivalrous code of the gallant officers and gentlemen of the Old South; as such he was the prototype of Col. John Sartoris, the revered ancestor of the Sartoris twins who figure in both the novel *Flags in the Dust* and the screenplay *War Birds*. Although Colonel Falkner went into business after the Civil War, his avocation was writing, another thing about him that profoundly impressed young William. The colonel's output was not large, but it did include one bestseller, a romantic novel entitled *The White Rose of Memphis* (1880), which went through no less than thirty-five printings.

A year after William's birth, the family moved to Ripley, Mississippi, and then in 1902 to Oxford, thirty-five miles from William's birthplace. After operating a livery stable in Oxford for some years, his father became business manager of the University of Mississippi at Oxford. The Falkners' first home was on what is now South Eleventh Street; a few years later they moved to a house on what is now South Lamar Avenue, near the home of the Oldhams, whose daughter Estelle would later be William's high school sweetheart and eventually his wife.

William was a good student in grade school, even then manifesting a talent for storytelling. A classmate remembered that whenever a teacher asked each student to tell the rest of the class what they hoped to be when they grew up, Billy, as he was called then, would invariably reply when his turn came, "I want to be a writer like my great-grandaddy."[2] As Faulkner grew older, he began to take his formal studies less and less seriously. By the time he was in high school, he regularly slighted routine assignments in favor of reading books of his own choosing and developing his talents as a writer, especially by writing poetry. But no-one was ever able to inspire young Faulkner to improve his scholastic record, and he dropped out of Oxford High School in the eleventh grade. He did respond positively to the influence of Philip Stone, a college graduate four years his senior, who was going to be a lawyer. Phil Stone, on whom Faulkner would later model the character of lawyer Gavin Stevens in his fiction, was an urbane, intellectual man. He earned the adolescent Faulkner's lasting gratitude by being the first person of any consequence, besides Faulkner's mother, to take a serious interest in his literary ambitions.

Miss Maud, as Faulkner always called his mother, had told Phil Stone's mother about her own son's penchant for writing poetry; and when Phil, who had a lively interest in literature, heard about it, he decided to drop by and talk to Faulkner about his literary aspirations. In the course of their conversation, Stone looked over some of Faulkner's verses and was much impressed by what he saw. "Anybody could have seen that he had a real talent," Stone recalled afterwards, and he told Faulkner that. From then on, Stone staunchly encouraged Faulkner to develop his abilities as a writer, and the pair developed a lifelong friendship.

After Faulkner quit school, it became increasingly apparent that he was developing a serious drinking problem. He turned to liquor, Blotner observes, not only "to overcome his habitual shyness" at social gatherings but in many other circumstances as well; even at this early date, Faulkner already had begun to use alcohol to help him endure any situation he detested, "until he could escape it."[3] Like other men in the family, all the way back to Colonel Falkner himself, William Faulkner became a heavy drinker; as we know, this dependence on alcohol would last the rest of his life.

Throughout the time that Faulkner and Estelle Oldham were dating — that is, throughout their high school years and after — she continued to go out with other young men as well. Finally, in spring 1918, after much hesitation and indecision and with her parents' open encouragement, she made up her mind to break off her longstanding relationship with Faulkner and marry a promising young lawyer named Cornell Franklin. Estelle Oldham could hardly be blamed for turning down an unpromising suitor like Faulkner, an unpublished author who was hardly likely to prove a responsible husband and father. Faulkner was shattered at losing the woman he loved to someone with better prospects. Of course at the time no-one, least of all Faulkner himself, could have guessed that little more than a decade would elapse before Estelle and her first husband would drift apart; or that, after divorcing Cornell Franklin, she would finally marry William Faulkner on 20 June 1929. All of that was in the unforeseeable future. Given the way things were in the painful present, however, Phil Stone, who was studying law at Yale at the time of Estelle's marriage to Franklin, thought it a good idea to invite Faulkner up to New Haven for a visit.

Before leaving Oxford for New Haven, Faulkner had tried to join the aviation branch of the United States Signal Corps, but in spite of the desperate need for volunteers during World War I, which was then in progress, he had been rejected. At 5 feet, 5½ inches, Faulkner was not tall enough to meet the corps' specifications. Stone advised him to try the Canadian Royal Air Force, which might take him despite his lack of height. Faulkner accordingly went to New York City in summer 1918 to attempt to enlist in the Canadian RAF. Fearing that his real nationality would prove an obstacle to his joining the Canadian armed forces, he affected a bogus English accent for the occasion, in an effort to convince the recruiters that he was British-born. It was at this time too that he reinstated the "u" in his last name, hoping that this would make his surname appear British. In any event, he was accepted by the Canadian recruiters, who neither balked at his shortness nor made a serious issue of his nationality. Faulkner, as we know, subsequently retained the "u" in his family name when he began writing for publication. As John Faulkner has explained, his brother Bill believed that most people assumed that the family name was spelled with a "u" anyway, and it was easier for him to change than to expect everyone else to.

On 11 November 1918, while Faulkner was still in training, the war ended, and he was back in Oxford by December. Because he never saw any action overseas, Faulkner would later give to the Sartoris brothers, and the other World War I fighter pilots who figure in his fiction and film scenarios, the adventurous wartime experiences he was denied.

The television documentary on Faulkner's life and work scripted by A.I. Bezzerides succinctly covers the immediate postwar years of Faulkner's life in these words: "Even though he had not graduated from high school, he registered at the University of Mississippi under an exception granted discharged soldiers. He spent his time writing one-act plays, an occasional review, and pursuing his interest in drawing by making illustrations for college publications."[5] In addition, he tried his hand at short fiction. His first published story, "Landing in Luck," not surprisingly about a cadet in flight training, appeared in the campus newspaper, *The Mississippian*, on 26 November, 1919. But Faulkner's interest in college turned out to be just as shortlived as his interest in high school had been, and he dropped out of Ole Miss on 5 November 1920. Because he graduated from neither high school nor college, Faulkner would ever after refer to himself as the world's oldest sixth grader.

In 1921 Phil Stone was instrumental in obtaining for him a steady job as the university postmaster, but the aspiring author preferred reading and writing in the back room of the post office to sorting the mail. In the face of mounting complaints about his studied indifference to his job, Faulkner was finally relieved of his duties in fall 1924. Asked by a friend how he felt about his dismissal, Faulkner responded that he was fully aware that all his life he would probably have to defer to people who were better off than he was, but, he added, "I refuse to place myself at the beck and call of every son-of-a-bitch with the price of a two-cent stamp."[6]

In 1925 Faulkner moved to New Orleans and joined the literary circle there presided over by novelist Sherwood Anderson, who lived in the French Quarter. Faulkner later remembered how impressed he was by the lifestyle Anderson had established for himself as a professional writer. Anderson "would be in seclusion all forenoon—working. Then in the afternoon he would appear, and we would walk about the city talking. Then in the evening we would meet again, with a bottle now, and now he would really talk; . . . whereupon I said to myself, 'If this is what it takes to be a novelist, then that's the life for me.'"[7]

The Early Novels

During much of this six-month stay in New Orleans, Faulkner lived in a ground-floor apartment in Orleans Alley, a narrow little street off Jackson Square in the Quarter. It was there that he wrote for the feature section of *The Times-Picayune* some short fiction which constituted the first stories he ever sold for commercial publication. In July 1925, he set sail for Europe, where he settled for a time in Paris, temporarily becoming part of the colony of bohemian artists on the Left Bank. While in Paris, he continued working on his first novel, *Soldiers' Pay*, begun in New Orleans; it was published, largely through the auspices of Sherwood Anderson, on 25 February 1926, shortly after its author had returned to the United States.

Soldiers' Pay, which deals with a disabled veteran of the First World War, collected a respectable sheaf of notices; but Faulkner's second novel, *Mosquitoes* (1927), about the New Orleans literary scene of which he had been so much a part, was not as well received. Then it was that Faulkner remembered those long talks he had had with Anderson before his trip to Europe. Anderson had emphasized that, to be a good writer, one must never forget one's roots, the milieu in which one was born and raised. "You have to have somewhere to start from; then you begin to learn," Anderson told the neophyte novelist. "It don't matter where it was, just so you remember it and ain't ashamed of it. Because one place to start from is just as important as any other. You're a country boy; all you know is that little patch up there in Mississippi where you started from. But that's all right too."[8]

In Faulkner's next novel, *Flags in the Dust* (1929), he clearly set out to follow Anderson's advice; although the book focuses on the Sartoris clan in particular, the novel paints a panoramic picture of that part of the Deep South where Faulkner not only had spent his youth, but which he would call home for the rest of his life. Faulkner christened the mythical county in which this novel and most of his subsequent novels are set Yoknapatawpha, the old Chickasaw name for a river near Oxford; and he named its county seat Jefferson. It goes without saying that Jefferson, Mississippi, and the rest of the county very much resemble Oxford, Mississippi, and its environs. In writing *Flags in the Dust*, Faulkner populated Yoknapatawpha County, of which he proudly called himself the sole owner and proprietor, with a host of characters who would reappear in his fiction for the rest of his creative life. That novel, he later said, contained the germ of the other books he was to write about his apocryphal county, because he put "enough people in it" to keep him busy from then on, trying to write about them all. Indeed, even while he was composing the novel, he had a striking revelation: "I discovered that my own little postage stamp of native soil was worth writing about, and that I would never live long enough to exhaust it. . . . I created a cosmos of my own."[9]

Sanctuary: The Novel

Faulkner's next novel in the ongoing saga of Yoknapatawpha County, *The Sound and the Fury* (1929), which will be treated later, was a *succès d'estime.* *Sanctuary* (1931), on the other hand, was a *succès de scandale* which Faulkner later admitted he had deliberately composed in order to make a profit. His previous books had not sold well, and his financial resources were dwindling fast. He was growing weary of writing books that "got published but not bought," he confides in the introduction to the 1932 Modern Library edition of the novel; so, although he envisioned the book as a serious work of fiction, he "invented the most horrific tale" he could imagine in order to create a certain bestseller. But his publisher found the book so shocking that he was afraid to print it: "Good God, I can't publish this," he advised the author. "We'd both be in jail."[10] Discouraged by his publisher's negative reaction, Faulkner put the novel aside for the time being and went on to other projects. To his great surprise, in late autumn 1930 he received the galleys of *Sanctuary* from his publisher, who obviously no longer deemed it imprudent to market the book just as it was. When Faulkner read through the galleys, however, he was so thoroughly dissatisfied with the novel that, even though he had labored for months on its composition, he considered shelving it indefinitely. On second thought, he realized that he literally could not afford to do that, since by then his financial status was worse than ever. He would not get his first chance to augment his income by screen work until 1932.

He had married Estelle Oldham Franklin a year earlier and now had a wife and two stepchildren, Malcolm and Victoria, to support. Besides, he had recently bought an antebellum mansion on the outskirts of Oxford, which he named Rowan Oak after the tree of good luck in Scottish lore. There he would live for the rest of his life. The venerable mansion and its wooded grounds not only afforded Faulkner a secluded place to write but also, as Jack Cofield notes in his book on Faulkner, enabled him to create for himself and his family "the beginnings of a stately, graceful, Southern lifestyle," which, as a born-and-bred southerner, he saw as "his ideal way of living."[11] Still, the dilapidated old house was badly in need of extensive renovation, and hence would be a considerable drain on his finances for some time to come. Given his need for funds, Faulkner could not simply scrap *Sanctuary* and with it the hope of royalties. He consequently opted to revise the galleys substantially before returning them to the publisher.

Although *Sanctuary* is a deeply serious work of art, there are, to be sure, some "horrific" elements in the novel, founded mostly on conversations Faulkner had had during his occasional tours of some of Memphis's shadier nightspots. In one nightclub he met a young woman who told him all about a bootlegger named Neal "Popeye" Pumphrey. The young gangster, who was thought to be impotent, had allegedly raped a girl with his revolver or some other gruesome instrument, and then kept her for a period of time in a bordello. This grisly tale became the basis of the novel's central episode. Many readers of Faulkner's introduction to the book have assumed that his revisions of the original version of the novel, which critic Michael Millgate has tagged the *Ur-Sanctuary*, were aimed solely at toning down the more lurid details of the story which had initially upset his publisher. On the contrary, in reworking the novel at the galley stage, Faulkner made little effort to modify the unsparing picture of the underside of human existence which the book presents. As we shall see, he revised the novel because he thought the original version was artistically flawed, not because it was immoral.

The fundamental storyline is essentially the same in both versions of the novel. Temple Drake, a frivolous, flirtatious female college student, is escorted by her beau, Gowan Stevens, to a dance; as the evening wears on, Gowan gets drunk. In search of more liquor, Gowan takes Temple with him after the dance to the Old Frenchman's place, a ramshackle country house that has served as a haven for bootleggers since the advent of Prohibition. The drunken Gowan wrecks his car en route, but he and Temple make it to the house all the same. Later on the cowardly Gowan sneaks back to town without Temple, leaving her stranded with the inhabitants of the Old Frenchman's place: Lee Goodwin, who runs the place; his common-law wife Ruby and their infant; Tommy, a mentally retarded handy man; Popeye Vitelli, a racketeer; and a couple of other hoodlums.

Temple beds down in one of the rooms in the house for the night; but Ruby, fearing what may happen to her at the hands of one of the lecherous mobsters, sequesters her in the barn, where the girl is guarded throughout the night by Tommy. Temple is safe till morning, when Popeye gains entrance to the corn crib in which Temple is hiding. Popeye shoots Tommy when the latter tries to interfere; and, because he is impotent, Popeye rapes Temple with a corn cob. Afterward Popeye takes the unresisting Temple with him to Miss Reba's whorehouse in Memphis, where he hangs out whenever he is in town. He then provides Temple with a companion known as Alabama Red, so that he can derive vicarious pleasure from watching them together. Temple stays on at the brothel for a time because of her morbid fascination with Popeye's perverse world. This strange *ménage à trois* is destroyed, however, when Popeye discovers that Red has "cheated" on their arrangement by seeing Temple privately, and kills him.

Meanwhile, Lee Goodwin is accused of Tommy's murder; and a well-meaning but inept lawyer named Horace Benbow, whom Faulkner had introduced in *Flags in the Dust*, agrees to defend him. Goodwin, terrified of savage reprisals by the ruthless Popeye, will not even admit that the mobster was present when Tommy was shot, much less that Popeye did the deed. Horace eventually tracks Temple down at Miss Reba's; but Temple ultimately refuses to testify for the defense that it was not Lee but Popeye who not only murdered Tommy but violated her as well. Temple fears the scandal that will result if all of the facts of the case, including the unspeakable nature of her continued association with her rapist, should be revealed in open court. She consequently appears as a witness, not for the defense but for the prosecution, and crassly perjures herself by swearing that Lee Goodwin is guilty as charged. She in no way implicates Popeye in either Tommy's murder or her rape, and cryptically suggests that she spent the weeks since her disappearance from Jefferson in seclusion in Memphis, while she was awaiting the day of her court appearance. After the trial Lee Goodwin is lynched by an angry mob before his death sentence can be carried out. Nevertheless, Temple goes on playing the injured innocent, despite the cruel injustice she has visited upon Goodwin by her perjured testimony, and goes off to Europe with her father for a rest. As for Popeye, after getting away with the murders of both Tommy and Red, he is, ironically enough, executed for a killing he did not commit.

Perhaps the most crucial flaw that Faulkner identified when he examined the galleys of *Sanctuary* centered on his extended treatment of the character of Horace Benbow. In the novel's original form, a considerable amount of space was devoted not just to Horace's attempts to defend his client, but also to his attempts to cope with his private emotional conflicts, which by turns involve his invalid mother; his selfish, manipulative sister; his coarse, domineering wife; and his spoiled, defiant stepdaughter. It was not entirely clear whether Horace or Temple was supposed to be the principal protagonist of the *Ur-Sanctuary*, since the story focuses a great deal of attention on both characters.

In his revisions of the galleys, Faulkner cleared up this confusion by somewhat reducing Horace's role in the action, especially where the portrayal of his personal problems with his family was concerned. As Noel Polk writes in his afterword to the published edition of the original text, Horace's relationships with his relatives were dealt with "much more specifically and at considerably greater length" in the first version of *Sanctuary* than in the second.[12] In other words, the primary result of Faulkner's reworking of the galleys of *Sanctuary* was, as Malcolm Cowley puts it, that the published novel became truly what the title of the first movie adaptation of the book said it was: *The Story of Temple Drake*.

If Faulkner felt that Horace Benbow had played too large a part in the original text of the novel, he also believed that he had not devoted enough space in the *Ur-Sanctuary* to one of the novel's other main characters, the villain Popeye. At the galley stage, therefore, Faulkner gave greater depth and dimension to his characterization of Popeye. For example, he inserted into the revised text a flashback delineating Popeye's grim formative years, which started him on the road to becoming the sadistic, depraved criminal he eventually turned out to be. In this way Faulkner helps the reader better comprehend one of the most diabolical figures he ever depicted.

In sum, the conscientious care with which Faulkner revised *Sanctuary* at the galley stage suggests that he regarded the novel as a literary work of some substance, and not merely as a book designed to make a fast buck. In fact, it actually cost him money, in terms of extra typesetting fees, to revise his work so extensively in galleys, because the text had already been set in type. As he said, "I had to pay for the privilege of rewriting it." But his reworking of the novel was surely worthwhile in the long run, because in retrospect he believed that, after all was said and done, he had done "a fair job" of improving the book.[13] Indeed, a quarter of a century later he said that, in revising the novel, "I did everything possible to make it as honest and as moving and to have as much significance as I could put into it." There is no doubt that *Sanctuary* is the better for Faulkner's eleventh-hour revisions.

Sanctuary, as noted before, is a superficially sensationalistic tale which nevertheless has thought-provoking implications. Faulkner once explained that in writing the novel he felt compelled to present "an exposition of the terror and injustice which man must face, and which he must combat if he is to live with himself, in his soul; if he is to sleep in peace at night." The title of the book means that "everyone must have some safe, secure place to which he can hurry, run, from trouble."[14] The irony of the title in Temple's case is, of course, obvious, and is further underlined by her first name; for she is a desecrated temple who finds her "sanctuary" in a Memphis sporting house. Critic Dorothy Tuck fittingly comments that in a world where there is no justice, there can be no true sanctuary.

When *Sanctuary* was published on 9 February 1931, many critics and most readers missed these deeper implications of the story, and the novel achieved something of a notorious reputation in literary circles. Even Faulkner's own father disapproved of the book. "*Sanctuary*, even though it made Bill money and brought him recognition, distressed Dad a great deal," John Faulkner remembered. Miss Maud apparently better than his father understood the dark vision of a cruel and unjust world her son had been moved to depict in *Sanctuary*. "Mother said, 'Let him alone. . . . He writes what he has to.'"[15]

The Story of Temple Drake: The Film

Because of the book's popularity, Paramount Pictures purchased the screen rights to *Sanctuary* for $6,000 in spring 1932. Protests from women's clubs were being registered across the land, and the studio was almost immediately subjected to press attacks urging that the production be abandoned in view of the novel's notoriety. After the picture was completed, the outcry continued; in fact, the president of Paramount was even urged to burn the negative of the finished film in order to keep the movie from ever being exhibited. William K. Everson points out that when the film was eventually released in May 1933 (a month after *Today We Live*), it gained the dubious distinction of being one of the last straws "that almost single-handedly brought the crackdown" by the administration of the Motion Picture Production Code which resulted in the filming of all of those family classics of the later 1930s, such as *David Copperfield* and *Pride and Prejudice.*[16] This seems somewhat surprising today, not only because of the permissiveness of the contemporary screen but also because the film was given the mild title of *The Story of Temple Drake* in order to dissociate it from the novel, and because the sexual abnormalities on which its reputation was largely based were kept out of the screenplay. Yet the film still effectively captures much of the horror and suspense of the original story; and to that extent it is true to Faulkner's novel.

Even though Faulkner had no part in the composition of the script, more than one commentator on the film has erroneously stated that he did collaborate on the screenplay of *Temple Drake;* probably the confusion results from the fact that he worked on the film adaptation of his story "Turn About" as *Today We Live* at MGM at about the same time that the *Sanctuary* adaptation was being done at Paramount. Frederick Hoffman compounds the muddle by asserting in his critical study of Faulkner that, during the novelist's first visit to Hollywood, he adapted *Sanctuary* "for Joan Crawford in a film called *The Story of Temple Drake.*"[17] Crawford, of course, starred in *Today We Live*; it was Miriam Hopkins who played the title role in *Temple Drake.*

The first film adaptation of *Sanctuary* is a model of compression: in seventy-one minutes of screen time, director Stephen Roberts (*The Man Who Broke the Bank at Monte Carlo*) manages to tell the basic story of the novel, complete with an ending manufactured to be acceptable to the Production Code. The screenplay by Oliver Garrett is particularly adept at giving

Cinematographer Karl Struss, director Stephen Roberts, Jack La Rue (Trigger), and Miriam Hopkins (Temple Drake) on the set of *The Story of Temple Drake* (1933), based on *Sanctuary*. The film's frank storyline almost single-handedly brought about a tightening of censorship regulations in Hollywood. (Movie Star News)

thumbnail sketches of characters establishing their personalities. The open-ing courtroom scene depicts Stephen Benbow (William Gargan) as a lawyer of tenacity and resourcefulness, thus providing the film with the kind of impressive hero that Horace Benbow, his counterpart in the book, never musters sufficient courage to become. In passing sentence on Stephen's cli-ent at the end of a trial, the judge remarks that Benbow should not be crit-icized for defending such a disreputable man as his client, since he was called upon by the court to do so. Stephen objects to this, saying that he took the case precisely because he wanted to see to it that the defendant got a fair hearing. After court is adjourned, Stephen happens to meet Judge Drake (Sir Guy Standing), who tells the admirable young attorney that he wishes that his granddaughter Temple would become interested in some-one like him. Stephen replies that he has tried unsuccessfully to win Tem-ple's affections. This scene in the film establishes Stephen's love for Temple, whereas in the novel Horace Benbow has no serious romantic aspirations where Temple is concerned. That Stephen Benbow does will be important later in the movie.

In *The Story of Temple Drake*, Judge Drake – not the judge presiding in the trial – is Temple's grandfather instead of her father, possibly to emphasize that he is ineffectual in his efforts to control Temple's behavior. Roberts, for example, begins the next scene with a closeup of a grandfather clock showing the late hour. Then the camera pans to the front door, which is slightly ajar; on the other side of it we hear Temple flirting with a beau. Her hand coyly curls around the inside doorknob, and finally she comes inside and closes the door. The judge confronts Temple on the stairs and warns her about her late hours, but she is able to charm him in a fashion similar to that just used with the lad at the door. As Temple goes upstairs to bed, the camera stays behind on the staircase and holds momentarily on the portrait of one of the Drakes' female ancestors, who is wearing a frown that seems to imply her disapproval of Temple's behavior.

That note of disapproval is elaborated in a series of brief scenes in which various people who know Temple comment on her coquettish ways. One of the most notable of these vignettes shows Judge Drake's housekeeper ex-amining a torn piece of Temple's lingerie as she quips, "If Judge Drake did the laundry, he'd know more about Miss Temple." Another scene depicts Stephen's Aunt Jenny (Elizabeth Patterson) ruefully telling her nephew that Temple has a wild streak that may soon get her into trouble. Aunt Jenny's remarks about Temple's wild streak are echoed in the next scene, which shows Stephen reading a bawdy verse about Temple scrawled on a men's room wall, before he erases it in disgust and disbelief: "Temple Drake is just a fake. She wants to eat and have her cake." This scene is pointedly intercut with one in which Temple is leading on Toddy Gowan (Gowan Stevens in the novel) as they neck in his car.

Later on, after they have arrived at the Old Frenchman's place, Temple's penchant for flirting with trouble finally does lead to disaster, just as Aunt Jenny had warned it might. The sequence of events at the Frenchman's place develops much as it does in the book. When Toddy Gowan leaves Temple in the lurch, Ruby (Florence Eldridge) puts her to bed and turns off the light, wondering if she will be safe till morning. Trigger (the novel's Popeye, played by Jack La Rue) enters the room smoking a cigarette and shuts the door. In the darkness only the pinpoint glow of his cigarette, as it moves across the room in the direction of Temple's bed, is needed to suggest what he is up to, since there is no indication whatever in the film that Trigger is impotent. But the canny Ruby puts on a lamp, diverting the startled Trigger from his purpose; she then takes Temple to the barn where Tommy can guard her.

The next morning Tommy, still playing sentinel, assures Temple that she has nothing to worry about. Behind him in the background, however, the viewer can make out the figure of Trigger climbing a ladder to the loft above them. When he lets himself down into the stall where Temple is hiding, Tommy tries to bar his way, and Trigger shoots him dead. As Trigger advances toward the camera, we hear Temple scream and the screen goes black. All in all, this is a very effective way of staging the film's crucial rape scene, with Roberts and his cameraman, Karl Struss, managing, in Everson's phrase, to "suggest everything while showing nothing."

As a matter of fact, Roberts had originally planned to portray the rape scene somewhat more directly. Assistant producer Jean Negulesco, later a director himself (*Johnny Belinda*), made some preliminary sketches which showed, he recalls, "how the scene could be managed so as to pass the censors: it was suggested with hands, fingers, and so on."[18] But this depiction of the rape scene apparently did not receive the approval of the industry censor after all, since the scene as filmed ends with a blackout before the assault takes place.

Because in the film Trigger is not impotent, it is with him and not Alabama Red that Temple carries on an affair during her extended sojourn at Miss Reba's bordello in Memphis. After Temple has been away from Jefferson for a while, an article appears in the local newspaper stating that Miss Temple Drake is visiting friends in Philadelphia. Another succession of short scenes, similar to the group earlier in the movie, indicates how the spurious newspaper piece simply furnishes more fodder for the gossip-hungry townspeople. One of these vignettes constitutes a telling satirical comment on the gossipy townsfolk: an elderly woman mindlessly prattles on the telephone about Temple while stroking a cat, which finally sneers at its mistress with a sardonic meow.

After Stephen fails to get Lee Goodwin (Irving Pichel) to divulge the true facts about Tommy's death, Ruby herself informs Stephen where Temple can be found, so that Temple can exonerate Lee. This is a nifty simplification of the complicated circumstances in the book; there Horace learns of Temple's whereabouts by the desperate expedient of bribing a state senator to reveal that he has himself seen Temple at Miss Reba's.

Since the movie dispenses with Red and with his murder by Popeye, Roberts is able to wrap up the plot of the novel from this point onward with great dispatch. When Stephen visits Temple at Miss Reba's in the movie, she refuses to agree to testify for Lee Goodwin, not only because she fears for her own reputation, but also because she is afraid that the jealous Trigger will suspect that Stephen is in love with her and kill him. Her genuine concern for Stephen is the first glimmer we have that the film's Temple is going to turn out to be a better woman than the novel's Temple. Her conversation with Stephen has enabled her to see Trigger for what he is; and after Stephen departs, she tells the gangster that she is leaving him. They quarrel, and Trigger brutally strikes her while vowing that he will never let her go. She snatches his gun from the bed and fires. The scene concludes with a closeup of his hand crushing out a cigarette in an ashtray and then going limp in death.

We now witness in the film the moral regeneration of Temple Drake that anticipates Faulkner's sequel to *Sanctuary, Requiem for a Nun*. Before Temple goes into court to testify at Lee Goodwin's trial, she begs Stephen not to make her reveal the truth about what she has done. Stephen counters sympathetically but firmly, "It's our duty before God. Here's the chance for you to destroy that evil streak in you forever." In a supremely ironic moment, the judge says to Stephen, as Temple takes the stand, "It isn't necessary to establish the character of the witness. It hasn't been questioned, and I assume that it won't be."

Stephen makes a desperate effort to inspire Temple to speak the truth willingly by recalling the traditions of her family: "Your father died serving his country in the World War. You are proud of your family—their courage, willingness to sacrifice, their love of truth. You're a Drake. Will you tell us where you were. . . . " Stephen's voice trails off into silence, and he excuses the witness. Because of his love for Temple, he cannot bring himself to put her through the ordeal that faces her, and excuses her from testifying. There is a suspenseful moment of hesitation after Temple leaves the stand, and then she blurts out that she wants to tell everything. And so she does. "I went to the city with Trigger and stayed with him until this week," she admits at one point. "As a prisoner," the judge suggests. When Temple does not answer, there is a closeup of Judge Drake, who is sitting in the courtroom, averting his eyes in shame. After she admits shooting Trigger, Temple faints; and Stephen carries her from the courtroom, saying to her grandfather, "Be proud of her, Judge. I am."

In the final analysis, Stephen Roberts, whose promising career as a director was cut short by his untimely death three years after the release of *Temple Drake*, deserves no little credit for bringing *The Story of Temple Drake* into line with the Motion Picture Production Code while at the same time endeavoring to remain faithful to the novel. Still, some reviewers complained that the film condoned Temple's killing of Trigger, even though, as one film historian notes, "this one was as condonable a murder as ever was."[19]

Requiem for a Nun: **The Novel**

The Story of Temple Drake ends with the redemption of Temple Drake that Faulkner himself did not bring about until he wrote *Requiem for a Nun*, published in 1951, twenty years after the appearance of *Sanctuary*. As we shall see, Twentieth Century–Fox produced a film version of *Sanctuary* in 1961, in which the plot of *Sanctuary* and its sequel were woven together into a single story, allowing Temple's regeneration to develop as Faulkner himself envisioned it.

Faulkner took the title *Requiem for a Nun* from a short story which he began writing in December 1933 but never finished. The "nun" of the novel's title, Nancy Manningoe, was a black woman who first appeared in Faulkner's 1931 short story, "That Evening Sun." Although in that story Nancy was a prostitute and dope addict, in *Requiem* she would be presented as a God-fearing woman living a reformed life. The attorney who plays an important role in the novel is Gowan Stevens's uncle, Gavin Stevens, a character whom Faulkner had been using in his short fiction since the early thirties. Gavin Stevens was most likely based on Faulkner's lawyer friend Phil Stone; as Carl Singleton observes in his thesis on Faulkner, both Phil Stone and Gavin Stevens attended Ivy League colleges, had an affinity for classical literature, and were incurably loquacious, after the stereotype of small-town lawyers. (Critic Irving Howe has called Gavin Stevens the biggest windbag in modern American literature.)

In brief, the cast of characters of *Requiem,* headed by Temple Drake, Nancy Manningoe, and Gavin Stevens, clearly demonstrates Faulkner's penchant for summoning characters he had employed before in his fiction to take part in later works. "These people I figure belong to me," he once explained, "and I have the right to move them about in time when I need them." Faulkner elected to carry Temple's story farther than he had in *Sanctuary,* because he wondered what her future might have been if Gowan Stevens were to marry her as his way of demonstrating to the gentry of Jefferson his willingness to make up for his shabby conduct in deserting her at the Old Frenchman's place. "What could a marriage come to," Faulkner asked himself, "that was founded on the vanity of a weak man?"

Although he considered *Requiem* a novel, Faulkner decided to cast the central action of the plot in the form of a three-act play, because he felt that the interaction of the principal characters "fell into the hard, simple give-and-take of dialogue."[20] Each of the acts, however, was to be introduced by what he termed a narrative "preamble." These prefaces were designed to place Temple's story against the backdrop of the legendary history of Yoknapatawpha County by recalling the days when the southern aristocracy still adhered to a chivalric code of conduct, to which succeeding generations have increasingly paid only lip service. This code of the Old Order, epitomized for Faulkner by his great-grandfather, glorified qualities of honor and integrity which too often seem utterly lacking in modern descendants of the old southern clans. By juxtaposing the past (the prefaces) with the present (the acts of the play), then, Faulkner was able to document the moral decline of the southern aristocracy from the antebellum period down to modern times. That decline reaches its nadir in people such as Temple Drake.

Because of its alternating sections of narration and drama, Faulkner described *Requiem for a Nun* as a three-act play whose plot unfolds "inside a novel," that is, within the context of the narrative introductions.[21] Each of the three prose overtures focuses on an edifice associated with the preservation of law and order in civilized society: courthouse, state house, and jail. These structures also provide the main settings for the dramatic action of the novel.

The story of Temple Drake, as continued in *Requiem for a Nun*, takes place in the late 1930s, about eight years after the events chronicled in *Sanctuary*. As the story opens, Nancy Manningoe, who after abandoning a life of vice served as Temple's housekeeper, has been convicted of smothering to death Temple's six-month-old daughter. Gowan's uncle, Gavin Stevens, the county attorney, had served as Nancy's defense lawyer, even though the murder victim was his own nephew's child. Shortly before Nancy's death sentence is to be carried out, Temple asks Gavin to appeal the verdict, on the grounds that Temple now admits she willfully withheld evidence at Nancy's trial. The lawyer in turn persuades Temple to drive with him to Jackson to see the governor about obtaining a pardon for Nancy. Unknown to Temple, Gavin has arranged to have Gowan secretly overhear his wife's story as she recounts it to the governor, since Temple up to now has refused to level even with her husband about the real facts of the case.

Temple confesses that a thug named Pete, the brother of her deceased lover Alabama Red, had contacted her with a view to blackmailing her, based on her relationship with Red. Temple and Pete were soon engaged in a clandestine affair, which culminated in Temple's decision to run away with Pete. As a matter of fact, on the night of her infant daughter's death, Temple was preparing to leave town with this hoodlum. Temple had planned to take her baby with her and to leave her four-year-old son behind with his father; but Nancy smothered the infant with a pillow in order to keep Temple from exposing the innocent and helpless child to the debased and perilous underworld existence that her mother would be bound to lead with the vile hoodlum Pete. As Nancy saw it, if she could not keep Temple herself from surrendering once more to evil, and could not convince Temple not to take her little daughter with her, then the infant was better off dead.

After hearing Temple's story, the governor refuses to pardon Nancy. He realizes that since Nancy has known all along that taking the life of the child would cost her her own life, she is fully prepared to carry through her sacrifice to the end. As Faulkner himself has commented, "She was capable within her poor dim lights and reasons of an act which, whether it was right or wrong, was of complete, almost religious abnegation of the world for the sake of an innocent child. It was paradoxical the use of the word *nun* for her, but to me that added something to her tragedy."[22]

In confessing before the governor her own responsibility for the things that have happened, Temple Drake for the first time has earned the right to be known as Mrs. Gowan Stevens, i.e., as an authentic wife and mother. She is no longer living a lie, and is now ready to begin building a new life with her husband, who is willing to take her back despite the fact that he now knows every detail of her ghastly past. As Gavin tells Temple, "the past is never dead. It's not even past" until it has been confronted and dealt with, as Temple has been compelled to do in the course of the story. "You—everyone—must . . . pay for your past."[23] Temple at last seems to have paid for hers.

In *Requiem for a Nun* Faulkner strikingly illuminates a theme that one often finds reflected in his fiction: only through suffering and self-sacrifice can one attain redemption. In the present instance, both Temple and Nancy rise above sinful pasts by suffering. This theme is perhaps best enunciated in *Requiem* toward the end of the drama, when Temple visits Nancy in the death cell. Nancy expresses to Temple her firm belief that God "don't tell you not to sin, He just asks you not to. And He don't tell you to suffer. But He gives you the chance." Nancy then goes on to explain to Temple that He is a forgiving God and wants to save Temple; Temple responds that while she would like to believe that such a compassionate God exists, she has her doubts. Nancy assures her that He does, but adds that on earth we can only know Him by the light of faith; she voices her fervent hope that Temple's faith in Him will grow stronger. In Tennyson's words: "We have but faith: we cannot know. . . . A beam in darkness: let it grow." In essence, Nancy urges Temple to place her trust in God "and He will save you." On this strong note of Christian affirmation, *Requiem for a Nun* comes to a close.

When *Requiem for a Nun* was published on 27 September 1951, not a few book reviewers wondered if the three-act play contained in the book could be effectively transferred to the stage. Both Faulkner and his long-time friend, actress Ruth Ford, believed that it could. Ford, who had dated Faulkner's youngest brother Dean in the early 1930s, had gotten to know the novelist when they were both working at Warner Brothers in the mid-1940s. At that time Ford had encouraged Faulkner to write a play for her, and he composed the three-act drama that is the heart of *Requiem* with a view to later adapting it for stage presentation specifically as a vehicle for

Ford. Faulkner made a couple of discouraging attempts at revising *Requiem* for the theater but finally decided that he was not enough of a playwright to do the job properly. So he eventually turned the task over to Ford, who willingly accepted it.

Requiem for a Nun: The Play

In order to make *Requiem* more viable as a stage work, Ford revised the text of the drama in various minor ways, such as judiciously condensing some of the longer passages of expository dialogue, so that a theater audience could more easily follow them. When this acting version of *Requiem* was eventually published in 1959, Faulkner appended an explanatory note in which he graciously said that *Requiem* truly became a play "only after Ruth Ford saw it as a play and believed that only she could do it right." What she brings to it, "to make it a better play, is Ruth Ford."[24]

Efforts to mount a production of the drama failed in America but succeeded abroad. *Requiem* opened in London at the Royal Court Theater on 26 November 1957, in a production staged by Tony Richardson and starring Ford as Temple Drake and her husband, Zachary Scott (*The Southerner*), as Gavin Stevens. By then the play had already been produced in other European countries. It was especially successful in Paris, in a translation by Faulkner's fellow Nobel Prize laureate, Albert Camus. The British production garnered fairly enthusiastic notices and played to packed houses for the whole of its one-month limited engagement in London. When the production premiered on Broadway on 30 January 1959 with the same director and stars, however, the New York reviews were less favorable than the London ones had been. The majority of the American critics complained that Faulkner's drama, even in Ford's revised version, still had too much talk and too little action. The Broadway production was by no means a sellout, closing after forty-three performances. The disappointing New York notices caused no little consternation at Twentieth Century–Fox, since the studio, presumably on the strength of the play's reception in London, had bought the film rights for *Requiem* before it opened in New York.

Nevertheless, Fox, which had also purchased the screen rights to *Sanctuary* from Paramount, went ahead with plans to make a film that would blend the two works together into a single motion picture under the overall title of *Sanctuary*. Faulkner personally received $81,000 as his share of the total amount Fox paid for the rights to the two works – the most money that he ever obtained from the sale of his work to the movies. *Sanctuary* was to be directed by Tony Richardson, a particularly felicitous choice given the fact that he had twice directed *Requiem* on the stage.

Sanctuary: The Film

It was producer Richard Zanuck – the son of Darryl Zanuck, for whom Faulkner had worked at Fox in the 1930s – who conceived the idea of making *Sanctuary* and its sequel into a single movie. Having first secured the rights to *Requiem for a Nun,* he decided that, since the New York critics had found the play static and wordy, it would be a good idea to include material from *Sanctuary* in the screenplay of the film as well, since the earlier book contained several action-filled sequences that would work well on the screen. Besides, Zanuck reasoned that the finished film's box office potential would be significantly increased by identifying the movie with *Sanctuary,* one of Faulkner's most popular novels.

"We wanted very much to talk to Mr. Faulkner," Zanuck told an interviewer at the time. "But we could never get to him." As a matter of fact, the studio representatives whom the producer dispatched to Mississippi to confer with the novelist about the script completely failed to locate him. "From what I understand," Zanuck commented, "Mr. Faulkner does his best to avoid Hollywood."[25] Zanuck was correct in his assumption that, at this point in his career, Faulkner no longer cared to have any professional association with the film industry, even when it involved the adaptation of his own work to the screen. Faulkner, as we have seen, gave up writing for motion pictures altogether after *Land of the Pharaohs* (1955), because by the mid 1950s his income from his publications and from movie sales of his work made it no longer necessary for him to engage in screen work. Indeed, from that time onward, he preferred to sell his work to Hollywood outright and to have nothing whatever to do with the preparation of the screenplay for a given film, even in an advisory capacity.

In scripting Fox's widescreen version of *Sanctuary* (1961) James Poe ingeniously merged the original plots of *Sanctuary* and *Requiem for a Nun* into a continuous narrative that smoothly elides incidents from the two books in a most inventive fashion. Both the murder of Tommy, called Dog Boy in this film, and the subsequent trial of Lee Goodwin for the crime drop out of the plot entirely, so that the trial of Nancy for killing Temple's baby serves as the focal point of the action of the entire film. Hence the movie opens with a pre-credit sequence that depicts Nancy (Odetta) being sentenced to the gallows for murder and muttering her prayerful response to the verdict, "Thy will be done. Thank you, Lord."

Gavin Stevens is called Ira Stevens in the film, probably to avoid the confusion of his name with that of his nephew Gowan. In the film's first scene following the credits, Ira (Harry Townes) visits Temple (Lee Remick) after the trial and informs her that he knows that a man was with her on the night of her baby's death, and that she can still help Nancy if she will tell the truth about the events of that night. After Ira leaves the house, Temple gazes on the empty crib in the nursery for a moment and then tells Gowan (Bradford Dillman), to his amazement, that she wants to save Nancy. She arranges with Ira to go to the home of the governor (Howard St. John), who in the film happens to be Temple's father, possibly to explain her easy access to a man in his position. Her father agrees to hear her out.

As Temple recalls, voice-over on the sound track, that fateful night eight years before when she was going to the dance with Gowan, we see a younger Temple standing in the doorway of the living room in which her older self had just begun recounting the story. She bids goodnight to her father and goes off to the dance with Gowan. Afterwards they move on to the Old Frenchman's place, where they meet Dog Boy (Strother Martin) and some of the bootlegging gang. In the present film Nancy replaces the Ruby character of the novel *Sanctuary* and the film *The Story of Temple Drake* as the woman who seeks to shield Temple from the gangsters at the Frenchman's place. At this point the film ominously foreshadows Nancy's later motivation for slaying Temple's baby, by having Nancy refer to her own infant, lying in a crib in the kitchen: "He's sick," she muses, "been sick all his life—ain't no place to raise a child up." Such a depraved atmosphere, she feels, can only stunt an infant's development; some eight years later she will take steps to see that Temple's child is not exposed to the same sort of environment.

Popeye, in this movie called Candy Man, is played by Yves Montand, whose native French accent is explained in the film by making Candy a Cajun from New Orleans. His name, Faulkner critic Pauline Degenfelder notes, suggests the dual underworld meaning of candy: "whiskey," indicating that he is a bootlegger, and "desire," implying his sexual prowess.[26] For

Temple Drake (Lee Remick) and Candy Man (Yves Montand) in *Sanctuary* (1961), based on both *Sanctuary* and its sequel *Requiem for a Nun*. (Movie Star News)

Candy, like Trigger, his counterpart in *The Story of Temple Drake,* is definitely not impotent, so neither Alabama Red nor his blackmailing brother Pete figure in the present movie. Candy demonstrates his virility unequivocally in the rape scene. Candy enters the barn where Temple is spending the night and finds it easy to overcome her resistance to his advances; at that moment the scene shifts to the following morning. Candy informs Temple that he is taking her with him to New Orleans, and that they might as well commandeer for the trip the car Gowan left behind when he made his retreat back to Jefferson. At Miss Reba's, Temple again meets the ubiquitous Nancy, who works there as a maid and offers to look after her. For his part, Candy promises to protect her and take care of her. "I was learning what it was like to be with a real man," Temple's voice comments over the sound track. "Next morning I woke to a different world: gin for breakfast, new clothes that Candy had bought for me. That dingy little room at Miss Reba's became for me a sanctuary of sin and pleasure." As she watches herself in the mirror taking a swig of gin, she says to her reflection with raffish glee, "Jazz Baby, you are low down."

Since the whole trial of Lee Goodwin has disappeared in Richardson's film, there is no lawyer to trace Temple to the brothel in the hope of convincing her to testify on Goodwin's behalf. Hence in the present film she must be discovered in another way. What happens is this.

Candy, once more driving Gowan's car, embarks on a bootlegging expedition with Dog Boy. The police are lying in wait for him along the highway, however, and take after him; the chase ends as Candy swerves off the road and crashes into a ditch, where the car bursts into flames. When Dog Boy's charred corpse is found in the wreckage, it is thought to be Candy's, and he is presumed dead.

"That's how they found me," Temple adds, voice-over on the sound track, "by tracing the car. It was the return of the innocent from the ranks of the damned. Of course it was hushed up, because the injured party might lose her reputation. And she said to herself, 'Here we are, back home, and that's that.' But she was still screaming under her skin for her lost love."

As this extended flashback—which covers the principal events of *Sanctuary*—comes to an end, we are back in the present, as she says to her father, "I let you have your own way, even to marrying Gowan; he felt responsible."

When Temple again takes up the narrative, we slip back into the past once more and see her hiring Nancy as a domestic servant. After all, she explains, Nancy was her only link with the past: "Nancy was kind and understanding to me when I needed kindness and understanding." Or, as Temple puts it more bluntly in *Requiem for a Nun*, Nancy "was the only animal in Jefferson that spoke Temple Drake's language." Significantly, Temple often refers to herself by her unmarried name in both *Requiem for a Nun* and in the movie because, as mentioned, she wishes to imply that at that point in her past life, she had not yet earned the right to be known as the responsible wife and mother signified by the name Mrs. Gowan Stevens. Emotionally she was still an irresponsible adolescent underneath her carefully cultivated veneer of respectability and maturity. This is demonstrated by her taking up with Candy once more, when he suddenly comes back into her life. Candy escaped from the auto accident in which he was thought to have perished and has been in hiding ever since. Thus it is Candy with whom Temple is going to run away in the Richardson film, and not Red's brother Pete as in *Requiem for a Nun*. This plot twist adroitly avoids the necessity of introducing an important new character like Pete so late in the film, since in the film there is only one gangster in Temple's life instead of two, and also helps to bind the plots of *Sanctuary* and *Requiem for a Nun* more tightly into a continuous narrative.

With the exception of the substitution of Candy for Pete, however, the events in the film proceed from this point onward pretty much as they do in Faulkner's work. In the film's final flashback, Nancy begs Temple to think of her child: "You can't take it with you when you run off, and you can't leave it here. The baby will wind up in the garbage can or an orphanage." When Temple still insists that she is taking her little girl with her, Nancy folds her hands in an attitude of prayer and whispers, "I've tried everything I know; you can see that." Then she disappears into the nursery. A moment later Temple enters the nursery to get the baby, but the camera stops at the doorway and does not follow her inside, as if recoiling from what has happened within. There is an instant of silence and then Temple's anguished scream.

"The rest you know," Temple says to her father and Ira, as the flashback concludes. "Candy vanished, and Nancy has been sentenced to hang; and all the time she has said nothing but 'Thank you, Lord.'" When the governor says that there is nothing that he can do for Nancy, Ira assures Temple that her painful admissions have nevertheless not been made in vain. "I brought you here to wipe the slate clean, to give you a chance to start again," he says. As Singleton comments, Ira's purpose in having Temple make this confession to her father, the governor, was not so much to save Nancy's life as to save Temple's soul. Then Ira goes off to see Gowan, who is not present to hear Temple's story as he is in *Requiem*. After relaying the facts to Gowan, Ira intercedes for Temple with her husband: "Out of what happened tonight could come a new beginning. Free her by standing by her to face the past. Face your own weakness, your own evasions." Gowan responds thoughtfully, "Sure—like the Good Book says, 'The Truth shall make you free.'"

The next scene is virtually an illustration of that Scriptural text. Set in Nancy's cell, the scene is played between Nancy and Temple, without lawyer Ira present as interlocutor, as he is in *Requiem*. The dialogue constitutes a neat distillation of the corresponding lines of Faulkner's dialogue at this point, and strike a similar thematic chord. Temple tells Nancy that she has confessed everything, and Nancy replies, "I gave up this life when I raised my hand against that child. You had to suffer through the telling of it – that's the way we get salvation."

"Salvation," repeats Temple. "We're all looking for some place to feel safe, a place to hide. We look for it in such strange places."

"Salvation means more than hiding," Nancy continues. "It means facing up to life, for your children now and those to come. You've got to believe that you are forgiven as I know I am forgiven." As in *Requiem for a Nun*, Nancy's parting assurance to Temple is that, if she places her trust in God, He will save her.

Temple emerges into the sunlight outside, where she finds Gowan waiting for her. They walk down the street together as the camera pulls back to show Nancy, with a serene expression on her face, gazing heavenward through the barred window of her cell. Getting all three of them into the same shot marks the most notable use by Richardson of widescreen cinematography in the entire picture. Happily the film is photographed in black-and-white, since the use of even the most muted color process would not be in keeping with the stark atmosphere of Faulkner's somber tale.

Although both critical and popular response to the picture was lukewarm, it has as much of the flavor of Faulkner as *The Story of Temple Drake* did. Both movies manage to reflect Faulkner's thematic concern with suffering, sacrifice, and salvation in a compelling manner. Nevertheless, one can still ask what sort of overall judgment can be rendered about the relative merits of the two movies, drawing as they both do on the same story material.

For one thing, Roberts' film, which was made on a relatively modest budget and runs only an hour and eleven minutes, tells its story in a brisk, straightforward fashion, with a minimum of character development. By contrast, Richardson's movie, a more expensive widescreen production, is technically a more polished piece of work than the previous movie; moreover, it is half an hour longer than the earlier film and therefore devotes more time to an in-depth examination of the psychology of character than was feasible in Roberts' shorter, sparer movie. On the other hand, Richardson's movie contains some slow-paced, talky stretches (mostly derived from *Requiem for a Nun*), one of the major faults that contemporary cinema critics found with the film. As a result, the viewer's interest occasionally tends to flag while watching Richardson's *Sanctuary*, something that never happens in the Roberts film.

In the final analysis, it seems that whether or not one believes that *The*

Story of Temple Drake is a better movie than *Sanctuary* depends on whether one prefers a fast-paced film that emphasizes action over character development to a slower but denser motion picture that probes character more deeply. My own capsule comment on the two pictures would be that Roberts' 1933 film is still the more entertaining of the two films, while Richardson's 1961 movie is more to be admired than enjoyed. But both remain worthy of the discriminating moviegoer's attention.

CHAPTER 4

Knight Without Armor:
Intruder in the Dust (1949)
and *Tomorrow* (1972)

> Justice is accomplished lots of times
> by methods that won't bear looking into.
> *William Faulkner*

> Gavin Stevens was . . . a county attorney,
> an amateur Sherlock Holmes, [not] a detective, . . .
> one of these tough guys that slapped women around,
> took a drink every time he couldn't think of what
> to say next.
> *William Faulkner*

While Faulkner was working on the script for *The Big Sleep* in fall 1944, Howard Hawks asked him why he didn't write a detective story. Faulkner replied, "I've been thinking of a nigger in his cell trying to solve his crime," that is, trying to figure out who committed the homicide with which he has been charged.[1] One of the central characters Faulkner planned to include in the story was Faulkner's ubiquitous lawyer, Gavin Stevens, who was to serve as the black man's attorney.

Intruder in the Dust: The Novel

Actually the plot of *Intruder in the Dust,* as the novel would be called, had been germinating in the novelist's imagination for some time. As early as

1940, he mentioned in a letter to his publisher that he had in mind "a blood-and-thunder mystery novel which should sell (they usually do)." But at the time Faulkner was occupied with other projects, and he did not get around to writing *Intruder* until 1948. When he began the book in January of that year, he envisioned it as a novella of around one hundred pages. But as he continued working on it, he realized that the story was growing into a full-fledged novel. By the time he had finished it in April, the book was more than twice the length he had initially projected. Having decided to make Gavin Stevens' nephew, Chick Mallison, a key character, Faulkner now saw the story not as a simple whodunit, but as "a pretty good study of a sixteen-year-old boy who overnight became a man" by doing his part to help save the life of an aging Negro prisoner, Lucas Beauchamp.[2]

Chick initially becomes involved in Lucas Beauchamp's plight when Lucas asks him to notify his uncle that he wants Stevens to take his case. Later on, Lucas calls on the lad again, this time with a far more serious request: to disinter the body of Vinson Gowrie, the white man Lucas is supposed to have shot, in order to prove that the bullet that killed Gowrie did not come from his gun.

In an extended flashback Faulkner dramatizes how the paths of Chick and Lucas first crossed. The latter, it turns out, is part white, as a result of the miscegenation practiced by previous generations of slaveholders in the South. He is proud of the fact that he has a little farm of his own, bequeathed to him by one of his white forebears, because that means that he is a landowner like his white relatives, the McCaslins—a status enjoyed by no other local black. One wintry day four years before Lucas got into his present trouble, Chick had fallen into an icy creek near Lucas' farm. The dignified old patriarch had graciously invited the boy back to his cabin to dry out at his fireside and then given up his own dinner to let the lad have it. Before leaving for home, Chick condescendingly had offered Lucas his spare change, as if he were paying for the services of a black domestic servant instead of accepting hospitality extended by a generous host. Lucas, who always conducted himself as the equal of any white person, spurned the coins. Ashamed of his behavior, Chick subsequently tried by various token gestures to make amends for the insult he had offered Lucas, but never felt that he had actually succeeded in doing so. Hence, when Lucas asks Chick to help clear him of the murder of Vinson Gowrie, Chick finally sees a way of discharging his obligation.

In uncovering the evidence that eventually establishes Lucas's innocence, Chick is aided by his sidekick Alec Sander and by Miss Eunice Habersham, a venerable spinster who was a lifelong friend of Lucas's deceased wife Molly. Indeed, by intruding in the dust of Vinson's grave, Chick and his confederates save Lucas from being strung up and set on fire by the lynch mob that, spurred on by the Gowries—a savage horde of "white trash" living on the outskirts of Jefferson—was preparing to take the law into its own hands.

In coming to terms with the emotional conflict with which he is confronted when he is called upon to help save Lucas's life, Chick grows to maturity in the course of the novel. For Chick must summon the courage to defy the whites of the town by standing up for a black man they have already decided is guilty of murdering one of their own. Thus, besides being the detective story Faulkner originally conceived, *Intruder* is also, as he himself affirmed, the story of Chick Mallison's psychological evolution toward manhood.

After Chick has done all he can to aid Lucas, Gavin Stevens is spurred by his nephew's tenacity and fortitude to demand belatedly that an official autopsy be performed on Vinson Gowrie's body. The bullet that is extracted from the corpse is discovered to have come, not from Lucas' pistol but from a gun belonging to Vinson's brother Crawford. It seems that Crawford had cheated Vinson out of a substantial sum of money. In order to avoid a showdown with Vinson that Crawford feared might end with his own death, he murdered Vinson and framed Lucas Beauchamp, banking on the likelihood that Lucas would be lynched for killing a white man before the case ever came to trial, and that the matter would end there. When Crawford's guilt is unearthed by Chick and the others, his crime of fratricide is too much even for the vile Gowrie tribe to countenance, and Crawford is excommunicated from the clan. The outcast, who feels that he has the curse of Cain upon him, takes his own life with the same gun he had used to shoot his brother.

If Chick Mallison changes in the course of the novel, so does Gavin Stevens; the latter's attitude toward race relations in the South broadens considerably as the plot unfolds. True, at the outset of the novel Gavin's racial views are already sufficiently advanced to allow him to undertake the defense of a black man, just as he was willing to defend Nancy Manningoe in *Requiem for a Nun*. Nevertheless, as David Minter writes in his critical biography of Faulkner, in the course of the story Gavin's attitude toward race is further broadened by observing and reflecting upon both the stoic endurance of Lucas Beauchamp in the face of adversity and the faith of his nephew, who believes in the black man's innocence before Gavin does. Gavin accordingly revises his outlook on the whole question of race and articulates his more enlightened views most forthrightly in the course of the book.

When some reviewers of the novel jumped to the conclusion that Gavin was Faulkner's spokesman on race, he replied that Gavin was not his mouthpiece, just a good specimen of the white southern liberals of the 1930s, the time when the story takes place. Although the opinions Gavin expresses on racial issues in his typically inflated rhetoric are decidedly moderate by today's standards, they angered a number of southern readers when the book came out. One of these was the novelist's uncle, John Falkner, himself an attorney. Asked if he thought that he had in any way inspired the character of Gavin in *Intruder*, the outspoken attorney vociferously denied that there was any connection whatever between himself and what he termed a "nigger lover" like Gavin Stevens.[3]

Interestingly, the controversy over Gavin's views on race stirred up when *Intruder* first appeared helped rather than hindered the novel's sales, and it became Faulkner's first bestseller since *Sanctuary*, published nearly two decades earlier. Given the book's commercial success, it is not surprising that *Intruder in the Dust* also became the first of Faulkner's novels since *Sanctuary* to be bought by the movies. Metro-Goldwyn-Mayer, the company that had produced *Today We Live* back in 1933, acquired the screen rights to *Intruder* for $50,000 in July 1948, more than two months before the book's publication on September 27. When a relative dropped by his home to congratulate Faulkner on this enormous financial windfall, she found him dancing tipsily around the room barefoot. "Anyone who can write a book and sell it to Hollywood for $50,000 has a right to get tight," he explained, and to dance a jig with his shoes off.[4]

Intruder in the Dust: The Film

The motion picture version of *Intruder in the Dust* (1949) was in the capable hands of producer-director Clarence Brown (*The Yearling*). Brown, who had made his first movie in 1920, was one of MGM's senior directors, and it was he who had persuaded the front office to purchase the rights to *Intruder*. A native southerner, Brown's interest in the book was ignited by his vivid memories of a brutal Atlanta race riot lasting more than a week, that he had witnessed in 1906.[5] As a result of this dreadful experience, Brown for many years had wanted to make a film that examined the racial tensions in the South, and he was confident that Faulkner's controversial mystery novel would allow him to do just that. Brown communicated his eagerness to make the movie to Metro's production chief, Dore Schary, who shared his enthusiasm; and plans for the production moved ahead.

Screenwriter Ben Maddow (*The Asphalt Jungle*) was assigned to adapt *Intruder* for the screen. After discussing the film's storyline with Clarence Brown, Maddow hammered out a preliminary treatment which was readily approved by the studio. He then went on to write the screenplay itself which he worked on between November 5 and November 29. While the script was still in preparation, Maddow and Brown continued to hold script conferences in which writer and director traded ideas about plot and dialogue; and Maddow reworked the screenplay accordingly. Maddow and Brown sagely agreed, for example, to simplify the novel's complicated plot by eliminating the episode in which Crawford Gowrie kills a blackmailer who has figured out the true identity of Vinson's murderer.

Whenever he could, Maddow interpolated into the script portions of dialogue taken directly from the novel. Thus, Gavin caustically reminds Lucas that, if he had shown a little more respect for whites in the past instead of insisting on behaving like their social equals, they might not hate him so bitterly and be so determined to take the law into their own hands and lynch him for killing a white man. Lucas would have been the first to concede that his proud, independent ways had long been a source of friction between himself and the townspeople, who deeply resented him as a threat to white supremacy. Nevertheless, he points out to Gavin, it is too late for him to change his ways even if he felt inclined to do so: "So I'm to commence now. I can start off saying mister to folks who drags me out of here and builds a fire under me." Gavin has no answer for that. In short, by working Faulkner's dialogue into the script and by other means as well, Maddow endeavored to make the screenplay of *Intruder* as faithful as possible to Faulkner's novel. As he told an interviewer, fidelity to Faulkner was the guiding principle of his work on the screenplay.

The shooting script for *Intruder in the Dust* was officially approved for production on 8 December 1948. With that, Maddow's job was finished, but Brown's had just begun. Brown had managed to convince the front office to allow him to shoot the bulk of the movie on location in Faulkner's

The citizens of Faulkner's hometown of Oxford, Mississippi, participating in a mob scene for *Intruder in the Dust* (1949), in Court House Square, immortalized in Faulkner's fiction. (Museum of Modern Art/Film Stills Archive)

own hometown of Oxford, Mississippi, in order to lend the film a sense of authenticity. When news reached Oxford that a film unit would soon be arriving to shoot location scenes for the movie, the reaction of the populace was not uniformly enthusiastic. As Faulkner phrased it to a friend, some of the locals were saying, "We don't want no-one comin' into our town to make no movie about lynchin'."[6] But when Brown arrived in Oxford in February 1949 to make preparations for location filming, he was able to win the support of the Oxford Chamber of Commerce by assuring its membership that, as a southerner himself, he would see to it that *Intruder* would reflect the true southern viewpoint on race. That Brown had won his case became evident not long afterward, when a full-page advertisement appeared in the *Oxford Eagle*, endorsed by forty local merchants who pledged the picture people their full cooperation.

Brown accordingly went ahead with preproduction planning for the movie. By March 10, the first day of location shooting in Oxford, the full production unit of more than fifty actors and technicians had all arrived to begin filming in earnest. The unit was working on a thirty-one-day shooting schedule while in Oxford, and during that time Brown and Faulkner developed a genuine respect for one another. Hence, although Faulkner rarely visited the set to watch the filming or came to view footage already shot, he did try to cooperate with the making of the picture in any way he could. Faulkner helped Brown scout locations and advised him on the final casting of the picture. By and large the novelist went along with the director's choice of players, both for the principal characters, which were to be enacted by Hollywood professionals, and for the bit parts to be taken by local residents.

But he did recommend one crucial casting change, with which Brown readily concurred. The role of Crawford Gowrie was originally entrusted to Dan White, who had played villains effectively in other films. Faulkner felt that because the actor too obviously looked like a typical movie "heavy," the audience might guess that he was the villain too early in the picture. The kind of actor needed for the part, said Faulkner, was someone who would not be so easily identifiable as the culprit. He should appear on the surface to be a chubby, sweaty, commonplace type of person, whom the audience would not immediately suspect of being the guilty party. Consequently Brown assigned the part to Charles Kemper, who had played the plump, good-natured buddy of the hero in *The Southerner* and who fit Faulkner's specifications perfectly. He then gave the role of Will Legate, a sheriff's deputy to White, thereby shrewdly casting both actors against type. As for the rest of the cast that Brown had assembled, Faulkner was particularly impressed by Juano Hernandez, who was to play Lucas Beauchamp, and willingly coached the actor, who was of Puerto Rican descent, in mastering an authentic southern accent.

Besides assisting the director with casting and location hunting, Faulkner also accepted Brown's invitation to touch up the final shooting script for the film. But he received no acknowledgment in the screen credits for his contributions to the screenplay, because his contract with Warner Brothers had not yet expired. In spite of the fact that by this time Warner's had all but ceased to call upon his services as a screenwriter, the fact remained, as Ober reminded him, that "if you want to work [in pictures] you will have to work for Warner's, as they could probably prevent your working for another studio."[7] Consequently, although Faulkner did in fact make some alterations in Maddow's screenplay, he could not receive official recognition for his efforts.

After Faulkner had gone over the script, he wrote to his publisher, Bennett Cerf, that he found much that he admired in the screenplay, and little that he wished to change. In this same letter, Faulkner goes on to say, "I rewrote, rearranged, the dialogue in the jail cell sequences, and rewrote the scene in the sheriff's kitchen, . . . and straightened out the tag; but that was all."[8] Faulkner wrote out his proposed revisions of the screenplay in his own hand, and the seven pages which comprise the emendations he made in the script are part of his private papers in the University of Virginia's Alderman Library.

Most of Faulkner's revisions of the script were accepted and duly incorporated into the final shooting script on two pages dated 19 March 1949, and on five pages dated 21 March 1949. (Additional pages of last-minute revisions which are inserted into a shooting script are customarily dated in order to indicate that they supersede earlier versions of the same material.)

The first two pages, dated March 19, are a rewrite of a dialogue passage which occurs as part of what Faulkner refers to in his letter to Cerf as "the jail cell sequences." The interchange between Chick (Claude Jarman, Jr.) and lawyer Stevens (David Brian), called John rather than Gavin in the film, takes place outside the jail house just after their first talk with Lucas. Faulkner added some lines in which Gavin tells Chick that he took Lucas's case because he wants to ensure that the black man gets a fair trial, even though he personally believes that Lucas is guilty as charged. "He killed

Vinson Gowrie," Gavin contends. "No matter what the provocation, and
he probably had plenty—nevertheless, he killed a man." In these additional
lines of dialogue Faulkner wanted to stress the fact that Gavin at first is
convinced of Lucas's guilt and will have to be persuaded to the contrary.

By contrast, in the five-page March 19 revision of another passage, Faulkner makes it clear that Gavin is the first to admit that it was wrong of him
to assume Lucas's guilt without knowing the facts. The scene in question
takes place right before Gavin and Sheriff Hampton (Will Geer) go out to
the cemetery to make an official examination of Vinson's grave. Their purpose is to follow up on Chick's unofficial foray to the cemetery with Alec
Sander and Miss Habersham the night before, which had revealed that the
real murderer had stolen Vinson's body in order to avoid the possibility of
an autopsy, which would inevitably establish Lucas' innocence. In the new
dialogue Faulkner added to the kitchen scene, Gavin generously acknowl-
edges that this unlikely trio of gravediggers has manifested a compassionate
belief in Lucas' innocence, which he himself obviously lacked until they
made it clear that the actual culprit is bent on trying to thwart any further
investigation of his crime. "If you want to get anything done," he comments, don't bother the men folks with it. They're too cluttered up with
facts. Get the women and children to working on it." His point is that
women and children do not get bogged down in analyzing the facts of the
matter the way men tend to do, but rather act on intuition and get things
done.

In short, Faulkner's revisions made the two scenes, outside the jail and
in the kitchen, complement each other nicely by vividly dramatizing the
shift in Gavin's attitude toward his client. "These pages," Regina Fadiman
writes, "clearly emphasizes Stevens's change from the stubborn certainty
that Lucas was guilty to a baffled regret that he, Stevens, could have been
so wrong."9

Faulkner's alterations in what he termed "the tag" of the screenplay were
the only ones he submitted to Brown that were not inserted into the shooting script. Faulkner's intent in modifying the movie's last scene was to
make the movie's racial message less explicit than it was in the shooting
script. As it happened, the lines in the final scene which Faulkner wanted
to change had been written into the script at the behest of Dore Schary.
A movie executive known for his predilection for "message pictures," Schary
had specifically ordered Maddow to explicate the movie's racial theme at
the end of the picture. Maddow had balked at having Gavin and his nephew

both solemnly refer to Lucas as the keeper of their white consciences. Like Faulkner, Maddow thought that the new lines would render the ending of the film too preachy and thus give the whole picture what he called "a falsely sentimental turn"; but he had been overruled by Schary.[10] It was most likely Schary, therefore, who ultimately overruled Faulkner as well.

Faulkner's judgment, and Maddow's too, were subsequently vindicated when not a few critics singled out the explicit moralizing at the movie's finale as the only wrong note struck in the entire picture. Perhaps Pauline Kael put it best when she wrote, "Fortunately the character of Lucas is so dominating that what we have witnessed cannot be reduced to such commonplaces"; the viewer knows, without being told, "that Lucas has won; that the sheepish, guilty townspeople will now have to accept him on his own terms."[11]

Furthermore, the movie's racial theme is expressed more subtly and movingly earlier in the film than it is in the movie's last scene. At the beginning of the picture, Brown's camera focuses on a church spire and then pans slowly downward to take in some Sunday worshippers about to enter the church. Hymns can be heard from inside as the group stands around Jefferson's town square, where the lynch mob, including some of these same townspeople, will soon gather. As film historian Alan Estrin notes, in the film's very first sequence "the director anticipates the contradictions that will run like a strong undercurrent throughout this film: how can people who profess to follow the teachings of Christ treat their fellow men . . . so barbarously?"[12] The film's racial concerns are also present in the scene in which Sheriff Hampton escorts Crawford Gowrie to the jail after his arrest. When one of the crowd in front of the jail asks the sheriff if it is true that Crawford murdered Vinson, he replies, "That's right. He's the one. The man that killed his brother." The emphasis on the word *brother* implies that any man who kills another commits fratricide, because we are all members of the same human family; the mob's proposed lynching of Lucas Beauchamp would have been, symbolically speaking, another fratricide. In fine, the affirmation of human equality reverberates from the opening sequence throughout the film, and this overarching theme need not have been restated in so many words in the closing moments of the picture.

Even so, when the picture was finished, Faulkner personally was very pleased with it. He told Cerf in the letter cited above that Brown was one of the best directors he had ever worked with, adding that he deserved no credit for what he deemed his minimal contribution to the overall production. "I myself am so pleased with the job," he concluded, "that I would like all the credit to stay where it is: with Brown and the cast."

Faulkner had every reason to be satisfied with Brown's film version of his novel, and the movie is generally regarded as one of the best films that Brown directed in his long career. Having begun directing pictures in the silent era, Brown placed a great deal of importance on telling a story visually, and there are many instances in the film which demonstrate his capacity to think in visual terms rather than relying on dialogue to make a point. Take, for example, the scene in which Chick arrogantly insists on paying Lucas for his hospitality. When his black host refuses the coins which Chick is holding out to him, there is a closeup of the lad's hand as he angrily clenches it into a fist and then contemptuously drops the money on the floor. This single image tells us more about the way in which the doctrine of white supremacy has been ingrained in Chick than several lines of dialogue could.

Another expertly directed sequence which highlights the visual over the verbal takes place the day after the discovery of the empty grave. Chick returns to the burial site in the company of his uncle and the sheriff, with the aim of tracking down the vanished corpse. Their search party is soon joined by the head of the Gowrie tribe, Nub Gowrie (Porter Hall, in an immaculate performance); his twin sons; and his passel of bloodhounds. Together they explore the nearby swamp, where they suspect the murderer frantically stashed Vinson's body. Their suspicions prove correct, for the group eventually finds the corpse submerged in quicksand and brings it back to dry land.

Then, in one of the picture's most moving moments, Nub Gowrie, fighting back tears, mutely bends over his dead son and, in the absence of a handkerchief, jerks out his shirt tail and wipes the crusted sand from Vinson's face, manifesting a tenderness no-one would have suspected the gruff old man to be capable of. A sequence such as this one, with its emphasis on visual storytelling, could have come from one of Brown's silent movies.

Brown's sure visual sense is also very much in evidence in the scene which immediately follows the discovery of the missing corpse. It begins with a superbly executed long take. In the course of one uninterrupted shot, the camera roves all around the town square to record the gathering of the people of Jefferson for the lynching which they assume is shortly going to take place. The milling crowds, along with loudspeakers blasting frenetic swing music, create a gaudy carnival atmosphere. The camera glides unobtrusively from one group to another, pausing to capture a fleeting remark or gesture, such as a woman casually applying lipstick in the sideview mirror of a truck, then continuing on its way. At last the camera halts as a woman carrying a baby in her arms, as nonchalantly as if she had brought her child to see a circus parade, walks up to Crawford Gowrie and inquires when things are going to get started. Both Brown and his Oscar-winning cinematographer Robert Surtees (*King Solomon's Mines, The Bad and the Beautiful, Ben Hur*) could be proud of this brilliant bit of camera work.

Crawford then approaches Miss Habersham (Elizabeth Patterson), who is resolutely sitting just inside the door of the jail with a sewing basket beside her, ostensibly concentrating on her mending. Actually she is silently, defiantly guarding the passage to Lucas' cell against Crawford and his surly henchman, even though a flimsy screen door is the only barrier that stands between her and them. At first Crawford threatens to remove her from the doorway by force; then he backs off, but not before issuing a warning. He reminds her that she is, after all, a frail old lady; sooner or later she will grow weary from her vigil, and when she does, he and his men will move in and take Lucas. But Miss Habersham, who spunkily tells Crawford that she is going on eighty and is not tired yet, valiantly manages to hold out until Vinson's body is brought into town and the telltale bullet removed from it. In tribute to her courage, Gavin later remarks, "She's the only lady anywhere that ever held a jail with a twenty-gauge spool of thread."

After Crawford—who does not commit suicide in the movie—is locked up and Lucas is freed, Lucas appears in Gavin's office to pay the lawyer his fee for getting him released from jail. But Gavin graciously responds that his client owes him nothing, since it is really Chick, also present at the interview, who actually saved Lucas' life. When Lucas stubbornly insists on paying his attorney something, Gavin finally settles the matter by accepting two dollars for "expenses"; whereupon Lucas demands a receipt for his money. Lucas is here turning the tables on Chick, who had earlier attempted to pay him for "services rendered." The old man is in effect teaching the lad a lesson by implicitly reminding him that there are some acts of generosity which are literally priceless and hence beyond repayment; Chick could no more pay Lucas for rescuing him from the frozen pond than Lucas himself could pay Chick for saving him from a lynching. In absorbing this lesson, Chick, in the film as in the novel, takes a giant step toward becoming a mature adult.

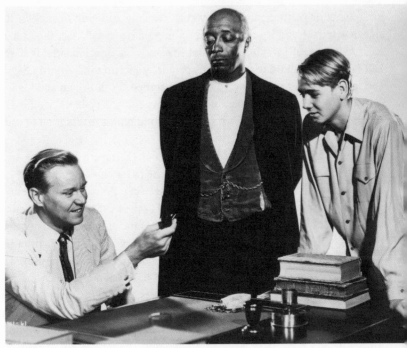

John Stevens (David Brian), Lucas Beauchamp (Juano Hernandez), and Chick Malliso[n] (Claude Jarman, Jr.) in *Intruder in the Dust,* the most faithful film version of a Faulkne[r] work. (Museum of Modern Art/Film Stills Archive)

The deft ensemble acting in this serio-comic scene – which Cleanth Brooks wrongly asserts is not in the film – shows that Clarence Brown, besides knowing how to use a camera, could also handle actors. Pauline Kael attributes the uniformly fine performances in the movie to Brown's long-standing ability to coax screen actors into giving their best. In the present instance, says Kael, "the performances Brown gets are astonishing"; and one need only think of Elizabeth Patterson (*The Story of Temple Drake*) as Miss Habersham confronting the lynching party, or of Porter Hall as Nub Gowrie in the quicksand sequence, to substantiate this statement.[13]

Faulkner initially was reluctant to participate in the festivities surrounding the film's world premiere in Oxford on 9 October 1949, because he hated the "hullabaloo" associated with such events. Nevertheless, once his family prevailed on him to take part, he took advantage of the occasion to voice publicly the praise of Brown and of the movie which he had expressed privately to people such as Bennett Cerf. Thus, when a reporter inquired what particularly impressed him about the picture, Faulkner responded, "Well, I liked the way Mr. Brown used bird calls and saddle squeaks and footsteps in place of a lot of loud music telling you what emotions you should be experiencing."[14]

In point of fact, the film has virtually no musical score at all, since, as Faulkner observed, Brown relied mostly on sound effects instead of background music to help create the mood of a scene. Aside from the music accompanying the movie's opening and closing credits, just about the only other music heard in the film is source music—that is, music that occurs as a natural part of the action and whose source is identifiable in a given scene. Such music includes the hymns employed in the film's opening church sequence and the jazzy tunes blaring from loudspeakers in the mob scene. An excellent example of Brown's utilization of sound effects in place of mood music, noted by Regina Fadiman, comes at the close of the quicksand sequence. While Nub Gowrie brushes away the sand from Vinson's face, the mournful howling of the Gowrie hounds expresses the old man's inarticulate grief. This sad sound is more effective at this point than any underscore could have been. In summary, Brown's use of natural sounds instead of incidental music whenever he could contributes significantly to the austere realism that characterizes the whole movie.

After the movie's premiere, Faulkner wrote to Sam Marx, for whom he had worked during his largely unsuccessful stint at MGM in the early 1930s, that his conscience had continued to bother him in the intervening years because he had not given the studio more for its money. But after seeing *Intruder,* his guilt feelings had abated somewhat: "I may still be on MGM's cuff, but at least I am not quite so far up the sleeve."[15]

Intruder in the Dust consistently received critical plaudits during its original run; yet it did not win a wide audience. Unfortunately it was one of four films dealing with the Negro question that appeared in 1949. The other three—*Home of the Brave, Pinky,* and *Lost Boundaries*—were certainly not without merit; but *Intruder in the Dust,* contemporary critics generally agreed, was the best of the lot. Nonetheless, because it opened after the other three, it failed to attract the public at large, which for the moment was surfeited with movies about racial problems. On the other hand, since the production was modestly budgeted at $500,000, its box-office returns were satisfactory.

In the years since its initial release, the film's critical reputation has steadily grown, and it continues to be exhibited in revival houses, on television, and in cinema classes. Fortunately, Clarence Brown lived to see *Intruder in the Dust* established as a film classic of enduring quality. He often commented in interviews in later years that he was delighted by the ongoing interest in the film, just as he had been happy to receive the British Academy Award for his direction of the picture at the time it first came out. But, as he testified around the time of his retirement from picture making in the 1950s, the praise he most cherished came from the novelist himself: "That Mr. Faulkner was well pleased with it has been one of the most gratifying rewards I have received in thirty-five years of making movies."[16]

"Tomorrow": The Short Story

Tomorrow, and tomorrow, and tomorrow,
Creeps in this petty pace from day to day
To the last syllable of recorded time,
And all our yesterdays have lighted fools
The way to dusty death.

                              Macbeth

Tomorrow (1972), a film derived from the Faulkner short story of the same name, marks the third appearance of Gavin Stevens in a Faulkner film, following *Intruder in the Dust* (1949) and *Sanctuary* (1961). In *Tomorrow* Stevens' name was once again altered, this time to Thornton Douglas. The reason in this instance was that Twentieth Century–Fox owned the rights to the character's name for its film *Sanctuary,* even though Stevens was called Ira instead of Gavin in that film. Because Stevens' name varies in the trio of films in which he is featured, it is not immediately apparent to filmgoers that the same character, Faulkner's favorite lawyer, figures in all three pictures. But each in turn shows Stevens, whom Faulkner affectionately described as his amateur Sherlock Holmes, coping with an intriguing murder case.

"Tomorrow," which was originally published in the *Saturday Evening Post* in 1940, later reappeared as part of the 1949 collection of Gavin Stevens stories, entitled *Knight's Gambit.* In these stories, Faulkner's not-so-super sleuth endeavors, with varying degrees of success, to handle six different cases. When a friend once asked Faulkner why he wrote these mystery stories, he responded, "No matter what you write, it's a mystery of one kind or another."[17] He probably meant that in his fiction he always explored the mysteries of the human heart, which could be as perplexing and disturbing as any murder mystery.

In the Faulkner works featuring Gavin Stevens, his efforts to solve a crime often turn into a knightly crusade to uphold individual human rights. For, as Stevens knows only too well, a strict, literal interpretation of the law does not always yield true justice in an individual case. It certainly does not do so in the case of Jackson Fentry, the protagonist of "Tomorrow," one of Faulkner's finest, most heartrending stories. A narrow application of the law to Jackson's situation unfairly deprives him of the one thing in life he genuinely cares about. In the words of a compassionate character in "Tomorrow," Jackson's plight proves that "this world ain't run like it ought to be run a heap more times than what it is."[18]

"Tomorrow," which is narrated principally by Chick Mallison, begins with Chick recounting how Gavin Stevens lost his first court case, one that, ironically enough, he thought he was sure to win. Stevens had defended a citizen of Jefferson named Homer Bookwright, who was charged with murdering Buck Thorpe, a drunken drifter who was about to run off with Bookwright's daughter, despite the fact that he was already married. Because Thorpe had in fact drawn a pistol on Bookwright at the time the latter shot him, the evidence seemed strongly to favor the defendant's acquittal. Stevens was keenly disappointed, then, when a lone juror, Jackson Fentry, steadfastly insisted on voting to convict Bookwright of murder, and the judge was compelled to declare a mistrial. With young Chick as his companion, Gavin Stevens tours the countryside, inquiring of people who know Fentry why they think a poor dirt farmer had taken it upon himself to hang the jury, in spite of the fact that Bookwright would surely go free after the retrial.

In piecing together the information he gleans from Fentry's neighbors, the Pruitts, and from Isham Quick, who had at one time employed Fentry as caretaker of his sawmill, Stevens learns the truth.

Years before, during the period when he had temporarily left his farm to serve as custodian at the sawmill, Fentry, a lonesome bachelor, had taken in a pregnant woman deserted by her husband. When she died in childbirth, Jackson determined to raise the baby boy as his own. And so he did, until one day five years later, after Jackson had returned to the farm, when the dead woman's two brothers, a couple of mean hillbillies, came to Jackson's place to claim the child as their own. They had every legal right to do this, as the sheriff, who came along with them, advised Fentry; yet it would seem that a truly humane interpretation of the law would dictate that the child should remain with the man who had been both father and mother to him from birth. Nonetheless, the hardboiled Thorpes remained adamant, even when Isham Quick, who happened to be present, urged on them Fentry's claim that he had married the boy's mother on her deathbed. Their coldblooded response to Quick's entreaty was instantaneous. "He couldn't marry her," one of them replied. "She already had a husband. We done already attended to him." Just how they "attended" to their brother-in-law, no-one present dared to ask.

With a ferocity born of desperation, Jackson tried to drive the Thorpes off his place without the boy; finally the sheriff had to intervene and force Fentry to give the lad up. A number of years later, that same youngster, whom Fentry had named "Jackson and Longstreet" after two Civil War officers, turned up in Jefferson as Buck Thorpe, the reckless scoundrel whom Bookwright stopped with a bullet.

Once Stevens is in possession of all the facts, he is in a position to figure out precisely why Fentry refused to vote for Bookwright's release. "Of course he wasn't going to vote Bookwright free," Stevens reflects, "because somewhere in that debased and brutalized flesh which Bookwright slew there still remained, not the spirit maybe, but at least the memory of that little boy, that Jackson and Longstreet Fentry, even though the man the boy had become didn't know it, and only Fentry did." What Stevens is saying is that Bookwright had killed all that was left of the lad that Fentry had loved like a son; and even though Fentry was well aware that Bookwright would certainly be exonerated when the case was retried, by refusing to vote for Bookwright's acquittal in the first trial, he at least would not personally have had a hand in helping to set free the man who shot the only son he would ever have.

Stevens winds up his remarks with an allusion to Macbeth's famous soliloquy, quoted above, in which Shakespeare's tragic hero asserts his depressing conviction that human beings have little to look forward to in life, because tomorrow inevitably will be no better than yesterday: "The lowly and invincible of the earth—to endure and endure and then endure, tomorrow and tomorrow and tomorrow." In alluding to *Macbeth*, Stevens suggests that, because Fentry thought of Jackson and Longstreet as his son, the boy was his sole hope for a better tomorrow. In other words, it had been Jackson Fentry's dream that the lad would grow up to perpetuate the Fentry name and to farm the land that had belonged to the family for generations. And so, once the youngster was taken from him, the childless bachelor would never again have reason to look forward to tomorrow. Hence Stevens admires Fentry for continuing to endure without complaint, even though, as critic Jack Barbera says, he is permanently bereft of the surrogate son who would have given "full meaning to his endurance."

Stevens's compassion for Fentry, despite the fact that Fentry has caused him to lose his first court case, undoubtedly elicits some admiration for him in his nephew. It is true that Stevens can be wrongheaded at times, as when he hastily assumed that Lucas Beauchamp was guilty of slaying Vinson Gowrie before all the facts were in; still, Chick implies more than once in the *Knight's Gambit* stories, he is aware that his uncle is a fundamentally decent man who does his duty as he sees it. Perhaps the most touching tribute ever paid to Stevens in Faulkner's fiction occurs in still another book in which Gavin Stevens and Chick Mallison both figure, *The Mansion.* In that novel Chick explicitly states his deep feeling for Gavin, despite his flaws. There is no better summation of the portrait that Faulkner painted of Gavin Stevens throughout his work than these words of Chick's: "He is a good man, wise too except for the occasions when he would abberate, go momentarily haywire and take a wrong turn that even I could see was wrong. . . . But he is a good man. Maybe I was wrong sometimes to trust him and follow him but I never was wrong to love him."[19]

Tomorrow: The Television Play

Two years after "Tomorrow" was published in *The Saturday Evening Post,* Faulkner considered writing a scenario for a film adaptation of the story which he would then submit to Warner's, where he was working at the time, or to any other studio that was interested. But he apparently never got around to pursuing this project. In fact, describing the tale in a letter six years later, he summarized the plot inaccurately, indicating that he had all but forgotten the story. As things turned out, the first adaptation of "Tomorrow" was not done for the big screen but for the small screen. Both the teleplay and the feature motion picture derived from the story were scripted by Oscar-winning screenwriter Horton Foote (*To Kill a Mocking-*

bird, Tender Mercies). Foote's first encounter with adapting Faulkner to another medium was his script for the ninety-minute television production of Faulkner's *Old Man* on *Playhouse 90* in 1958. About six months later, producer Herbert Brodkin commissioned Foote to dramatize "Tomorrow" for *Playhouse 90*. The production would be broadcast live, as was the custom in those days, before videotape came into general use in the television industry.

Adapting a short story to the screen, whether for a ninety-minute television program or for a theatrical feature, involves expanding the original material, as we have seen with *Today We Live*, the movie version of "Turn About." When a scriptwriter expands a short piece of fiction for a different medium, he must be careful to create the new scenes in such a way that they will be totally in keeping with the tone and style of the original author's work. In trying to put meat on the bones of Faulkner's spare plot line for a television series with a ninety-minute format (actually seventy-two minutes of air time), Foote found that the character of the baby's mother deserved fuller treatment.

Even though Faulkner had only devoted a couple of paragraphs to the woman in the short story, Foote recalls that Faulkner "told me enough about her so that my imagination just began to work, and she became somebody I knew."[20] Foote named Faulkner's heroine, who is nameless in the short story, Sarah Eubanks, and set about dramatizing in detail her relationship with Jackson Fentry from the time she arrived at the cabin where Fentry was staying while acting as watchman at the lumber camp, to her untimely death a few months later.

To lead up to the presentation of these central events, Foote decided to begin the teleplay on the porch of the Pruitts' farmhouse, with lawyer Douglas (Charles Aidman) and his nephew Chick (Jimmy Baird) talking about Jackson Fentry with Ed Pruitt and his mother (Elizabeth Patterson, of *The Story of Temple Drake* and *Intruder in the Dust*). The teleplay then reveals Jackson's story in flashback, with Ed Pruitt (Chill Wills) acting as narrator, rather than Chick as in the short story. The teledrama ends back on the Pruitts' front porch, with Douglas' reflections, taken verbatim from Faulkner and quoted above, on the reasons for Fentry's behavior at Bookwright's trial.

Brodkin liked Foote's script very much and scheduled the production to be broadcast six weeks later, on 7 March 1960. The teleplay was directed by motion picture director Robert Mulligan (*To Kill a Mockingbird*), who had already done half-hour versions of two Faulkner short stories, which had been broadcast live on the *Suspense* series in 1954: "Smoke," another detective story from the *Knight's Gambit* collection, and "Barn Burning." Foote remembers that during a script conference with Mulligan about the television production of *Tomorrow*, the director asked him to consider starting out the drama with the trial, which would possibly make for a more interesting opening for the teleplay than beginning it on the Pruitts' front porch. Foote had initially thought of opening the television play with the trial but had decided that the restricted playing time of the teledrama would not permit the addition of the trial scene. Nevertheless, he endeavored once more to write the trial into the teleplay, while still keeping the script to the required length, but with no better results than before, "so it was agreed to return to what I had already written."[21]

With only sixteen rehearsal days and a budget of $113,000 at his disposal, Mulligan still managed to mount a first-class live television production of *Tomorrow*, in which he evoked poignant performances from Richard Boone and Kim Stanley, who played Jackson Fentry and Sarah Eubanks. Critics and viewers alike took the teledrama to their hearts; in fact, it drew one of the largest audiences of any production aired by *Playhouse 90* in its five-year run on CBS-TV. In addition, the success of the teledrama prompted the network to rebroadcast the show on 18 July 1961, by means of a filmed transcription of the original live transmission.

Sometime later, stage director Herbert Berghof got in touch with Foote and asked him to consider adapting his teleplay for an off-Broadway production of *Tomorrow*. The stage version was eventually produced in 1968, co-starring Robert Duvall and Olga Bellin. Foote's stage adaptation of *Tomorrow* stuck fairly close to the television script, so there is no need to give a detailed analysis of it here. One noticeable difference between the television play and the stage adaptation was that Thornton Douglas rather than Ed Pruitt served as the narrator of the stage play, so that Douglas could at times address the audience directly during the play, as if they were the jury. Two producers largely associated with the theater, Paul Roebling (Bellin's husband) and Gilbert Pearlman, saw the play on opening night, 15 April 1968; they were so impressed with the production that they subsequently told Foote that they wished to make a theatrical film of *Tomorrow*, with Foote once again supplying the script and the two stars of the stage production in the leads.

Roebling and Pearlman budgeted the production at a little over $400,000, not a handsome sum for a feature film by today's standards but about three times what CBS had spent on the live television production. Moreover, the producers planned to shoot the picture on location in Tupelo, Mississippi, Foote recalls, "to make it as authentic as possible."[22] All in all, it seemed like a promising project.

Tomorrow: The Film

Foote was obviously pleased with the prospect of doing *Tomorrow* as a feature picture, and went to work on the screenplay with great enthusiasm. The running time of the movie version was expected to be about half an hour longer than that of the teledrama; hence, in composing the screenplay Foote was able to expand the original short story even more than he had done for the television script. He fit the trial sequence into the film adaptation and restored some of the other scenes that had had to be dropped from the television play for lack of time. These included Fentry's long hike to the general store to buy Sarah a sack of hard candy, which is all he can afford to give her for Christmas, as well as Sarah's burial.

Foote decided to have Douglas, who had acted as narrator of the stage production, narrate the film as well. Since Ed Pruitt, the narrator of the teledrama, was not narrating the movie, the scenes with the Pruitts became superfluous and were eventually dropped from the movie adaptation. Chick Mallison, whose role in the teleplay was fairly tangential to the main dramatic action, likewise disappeared from the movie. When Foote finished the screenplay, which is dated 10 August 1969, he turned it over to the producers, who set about making preparations for shooting the movie in the South.

Before shooting began in spring 1970, Roebling, along with two assistants, spent six months in Tupelo, Mississippi (the birthplace of Elvis Presley), choosing locales, picking residents for bit parts in the film, and even recruiting a couple of harmonica players to add to the small group of musicians who would play the movie's simple background score on the sound track. In the meantime Joseph Anthony (*The Rainmaker*) had signed on to direct the picture. Roebling, who was familiar with Anthony's previous work on both stage and screen, has since said that Anthony was asked to direct the movie because he had already amply demonstrated that he had "a great feeling for simple people and simple circumstances; and what he did in *Tomorrow* proved me right."[23]

The movie opens with a brief pre-credit sequence which depicts the shooting of Buck Thorpe by Homer Bookwright. Then, while the credits roll, we witness Thornton Douglas' final plea to the jury for his client and watch as Jackson Fentry (Robert Duvall) hangs the jury. As the credits draw to a close, we hear Douglas (Peter Masterson), the film's narrator, voice-over on the sound track, declare that he intends to ascertain Fentry's motives for acting as he did: "You see, that was my first case, and I had to find out why I lost it. . . . " Fentry's story is then told in an extended flashback, after the manner of the television version of "Tomorrow."

All the key scenes from the teledrama turn up one way or another in the motion picture, including some material that Foote had expressly written for the television play but which had had to be excised for lack of time. One of the noteworthy scenes which Foote brought over from the television script virtually intact is the sequence set on Christmas Eve, in which Fentry gives Sarah a sack of sugar candy as a Christmas present, and she suddenly begins to weep softly. Embarrassed by her display of feeling, Sarah explains that she never used to cry much at all. Even when her father drove her from the house for marrying a man he disapproved of, she continues, she did not shed one tear, but simply faced up to the situation as best she could. But lately she seems to burst into tears at the slightest provocation. "I'm just tired and nervous," she says; nowadays "somebody will come up to me and say 'Good morning' or 'Good evening,' and I'll cry." Joseph Anthony notes that this scene exemplifies Horton Foote's talent for employing revelatory dialogue to illuminate very effectively a character's personality. "That whole scene," comments Anthony, tells us much that is relevant "about Sarah, about her past, and who she is, and the kind of person she is," and as such is of great dramatic value in the film.[24]

Several valuable new scenes were created specifically for the movie, but two of the scenes which Foote constructed especially for the film contain lengthy speeches which unfortunately slow the progress of the story. In each scene Sarah delivers a monologue about her girlhood, referring to her Bible-Belt religious training, her relationships with her family, and similar matters. Some of this material is helpful in further illuminating her background, but in these two particular instances, Sarah tends to ramble on for a little too long. In commenting on sparing use of dialogue in film, director Carol

Robert Duvall as the poor dirt farmer Jackson Fentry in *Tomorrow* (1972), Duvall's favorite among all his screen roles. (Cinemabilia)

Reed once told me, "It's a funny thing: a scene can be good at three minutes, but if it's over-written into four, the extra minute weakens it." This is precisely the problem with the two scenes in question; reviewers who found the film of *Tomorrow* tedious at times more than likely were thinking of these two monologues.

Nevertheless, most of the additional sequences enhance the film considerably. A montage of touching vignettes bridges the five years from Jackson and Longstreet's infancy to the time when his uncles come to claim him. Of this sequence, Barbera writes, "We have Fentry carrying the boy like a papoose, picking cotton with him, hugging him in bed, playing with him in tall grass, and catching fish with him." Foote no doubt had this series of vivid images in mind when he remarked in an interview about the movie, "In film, the visual, sometimes in subtle ways, really takes over. The visual has an emotional impact that you can't get in the theater, and you can get it better on film than on live television."[25]

Near its conclusion, the film returns to the courtroom where it began. After the judge dismisses the jury, Douglas watches Fentry leave the courthouse, get on his mule, and ride out of town. As Fentry goes on his solitary way, Thornton Douglas, still narrating, expresses on the sound track his explanation of Fentry's reasons for hanging the jury, much as he does at the end of the short story and the television play.

After Joseph Anthony shot the picture, Reva Schlesinger, the film's editor, put together a preliminary assemblage of the footage into a rough cut that ran for more than four hours. Everyone concerned with the movie agreed that the running time of the film would have to be cut in half, since, as Roebling puts it, the story was too fragile to hold an audience's attention for more than a couple of hours. After all, "no-one was burning down Atlanta."[26] Consequently, Schlesinger, in consultation with the director, producers, and screenwriter, spent several months trimming the film to a final running time of 102 minutes.

One of the sequences excised from the final cut of the movie portrayed a meeting between Jackson Fentry and the young adult Buck Thorpe. This episode had been in both the short story and the teleplay. Robert Duvall was keenly disappointed that this encounter was not preserved in the release prints of the movie. Duvall felt that this scene implies that Fentry's deep attachment to the young man still persists, because of the link between Thorpe and the little boy he once was. Hence Duvall contends that if this scene had not been deleted from the movie, "Fentry's decision not to acquit the man who killed the boy would have more meaning, make more sense."

Reva Schlesinger has explained how a scene that Duvall felt would have clarified Fentry's motivation wound up on the cutting room floor. "We used local people for a lot of the parts," she recalls, and some of them were marvelous. But the young man chosen for the role of Buck "just didn't have it"; as a result, the sequence in question was "so poor in comparison with the quality of everything else, we couldn't use it." Schlesinger concludes, "you can do millions of things in the cutting room, but you can't do what you don't have on film."

Robert Duvall still ranks *Tomorrow* as his own personal favorite among all his films. Nevertheless, because he has some reservations about the film, particularly the one just mentioned, his praise of the picture is not unqualified. It was, he says, "a wonderful picture and a great part for me, but I think it could have been a greater movie."[27] All things considered, that seems a judgment with which one can easily agree.

The movie received several favorable notices when it opened in summer 1972. Critics pointed to the searching portrayals of Jackson and Sarah by Duvall and Bellin, Joseph Anthony's sensitive direction, Alan Green's flawless black-and-white photography, and Horton Foote's literate screenplay. Rex Reed even said that *Tomorrow* stands among the best American movies ever made. Yet the film did not receive wide distribution when it first opened. One reason was that none of the actors in the picture were major stars. Even Robert Duvall did not come into real prominence until after the two *Godfather* films (1972 and 1974). Therefore exhibitors tended to write the movie off as a low-budget picture with no big names able to attract a large audience. After some scattered playdates around the country, *Tomorrow* sank into obscurity. Like the screen version of *Intruder in the Dust*, however, the film's critical reputation as a screen classic continued to grow over the years. *Tomorrow* surfaced in a second release in major cities like New York and Chicago: when both Duvall and Foote won Oscars for *Tender Mercies* in spring 1984, there was renewed interest in their earlier collaboration. Some months later *Tomorrow* found a still wider audience when it was telecast for the first time on PBS network. And it now enjoys continued availability on videocassette.

It goes without saying that, regardless of some minor flaws, the motion picture version of *Tomorrow* is superior to the live television production. First of all, in revising his television script for the movie, Horton Foote was able to realize more fully the dramatic possibilities of the original story. Moreover, Joseph Anthony took full advantage of the opportunity to shoot the film version on location in Mississippi, capturing with compelling realism the austere atmosphere in which an impoverished farmer such as Jackson Fentry would live out his life.

One element of the story that has remained unchanged from one version of Faulkner's tale to the next is its theme. As elsewhere in his fiction, here Faulkner suggests that if some people are broken by suffering, others like Fentry can be ennobled by it. Joseph Anthony singles out the theme of "Tomorrow" as the primary reason for the lasting appeal of the story: "To me, the universality of its theme is the meat of it, the power of it. The tale of Jackson Fentry is a reminder for humankind everywhere about . . . the wonderful quality of human beings who can endure under degradation and still remain magnificent and unique." Faulkner's depiction of the indomitability of the human spirit in "Tomorrow" undoubtedly attracted Horton Foote to the story from the start. This theme has interested him all his life. "I've known people that the world has thrown everything at to discourage them, to break their spirit," he explains. "And yet something about them retains a dignity. They face life and they don't ask questions." Such a person is Jackson Fentry, and in Foote's mind no-one was better suited to play him than Robert Duvall. "He adds such a sense of dignity to that terrible expression, 'the little man,'" says Foote.[28]

Like Ben Maddow, Horton Foote believes very strongly that a screen adaptation of a fictional work must be faithful to the thematic intent of the original story, and he was gratified to learn that Faulkner, who lived to see the teledrama but not the film version of "Tomorrow," had liked the teleplay for that very reason. "People often ask my advice about dramatizing Faulkner," Foote has said. He always answers that the most essential thing to remember about doing an adaptation of a Faulkner work is that one must make sure that everyone involved with the production is committed to trying to reproduce Faulkner's personal vision as closely as possible. "I think Hollywood has so often failed with him because they insist on improving him—for whatever reasons: to make him more palatable, more popular, more commercial. I think it would be well for any dramatist to give up this approach. He can be dramatized; he can't be improved."[29]

CHAPTER 5

The Wild Blue Yonder:
The Tarnished Angels (1957)

> There was then in New Orleans a gang of barnstorm-
> ing aviators. They flew decrepit Wright Whirlwinds stuck
> together God knows how. [Faulkner and I] struck up a
> friendship with several daring fellows, who soon got
> themselves killed.
>
> *Hamilton Basso*

> Those frantic little airplanes which dashed around
> the country; and people wanted just enough money to
> live, to get to the next place to race again. . . .
> They were as ephemeral as the butterfly that's born
> this morning with no stomach and will be gone tomorrow.
>
> *William Faulkner*

During Faulkner's tenure at MGM in the early 1930s, one of his assignments had been to write a screenplay entitled *War Birds* which, we remember, he based on two of his stories about World War I pilots, "All the
Dead Pilots" and "Ad Astra." While he was busy with this project, a Faulkner short story about fliers, entitled "Honor" and published in *American
Mercury* in 1930, was being adapted for the screen by Harry Behn. Because
Howard Hawks sent Faulkner a preliminary treatment of the proposed
film, Todd McCarthy and others have assumed that Faulkner collaborated
on the scenario of *Honor*. But according to a letter from Faulkner to Sam
Marx dated 19 July 1933, he did little more than read through the treatment
and return it, since at the time he was too preoccupied with *War Birds*

to work on the script of *Honor*. As Bruce Kawin has shown in his book on Faulkner's Metro screen work, there is no convincing evidence in the files at MGM that Faulkner had any more to do with the project than he said he did. In any event, *Honor*, like *War Birds*, was never produced; but Faulkner's short story "Honor" is still of interest to us at this point because its plot has some affinities with Faulkner's 1935 novel *Pylon*, which was filmed more than two decades later as *Tarnished Angels*. "Honor" centers on Buck Monaghan, a minor figure in "Ad Astra," who is now a wing-walker in a flying act which he performs at air circuses with Howard Rogers, a stunt pilot. After Monaghan becomes romantically involved with Rogers' wife, he begins to fear that one day, while he and Rogers are doing their act, the pilot may get even with him by deliberately maneuvering the plane so that he will fall from the wing to his death. When Monaghan finally realizes that, for Rogers, it is a point of honor to protect his partner's life when they are in the air together, regardless of the personal conflicts that they may have when they are on the ground, Monaghan is ashamed of having come between Rogers and his wife. He accordingly walks out of their lives for good. This plot is paralleled in the novel *Pylon*. Similarly, Jack Holmes, a parachutist, is involved with Laverne Shumann, the wife of his pilot, Roger Shumann; and she has a child by one of them, though none of the three knows for certain which of the men is the father. That the last name of the pilot in "Honor" is almost the same as the first name of his counterpart in *Pylon* is a further, somewhat more obvious link between the two works.

The Flying Faulkners

Faulkner's interest in writing about barnstorming fliers was born of his own experiences as an aviator. In spring 1933, well over a decade after he had left the Canadian RAF in 1918, Faulkner resumed his training as a pilot, taking formal lessons in flying at the Memphis airport from Vernon Omlie, a veteran Army pilot and barnstormer. In the fall of that year, Faulkner bought a biplane of his own. It was not long before all four Faulkner brothers had followed his lead and learned to fly; they spent so much time in the air that their mother joked, "I don't have a son on earth!" By spring 1934, Faulkner, billed as "William Faulkner, famous author," was ready to participate in a flying circus staged at Ripley, Mississippi, by Vern Omlie and

Laverne Shumann (Dorothy Malone) and Burke Devlin (Rock Hudson) in *The Tarnished Angels* (1957), based on *Pylon*, Faulkner's study of barnstorming aviators. A pilot himself, Faulkner loved the movie's flying sequences. (Museum of Modern Art/Film Stills Archive)

Faulkner's youngest brother Dean. (Later on, when Faulkner occasionally participated in an air show with Dean, the brothers were sometimes billed as the "Flying Faulkners.")

Some months later a budding Southern writer named Thomas (later Tennessee) Williams passed through Oxford on a visit to his grandparents in Memphis. In a letter to a friend back home in St. Louis, Williams said that he had observed Faulkner on the town square but had not ventured to speak to him since he seemed somewhat aloof and preoccupied. When Williams was informed by the locals about Faulkner's fascination with aviation, his reaction was that flying was an interesting if curious pastime for a writer.[1] Yet, since Faulkner's avid interest in flying had often provided him with material for his fiction, aviation was not, after all, such an eccentric hobby for a writer to cultivate. *Pylon* is a case in point. That novel, as John Faulkner has written, was inspired by his brother's trip to New Orleans in mid-February 1934, to attend an air carnival. This particular flying show was being held to celebrate the dedication of Shushan Airport (now known as Lakeside Airport), which Faulkner would call Feinman Airport in the novel. "A part of what Bill writes about in *Pylon*," said John, "actually took place at that meet," which was scheduled to coincide with the Mardi Gras festivities that year.

Faulkner initially composed a short story entitled "This Kind of Courage," based on the New Orleans air circus. His decision to turn the story into a novel came about in this way. Faulkner was having difficulty making headway on his novel *Absalom, Absalom!* during this period. He mentioned this fact in a conversation with Howard Hawks while he was working briefly in Hollywood in July 1934. Hawks advised him to take a break from that project and write a novel about something other than what Hawks termed "those damned hillbillies" that his fiction was so often concerned with. Pursuing the point, Faulkner pressed him for a specific topic, and Hawks rejoined, "Well, you fly around; don't you know some pilots . . . that you can write about?" Faulkner answered that he already had a short story in the works, one suggested by the New Orleans flying circus he had attended a few months earlier; it was about some barnstormers who performed in shows of that kind. Hawks said, "That sounds good."[2] And so Faulkner decided to set *Absalom, Absalom!* aside for the time being and to expand "This Kind of Courage" into a novel called *Pylon*.

Pylon: The Novel

There are several parallels between incidents that actually happened during the New Orleans flying show that Faulkner went to and episodes that
take place in *Pylon* at the air carnival in New Valois, which is what he calls
New Orleans in the novel. But two particular incidents that occurred at
the New Orleans meet especially contributed to scenes in the novel. When
Charles N. Kenily, a young aviator, accidentally lost control of his plane
during one of the events, his aircraft plunged into Lake Pontchartrain adja-
cent to the airport. His body was never recovered. The day before the Kenily
catastrophe, another pilot, Capt. W. Merle Nelson, was likewise killed in
a crackup. Nelson had left written instructions that, in the event of his
death, his body should be cremated and the ashes scattered from a plane
over the lake, and his wishes were carried out.

In *Pylon* Faulkner worked elements of both these air tragedies into the
episode of Roger Shumann's death in a flying race. In the novel Schumann,
like Kenily, crashes into the lake, and his body is never found. In addition,
Merle Nelson's special funeral rites suggested to Faulkner the scene in the
book in which an aviator drops a funeral wreath from his plane over the
place where Roger and his aircraft had disappeared into the lake.

In addition to drawing on some of the events that happened during the
air carnival to fashion similar incidents in his book, Faulkner modeled
some of the characters in the novel on people he met at the flying circus.
Thus the newspaperman who covers the event for a New Valois daily in
some ways resembles Faulkner's friend Hermann Deutsch, who represented
the *New Orleans Item* at the air show; and one news story that Faulkner's
reporter writes for his paper is similar to an account written by Deutsch
for the *Item.* Deutsch has told Cleanth Brooks that, while there are some
similarities between himself and the reporter (who is never called anything
else in the novel), he "couldn't hope to measure up to the reporter's capacity, or even liking for, alcohol." That dimension of the reporter's makeup, of
course, was derived from Faulkner himself, according to Howard Hawks,
who said that Faulkner went on a drunk while he was at the air circus;
and so, when he wrote the novel, he told the story "through the eyes of
the drunken reporter" who overimbibes more than once in the course of
the story.

Another character in the novel taken from life was champion aviator
Matt Ord, inspired by Jimmy Wedell, one of the most admirable airmen

of his day, who chalked up a record-breaking win in one of the races during the New Orleans air meet. Faulkner paints Matt Ord as a levelheaded flier who consistently refuses to take the foolhardy risks that Roger Shumann does for the sake of winning a flying contest. In creating the estimable character of this flying ace, says Brooks, Faulkner simply wanted to suggest that "a man who knows and loves and flies planes does not have to be a romantic daredevil" like Roger.[3]

Faulkner found writing *Pylon* a relatively easy task, compared with composing a complicated historical epic like *Absalom, Absalom!* He began writing *Pylon* in October 1934 and finished the first draft on November 25. By mid-December the finished typescript was on his publisher's desk. Although Faulkner wrote *Pylon* fairly rapidly, that did not keep him from revising his work carefully before sending it on to his publisher. Nonetheless, when he received the galleys in January 1935, he discovered that his publisher's editorial staff had made several changes in the novel's text, sometimes accompanied by acrid comments such as "This sentence is cockeyed" or "Can't we have a paragraph in the next four pages?"[4]

Blotner and Polk, in their notes for the 1985 corrected edition of *Pylon*, explain that in his typescript Faulkner had placed a flashback that ran for four pages in a single extended paragraph, in order to set it off from the narration of the events in present time which the flashback interrupts. In the galleys, this long passage had been broken up into several individual paragraphs; but, as Blotner and Polk point out, Faulkner "did not try to restore the passage to its original form."[5] Instead he inserted a transitional paragraph at the conclusion of the flashback, to signal to the reader that the flashback was at an end.

Faulkner also acquiesced to some of the other modifications which the editors had made in the novel, such as the deletion of some four-letter words. The effect of the various editorial emendations made in the novel at the galley stage is that the text of *Pylon* as originally published in 1935 differs in a number of minor ways from the later corrected edition of the book. No other Faulkner novel bears the mark of editorial intervention to quite the same degree as this one.

Since Faulkner tells his story largely through the eyes of the reporter covering the air show for his paper, the reader gets to know the members of Roger Shumann's flying troupe as he does. The first two individuals he encounters are Jiggs, Roger's mechanic; and Jackie Shumann, Laverne's little boy. The meeting about when he observes Jiggs taunting Jackie with the gibe, "Who's your old man today, kid?" The six-year-old rushes at Jiggs and hammers at him "with puny and deadly purpose," until Jiggs "cries uncle," shouting, "I quit! I take it back!"[6] In this way the reporter gradually learns of the *ménage à trois* in which Laverne is involved with her husband and his partner, Jack Holmes, a parachute jumper. That the youngest bears Jack Holmes's first name and Roger Shumann's surname symbolizes the ambiguity that exists as to which of them is really his father.

To the reporter, Jackie's predicament is no laughing matter; his sympathetic concern for the boy initially triggers his keen interest in Roger Shumann's unorthodox "family" and their nomadic lifestyle. His fascination increases steadily during the remaining days of the meet. "They ain't human like us," the reporter tells his editor; Roger, Jack, and Laverne, who also does parachute stunts with Roger, couldn't routinely risk their lives in flying contests the way they do, if they had human blood in their veins. If one of them is in a plane crash, he continues, it is not human blood that they are bleeding when they are hauled out of the wreck; "it's cylinder oil the same as in the crankcase."

The reporter eventually becomes personally involved with Shumann's tribe to such an extent that he helps Roger pressure Matt Ord into selling him a plane that Ord is afraid is unsafe. Roger has already smashed up his own plane in one of the racing events and needs another in order to compete in the show's big trophy race. Ord suspects that the engine of his plane is more powerful than its body can support; but he finally relents and turns the aircraft over to Shumann in time for the trophy race, in part because he realizes that Roger and his clan are desperately in need of the prize money. When Ord's worst fears are realized during the race and the plane's fuselage begins to come apart in midair, Roger consigns himself to certain death by purposely crashdiving into the lake next to the airfield. He does so in order to avoid cracking up near the grandstands and possibly killing some of the spectators.

Laverne, who was powerless to keep Roger from imperiling his life by flying the faulty plane, cries out in her anguish, "Oh damn you, Roger!" As she rushes toward the lakeshore, clutching Jackie's hand in hers, she turns and screams at the reporter, who is running along beside them, "God damn you to hell! Get away from me!" The reporter understands her bitterness towards him, for he realizes that his well-meaning meddling has helped to bring grief and disaster on the woman to whom he was developing a secret attachment. Even after Laverne's acrimonious rebuff, he still temporarily nurtures a vague hope that at some dim future date he will be reunited with her and Jackie. But that hope is crushed when he learns that Laverne plans to deposit her son with Roger's parents and move on with Jack Holmes.

Still, the reporter makes what recompense he can for his part in helping Roger acquire the plane that destroyed him. He writes a heartfelt account of Roger's death for his paper, one that recalls Hermann Deutsch's actual writeup of Merle Nelson's funeral rites in the *Item* on 19 February 1934. When Roger Shumann flew his last race, the reporter writes, his only real competitor was Death; "and Roger Shumann lost. And so today a lone aeroplane flew out over the lake on the wings of dawn, . . . dropping a simple wreath to mark his Last Pylon." Believing that Hagood, his editor, will not accept a news story that smacks too much of poetry and sentiment, the reporter produces another, more perfunctory rendition of the facts. Yet, as literary critic Karl Zender comments, "his subsequent attempt to recount the event journalistically is also frustrated, for his disgust at converting the experience into mere newspaper copy breaks through in almost every phrase of the account he leaves on Hagood's desk."[7] The reporter weights down the typescript on the editor's desk with an empty whiskey bottle – not the only one he has finished off during the remainder of the air carnival – and goes off into the night.

The reporter, as Faulkner delineates his personality, is a hopelessly ineffectual man whom the novelist associates with the pathetic, benighted title character of T.S. Eliot's poem, "The Lovesong of J. Alfred Prufrock." Throughout the poem Prufrock consistently fails to gain any deep insight into his unhappy state of affairs. At the novel's end, the reporter is left to wander, like another Prufrock, through the dark, foggy night, an apt metaphor for his murky state of mind, as he gropes to find some meaning in the events of the preceding few days. He cannot articulate to Laverne either his guilt about the part he played in Roger's demise or his loving solicitude toward her and Jackie. Because he is at a total loss as to what to say to either of them, he does not even see them off at the train depot when they leave town with Jack Holmes.

Although the reporter is hardly an inspiring figure, the novel is not without a hero, or at least someone with positive human qualities. Olga Vickery reminds us in her Faulkner book that, after all, in flying Ord's faulty plane in the trophy race, Roger Shumann shows himself willing to risk his life in an unselfish attempt to provide his group with the funds necessary for its continuance. Moreover, he chooses to lose his life in a watery grave rather than endanger the lives of any of the bystanders watching the race. To some extent, Vickery asserts, Roger Shumann can therefore be seen as a casualty of our modern, mechanized world; but his death "also asserts the capacity for love, loyalty, and self-sacrifice within that world."[8] Hence, Faulkner implies at the end of the book, Roger genuinely deserved the tribute which the reporter penned in his honor but which regrettably wound up in the press room wastebasket.

The action of the novel takes place during Mardi Gras, as did the New Orleans air circus that Faulkner attended. Cleanth Brooks writes that "Faulkner brings his story to a conclusion just before the dawn of Shrove Tuesday, the last day of Mardi Gras." From this Brooks infers that "clearly he had no wish to exploit whatever symbolism might lie in the fact that the morrow of penitence follows the traditional day of revelry."[9] On the contrary, Faulkner implies that very notion in the novel's penultimate chapter. While waiting for Roger's corpse to be dredged up out of the lake, the reporter notes that some of the holiday decorations are already beginning to fade and fall from the buildings around the airport where they had hung throughtout the festive Mardi Gras season, as if the very bunting itself "had anticipated the midnight bells from town which would signal the beginning of Lent." Indeed, the kind of dissipated carnival existence that Laverne and Jack Holmes shared with Roger on the barnstorming circuit has already given way, in the wake of his death, to the Ash Wednesday of mourning for his loss.

Pylon drew a cool critical response when it was published on 25 March 1935. Some reviewers were offended by the sex and violence in Faulkner's narrative; others felt that the novelist's allusions to the Eliot poems like "Prufrock" were at times more pretentious than meaningful. Most agreed that *Pylon* could not be numbered among Faulkner's major novels, since it rarely rises above the level of routine melodrama; and one Nashville daily went so far as solemnly to pronounce that Faulkner's talent was spent. A minority report was filed by Ernest Hemingway when he remarked in an article in *Esquire* that he had been "reading, and admiring, *Pylon* by William Faulkner."[10] Since Faulkner by this time cared little what was said of him in print, he did not fret long about the book's negative notices, but simply got on with *Absalom, Absalom!*

A few months after the publication of *Pylon*, an actual incident occurred which grimly illustrated the old adage that life sometimes seems to imitate art, rather than the other way round. Faulkner, we know, would sometimes join his youngest brother Dean in putting on an air show in the greater Oxford area. On 2 and 3 November 1935, the "Flying Faulkners" performed at Marquette Field, and the following week, on the Armistice Day weekend, Dean was staging another air carnival in Pontotoc. On Sunday afternoon, 10 November, some time before the show was scheduled to start, Dean took a student flyer and two passengers up for a short ride in the biplane that he had bought from his brother Bill. When Dean failed to return in time for the show, a search party drove around the area looking for the plane. They found it cracked up in a pasture near Thaxton; Dean and the other three occupants of the plane were all dead. An investigation of the wreckage revealed that, in John Faulkner's words, Dean had done "something he shouldn't have, letting a student have the controls with passengers aboard." Apparently the student pilot lost control of the plane, and Dean was not able to intervene in time to avert a crash. "Dean's luck just ran out," John Faulkner concludes. "Mine, Bill's, and Jack's never did." The other three Faulkners never had a serious accident while piloting an aircraft.[11]

Dean Faulkner's shattered remains were buried the day after the crash, on Armistice Day, 11 November 1935. William Faulkner chose the inscription for Dean's tombstone, giving his brother the same epitaph, a paraphrase of Exodus 19:4, that he had originally fashioned for the deceased aviator John Sartoris in *Flags in the Dust*: "I bore him on eagles' wings and brought him unto me." Dean Faulkner's widow, Louise Faulkner Meadow, told me that her brother-in-law Bill felt personally responsible for Dean's death to some degree, because he had encouraged Dean to learn to fly in the first place and had sold him the plane in which he was killed. William Faulkner therefore took it upon himself to provide for Louise and her baby girl, who was born the following March. "After Dean's death," Mrs. Meadow concluded, "Bill never wrote another book about flying."

The Tarnished Angels: The Film

Although various studios showed some interest in it over the years, it was not until the mid-1950s that Hollywood bought the rights to *Pylon*. "Different people have been nibbling at this book for twenty years now," Faulkner wrote Harold Ober in 1956. "There must be something in it somewhere." Producer Albert Zugsmith (*Touch of Evil*) was convinced that the novel had the potential to make a good movie. According to George Zuckerman, the author of the film's script, it was Zugsmith who sold the idea of making the picture to Universal-International – although the studio brass had never heard of the novel and initially thought that "*Pylon* was a snake."[12] Faulkner was paid $50,000 for the screen rights to *Pylon,* the same amount he had received for the movie sale of *Intruder in the Dust* eight years earlier.

Zugsmith was able to persuade the front office at Universal to make the movie because he had put together a production package that included several key people who had been involved in his highly successful 1956 film, *Written on the Wind:* actors Robert Stack, Rock Hudson, and Dorothy Malone; screenwriter George Zuckerman; and director Douglas Sirk.

German-born filmmaker Douglas Sirk was enthusiastic about directing *Tarnished Angels* (1957), the title chosen for the movie. He had wanted to make a film of *Pylon* ever since he had first read the novel in 1936, while he was still making pictures in his homeland, before the onset of World War II forced him to leave Germany for Hollywood. In fact, Sirk recalled trying without success to interest UFA, the German studio for which he worked in the 1930s, to film the novel; "but they weren't interested in a flying picture."[13]

Zuckerman had also read the book when it came out and was delighted to have the opportunity to adapt it to the screen. There was one stumbling block he had to overcome at the outset, however, before he could get down to working on the script in earnest; and that was that the front office feared that the novel's plot might be too racy to pass muster with the industry censor. Zuckerman therefore composed "a two-page memo on how I could get the script to pass censorship."

In his memo Zuckerman suggested, for example, eliminating from the script the *ménage à trois* that is so central to the novel. In this and other ways he showed how it would be possible to bring the scenario into line with the censorship regulations. His ideas met with the approval of both the studio and the censor, and he accordingly went ahead with composing the screenplay.

For Zuckerman a significant theme in the novel, which he also wanted to come across in the film, was embodied in the lesson learned by the reporter, whom he named Burke Devlin, as a result of abetting Roger Shumann in his efforts to acquire the aircraft that killed him. "What he learns about himself," Zuckerman has explained, "is that one who plays God sometimes unwittingly plays Death."

Sirk too saw Devlin (Rock Hudson) as someone who learns something about himself and about life through his association with the devil-may-care gypsies of the air he meets at the air circus. "At first he is wide-eyed, rather innocent, just reflecting events," said Sirk. "But then his conscious-ness grows, it widens from a lame curiosity to fascination," and eventually he comes to understand and to sympathize with Shumann and his group.

Since Faulkner had associated the reporter with J. Alfred Prufrock, Sirk read some lines from the poem to Hudson on the set "in order to give him an idea of what Faulkner had in mind with the reporter's character." Sirk selected the passage in which Prufrock admits that he is not Prince Hamlet and was never meant to be, implying that he knows that he is not a tragic hero and that in life he will always play a supporting role for those who are. "You are not the prince in this movie," Sirk told Hudson. "That's Stack." His point was that Roger Shumann, who sacrifices his life for oth-ers, is the true tragic hero of the film; hence, despite the importance of Burke Devlin in the story, it is Shumann and not Devlin who is the pri-mary protagonist of the drama. "To my surprise, he understood," Sirk con-cluded; Hudson never sought to upstage Stack in the scenes they played together or in any other way to steal the picture.[15]

To ensure that Robert Stack grasped the significance of the role of Roger, during shooting Sirk in turn read to him an excerpt from Eliot's "Waste Land," to which Faulkner also alludes in *Pylon*. The lines he chose com-prise the fourth section of the poem, entitled "Death by Water," in which the poet pictures the ocean waters washing away the flesh of a dead man who in life had been handsome and tall. When these lines are applied to Roger Shumann, they emphasize that he too died in his prime; this thought makes the death by water of the film's protagonist all the more poignant.

Since there is no *ménage à trois* in the film, the Jack Holmes character does not appear in the picture as such. In the movie the role of Jiggs (Jack Carson) is something of a composite of the characters of both Jiggs and Jack Holmes as they appear in the novel: the movie's Jiggs is not only Rog-er's mechanic but also has a deep feeling for Laverne (Dorothy Malone). In the film, of course, there is no evidence that Jiggs is actually sharing Laverne with Roger, although a rumor to this effect circulates on the barn-storming circuit.

Consequently, in spite of the fact that in the film Jackie Shumann (Chris Olsen) is still teased by the grease monkeys around the hangars for having "two fathers," Jiggs is not really competing with Roger for Laverne. Nor has he done so since the night that he and Roger had a showdown over which of them was going to marry her and take responsibility for her unborn child. On that occasion Jiggs demonstrated his willingness to wed Laverne, not because there was any reason to suspect that he might be the father of the child, but because he was afraid Roger, the real father, could not be trusted to live up to his obligations to Laverne by marrying her himself.

The episode is presented in flashback in the movie, while Laverne narrates it, voice-over on the sound track, during a conversation with Devlin. Laverne discloses to Roger and Jiggs that she is pregnant as the trio sit together at a table in a dingy café, and Jiggs immediately demands to know if Roger plans to marry her. Roger's response is to take two sugar cubes from the bowl on the table and make a pair of dice out of them by dotting them with pencil marks; he then challenges Jiggs to roll the dice with him, to determine which of them will marry Laverne. After both men have taken their turns, Jiggs says, "I lose, I marry Laverne"; and Roger answers, "No, she marries the winner."

One infers that it is Jiggs's very willingness to marry Laverne if Roger does not, that shames Roger into taking responsibility for Laverne and for the child she is carrying. Sirk's subtle handling of the nuances of this flashback sequence make it one of the better scenes in the movie.

Elsewhere in the film, Sirk displays special directorial skill in employing visual imagery to make a symbolic point. For example, on the night before the big trophy race in which Roger will fly Ord's risky plane, Laverne and Burke are alone in his apartment discussing the impending event. The Mardi Gras season is in full swing, and a costume party is in progress in the adjoining flat. Hearing the noise, Laverne remarks forlornly, "That's the story of my life: the party is always next door." Suddenly a partygoer wearing a death's-head mask bursts into the dimly lit room. Both Laverne and Burke are frightened by the shocking sight, because this ghostly apparition of the Grim Reaper which materializes in the shadowy room seems to presage that Death may claim victory over Roger in the next day's flying contest. In the trophy race sequence itself, right after Roger's aircraft plummets into the lake, Laverne stands on the shore, looking toward the scene of the crash. Near her in the crowd of onlookers is a Mardi Gras reveler wearing a deathly white mask which recalls the one worn by the individual who appeared in Devlin's apartment the night before. At this point the grotesque visage confirms that Roger's only real competitor in his last race was Death itself; and Roger has lost.

Laverne (Dorothy Malone) and Roger Shumann (Robert Stack) before his fatal flight in *The Tarnished Angels*. (Museum of Modern Art/Film Stills Archive)

The dark, brooding atmosphere of the film, coupled with the somber vision of life reflected in this tale of disillusionment and death, marks *Tarnished Angels* as the kind of American movie French film critics christened *film noir* (dark cinema). This cycle in American cinema, which flourished during the 1940s and includes earlier Sirk films like *Lured* and *Shockproof*, was nearing its end when Sirk shot *Tarnished Angels* in winter 1956–57. The pessimistic view of the human condition exhibited in such movies was an outgrowth of the cynicism spawned by World War II and the period of uncertainty in its aftermath.

This bleak attitude toward life is very much in evidence in *Tarnished Angels*. In keeping with the conventions of *film noir*, the film is dominated by a spare, unvarnished realism expressed in the stark, newsreel-like quality of the black-and-white widescreen location cinematography, and especially in the grim scenes of Roger's crash and other crackups during the air races.

The prototypical milieu of *film noir* is shadows; it is exemplified in the present film in ominous night sequences such as the one in Devlin's dark apartment, in which Laverne and Burke look forward with foreboding to the death-defying flight that Roger is to make the next day.

Yet the ending of *Tarnished Angels* is not as dark and gloomy as that of many *noir* movies, or as that of the novel from which *Angels* is derived. At the end of *Tarnished Angels* Laverne Shumann is allowed the kind of regeneration that Faulkner denies her in *Pylon*. In the movie Laverne does not abandon her son in order to continue her itinerant existence with another man. True, she is tempted to accept Matt Ord's offer of a liaison with him—in the movie, he is not the decent fellow he is in the novel—but Burke Devlin persuades her instead to take Jackie and go back home to Iowa, where she can raise her son in the wholesome environment of a small farming community. Sirk presages Laverne's change of heart by emphasizing her predilection for the novel *My Ántonia*, by Willa Cather, whose fiction chronicles life in the American Midwest. More than once Sirk focuses his camera on Laverne reading or clasping a copy of this beloved novel. When Burke goes to the airport to bid farewell to Laverne and Jackie, he presents her with his own copy of *My Ántonia*, and requests that she return it to him some day—in person.

Then she boards the plane for Iowa with Jackie, and as it takes off one recalls an earlier scene which also prefigures Laverne's ultimate regeneration in the picture. In it Laverne is making a daring parachute jump from Roger's plane in one of the events at the flying circus. The announcer wonders over the loudspeaker whether or not she will safely survive this perilous jump, and then as he watches her descent affirms reassuringly, "Lovely Laverne Shumann is going to make it." Pauline Degenfelder comments that the physical stamina Laverne exhibits in this scene foreshadows the "moral resiliency" which she demonstrates at the movie's conclusion.[16] Laverne Shumann, we know by film's end, is going to make it.

George Zuckerman has averred that the studio's high command insisted on an upbeat ending of this sort for the film, because they believed that a happy ending would be more in harmony with the expectations of the mass audience of the time. If the movie's conclusion is not in keeping with the somber way in which Faulkner ended his novel, we are at least prepared for it to some degree during the film, especially through Laverne's nostalgic references to the rustic farm life of her youth, prompted by her reading of *My Ántonia*.

Furthermore, Pauline Degenfelder rightly observes that Sirk keeps the movie's positive conclusion from seeming too pat by casting doubt on the possibility that Laverne and Burke will ever meet again, much less become man and wife. "Will I ever see you again?" Devlin asks quizzically; and Laverne answers simply, "I don't know." It was wise to introduce this note of ambiguity into the film's finale, since otherwise it would have appeared that Laverne's spiritual rejuvenation was being almost instantly rewarded with the promise of a handsome husband waiting in the wings to replace Roger. That would have rendered the ending trite and sentimental in a way that the actual ending is not.

The picture raises some other critical questions. Pauline Kael has suggested that it was a mistake to allow the movie to run for another quarter-hour after Roger's death. Presumably she is questioning the relevance to the film of such items as Devlin's eulogy for Roger and the hero's wake which the other pilots accord their deceased comrade. As for Burke's eulogy for Roger, in the film he delivers it orally to his editor and does not attempt to put it on paper and submit it for publication. After reading over the pedestrian presentation of the facts about Roger's demise which his newspaper is going to print, Burke drunkenly tells his editor that no mere news story is worthy of Roger's noble death. With that, he extemporizes a deeply felt tribute to Roger Shumann, expressing sentiments similar to those reflected in his poetic obituary for Roger in the novel. Devlin concludes with the words, "Throw the dirt gently on his grave, bow your head, and read kindly his epitaph."

This eulogy is as important in *Tarnished Angels* as it is in *Pylon* because it reinforces the fact that Roger's heroic death redeemed an otherwise reckless and aimless existence. A similar case, however, cannot be made for the wake sequence, which, unlike the press room scene just described, was not in the novel. The wake scene seems superfluous in the picture, in that, by way of additional toasts and tributes, it makes essentially the same point about Roger's noble demise as Devlin's eulogy does. It is not Devlin's speech, then, but the wake sequence that makes the scenes following Roger's death less of an epilogue than an anticlimax. The last fifteen minutes of the film should have been trimmed but not eliminated altogether.

Faulkner's opinion of the movie, which he expressed shortly after its release in December 1957, was that, although the film departed from the book in some ways, he felt that "it was pretty good, quite honest." Not surprisingly, he especially liked the flying sequences. Sirk recalled that Faulkner told him personally how much he admired the simplicity of Rock Hudson's performance as Devlin: "He thought that perhaps this was a new Gary Cooper."[17]

In the years since the picture came out, critical opinion has tended to be registered largely in extremes. Jon Halliday, in his book on Sirk, rhapsodizes that *Tarnished Angels* is "outstandingly the best adaptation to the screen of any Faulkner story." At the other end of the spectrum, Pauline Kael remarks, "It's the kind of bad movie that you know is bad—and yet you're held by the mixture of polished style and quasi-melodramatics achieved by the director, Douglas Sirk."[18]

Obviously a true assessment of the film lies somewhere between these contradictory judgments. A more balanced appraisal would be that *Tarnished Angels* has some excellent scenes, many of which have been noted; but it does not often rise above the conventions of ordinary melodrama. But then, neither does *Pylon*, as literary critics pointed out when the novel first appeared. *Pylon*, after all, is generally considered to be one of Faulkner's minor novels. And, as French cinema critic Georges Sadoul has written, Douglas Sirk was a conscientious craftsman whose adaptations of fictional works were seldom any better than their literary origins. There is no valid reason to see *Tarnished Angels* as an exception to this rule.

CHAPTER 6

Hot Spell:
The Long Hot Summer
(1958 and 1985)

> The bottom is full of nice people;
> only cream and bastards rise.
>
> *Lew Harper, in the film* Harper

The Snopes clan, a horde of "poor white trash," surfaces often throughout Faulkner's fiction, and he devoted three novels especially to them. Although the three books were published over a span of nearly twenty years, from the first in 1940 to the last in 1959, Faulkner conceived the fundamental plot of the entire Snopes trilogy in a single burst of creative insight. "I thought of the whole story at once," he said at the time the second volume was published in 1957, "like a bolt of lightning lights up a landscape and you see everything; but it takes time to write it." And he was in no hurry to finish it.

The Snopeses were based on a group of sharecroppers who started moving into Oxford during the years that Faulkner and his brothers were growing up. "They were not content to live out their lives as their forefathers had done, scrabbling out less than a living from some washed-out hill farm," John Faulkner recalled; rather, they were upwardly mobile with a vengeance. "As Bill described them, they moved first into the edge of town, into jerry-built frame houses that rented for only a few dollars a month," John Faulkner continued; "they took menial jobs, then got into businesses of their own, like cafés and small grocery stores."[1]

The Hamlet: The Novel

Faulkner's initial attempt at writing the first volume of his trilogy was entitled *Father Abraham*, named for the Old Testament patriarch who led his people out of the wilderness and into the flourishing land of Canaan. Flem Snopes, the undisputed chief of the Snopes tribe, is a latter-day Abraham who is determined to lead his kinfolk out of the back country and into the villages and towns of Yoknapatawpha County, where, like the Israelites of old, they hope to prosper. Faulkner began writing *Father Abraham* in fall 1926 but abandoned its composition after a while in favor of finishing another work-in-progress, *Flags in the Dust*. He decided to publish as a separate short story what was at that point the most substantial episode of *Father Abraham* that he had so far completed. He entitled it "Spotted Horses," and it eventually appeared in *Scribner's* in 1931.

Over the next decade Faulkner continued intermittently to compose and publish short stories about Flem Snopes and his relatives in various periodicals, always with a view to weaving these tales eventually into the fabric of the uncompleted novel, which would ultimately be called *The Hamlet*, or into a later volume of the Snopes saga. Faulkner summarized the evolution of *The Hamlet*, which is set in the early part of the century, this way: "*The Hamlet* was incepted as a novel. When I began it [as *Father Abraham*] it produced 'Spotted Horses,' went no further. About two years later suddenly I had . . . 'Jamshyd's Courtyard'"; and so it went, "until one day I decided I had better start on the first volume or I'd never get any of it down. So I wrote an induction toward the spotted horse story," which included not only some previously published stories about the Snopses, but also a great deal of new material. "'Spotted Horses' became a longer story, . . . and [I] went on with 'Jamshyd's Courtyard,'" the final episode in the novel.[2] He divided this cornucopia of material into four large sections or books: "Flem"; "Eula," named for the girl who becomes Flem's wife; "The Long Summer"; and "The Peasants."

In late 1938, while he was working on *The Hamlet*, Faulkner sent his publisher an outline of the entire trilogy, which traces Flem Snopes's systematic rise to a station of wealth and power by means of treachery and cunning. Flem begins his climb up the ladder of success by working in a general store in the village of Frenchman's Bend in *The Hamlet* (1940); he moves on to the town of Jefferson where he becomes vice-president of a bank in *The Town* (1957); in *The Mansion* (1959) he finally attains the presidency of the bank and occupies the mansion previously owned by his predecessor, whom he has ruthlessly supplanted as bank president.

The Hamlet was originally going to begin with a chapter centering on Colonel Sartoris "Sarty" Snopes, the ten-year-old son of Ab Snopes, a dour tenant farmer who has rented a small farm from a landowner named Major de Spain. Because of a petty disagreement between Ab Snopes and the major, Ab decides to burn down de Spain's barn. Ab has often taken vengeance in this fashion on anyone he believes has wronged him; and the story depicts the endeavors of Sarty, who is fed up with his father's savage ways, to prevent him from carrying out his plan of destruction. But Sarty's efforts prove futile, and the incident concludes with the lad running away from his family, never to return. Faulkner decided, on second thought, not to include this episode as it stands in *The Hamlet*, most likely because it seemed inappropriate to open a three-volume *magnum opus* by spotlighting a character who would disappear from the trilogy in the opening pages of the first volume and never appear again.

Faulkner therefore published this episode in the form in which he had originally written it, as a self-contained short story called "Barn Burning," in *Harper's* in 1939. Except for a reference to Sarty's flight from his family, Faulkner wrote Sarty Snopes out of the story altogether in the condensed form in which "Barn Burning" appears in Book One of *The Hamlet*. He concentrates instead in the novel on Ab Snopes's propensity for employing arson to settle his accounts with anyone who he thinks has done him an injustice. This dimension of "Barn Burning" is crucial to the plot of *The Hamlet*, because Flem is later able to utilize his father's reputation as an arsonist to parlay his way into a decent job in the village, so that he can renounce the wretched existence of a sharecropper for good. This comes about after he and his father have begun farming a piece of land belonging to Will Varner, a local businessman and landowner. When Will finds out about Ab's falling out with Major de Spain, he accedes to Flem's request to employ him as a clerk in his general store, with the understanding that in exchange Flem will keep his father from ever setting fire to a Varner barn while Ab is sharecropping on Will Varner's land. This position in Varner's store gives Flem a foothold in the business life of the village hamlet of Frenchman's Bend, and, more importantly, allows him to take his first step toward eventually displacing Will's son Jody as the old man's closest business associate, a feat that he accomplishes by novel's end.

"Spotted Horses," which Faulkner considerably revised and extended when he incorporated it into *The Hamlet,* was inspired by an incident that had actually occurred when Faulkner once paid a visit to the small town of Pittsboro. Faulkner happened to be sitting on the front porch of the boarding house where he was staying, while some strangers auctioned off some unbroken calico ponies in the vacant lot across the street. "Just like in Bill's story," John Faulkner has noted, "the men sold all the horses, put the money in their pockets and left. When the buyers went in to get their purchases, someone left the gate open and those ponies spread like colored confetti over the countryside. Bill sat there on the porch and saw it all. One of them ran the length of the porch, and he had to dive back into the hallway to get out of its path."[3] Faulkner had a character in his story chased by one of the spotted horses in a similar fashion when he recreated this event in fictional form.

The incident of the spotted horses in *The Hamlet* begins when Flem shrewdly hires a wily Texan to conduct the auction of a string of untamed ponies he has imported from Texas. Flem instructs the auctioneer to announce that the horses belong to him and not to Flem, so that Flem himself can remain a silent partner in the venture. The purpose of this subterfuge soon becomes evident. When the locals fail to capture the wild horses they have foolishly bought, some of them demand their money back; Flem maintains that he had nothing whatever to do with the sale of the animals and advises them that they must seek a refund from the Texan – who, of course, by that time has left town. Even Mrs. Armstid, who goes to court over the matter, is unable to force Flem to return the money her improvident husband paid for a pony she knows she and her impoverished family will never see again.

The horse auction is only one of the Flem's schemes to better his financial and social status during the period he is living in Frenchman's Bend. But his biggest coup is marrying Eula Varner, the voluptuous daughter of his employer, Will Varner, after Eula has become pregnant by her sweetheart, who has deserted her. This unexpected windfall enables Flem to become a member of the most well-to-do family in the village, and hence to take an important step up the social ladder he has been steadily climbing ever since he arrived in the hamlet.

The novel ends with Flem perpetrating one last fraud before leaving the village of Frenchman's Bend and moving on to the town of Jefferson. This final episode is a reworking of the short story "Lizards in Jamshyd's Courtyard," which Faulkner originally published in the *Saturday Evening Post* in 1932. It revolves around the Old Frenchman's place (in *Sanctuary*, the site of Lee Goodwin's bootlegging operation), which was deeded to Flem when he married Eula by her father, the owner of the property. Once the Frenchman's place is in his possession, Flem decides to take advantage of the old legend that a treasure may be buried on the grounds of the ramshackle mansion. This treasure, said to consist of several sacks of silver coins, was supposedly hidden there during the Civil War by the family that owned the place at the time, to protect their fortune from the invading Yankees. In order to implement his devious scheme, Flem slyly gives the impression to three townsmen that he has hunted for but failed to unearth this fabled treasure, and is willing to sell them the property, should they like to try their luck at finding and mining the buried silver. In reality he is perpetrating a hoax known as "the salted mine"; he has salted the grounds of the Frenchman's place with some coins the men can easily dig up. Before closing the deal with Flem, the trio goes on a preliminary digging expedition, just as Flem knew they would; and in due course they discover the coins Flem had planted there for them to find. They naturally assume that their discovery means they are well on the way to uncovering the whole treasure hoard, and eagerly buy the Old Frenchman's place from Flem. Only too late do they learn that they have been cheated by a practiced swindler.

As Millgate has shown, the theme that links the novel's varied incidents, including those of the Texas ponies and the salted silver mine, is the way that greed and self-interest infect human behavior. Faulkner must have conceived this theme at the very inception of the Snopes saga, since it clearly dominates the earliest material he composed about the Snopses, starting with *Father Abraham* in 1926. Even the marriage of Flem and Eula Varner revolves around this theme of greedy self-interest, since Flem agrees to wed Eula and give her unborn child a name in exchange for cash and some of Will Varner's real estate holdings. So in the world of *The Hamlet* even marriage is reduced to a crass business transaction. Millgate comments that at the conclusion of the novel, when Flem moves to the town of Jefferson where he plans to exploit the citizenry in much the same way he has conned and cheated the villagers of Frenchman's Bend, "we see that in linear terms *The Hamlet* can be simply and accurately described as the story of Flem's upward progress from near-rags to near-riches, from a dirt farm to the ownership of a substantial bank balance."[4]

The spotted horses incident in the novel is considered to be among

Faulkner's finest achievements as a fiction writer. It manages to encompass within the boundaries of one episode not only the farcical comedy inherent in the fruitless endeavors of the villagers to catch the mad steeds they have purchased, but also the pathos of the equally hopeless efforts of Mrs. Armstid to reclaim from Flem the money her husband wasted on the pony he bought. When Faulkner was asked whatever possessed these poor peasants to compete with each other at an auction for the dubious privilege of buying wild animals they could never hope to corral, much less tame, he answered that the variegated ponies "symbolize the hope, the aspiration of the masculine part of society that is capable . . . of committing puerile folly for some geegaw that has attracted him."[5] Putting it another way, the spotted horses represent the common tendency in human beings to buy what they do not need, with money they cannot afford, in order to impress others who, likely as not, are no better off than they are. And it is this human frailty that Flem pitilessly exploits for his own gain in the people of Frenchman's Bend during his tenure there.

The pervasive theme discussed above, which ties together the novel's different episodes, was not obvious to many of the critics who reviewed *The Hamlet* when it was published on 1 April 1940. More than a few reviewers confessed sheer bafflement over the novel; its multifaceted plot seemed to be what one critic termed a collection of episodes strung together like so many beads on a string, with no strong unifying theme. *Time* even wondered if the author himself really knew what the novel was all about. As a consequence of the tepid critical response to *The Hamlet*, it was not a bestseller. Hence no immediate interest was shown in the novel by any Hollywood studio; nor would there be for some years to come.

The Long Hot Summer: The Film

In 1955, Jerry Wald, for whom Faulkner had worked at Warner's, optioned the movie rights to both *The Hamlet* and *The Sound and the Fury*. Wald, who was an admirer of Faulkner and his work, was now producing pictures at Fox; and he succeeded in persuading the studio to pay a total of $50,000 for the movie rights to both of these novels. This was actually a bargain price, since Faulkner had received $50,000 apiece for the movie rights to *Intruder in the Dust* and *Pylon*. Wald decided that the film versions of both *The Hamlet* and *The Sound and the Fury* would be shot in widescreen and

Paul Newman as the quintessential outsider Ben Quick in *The Long Hot Summer* (1958), based on *The Hamlet*. (Movie Star News)

color. He opted to put *The Hamlet* into production first, borrowing the film's title, *The Long Hot Summer,* from Book Three of the novel, "The Long Summer." "We changed the name," director Martin Ritt (*Hud*) explained at the time, "so people wouldn't confuse it with that other *Hamlet.*"[6] Because of the movie's title, George Sidney and some other Faulkner commentators have assumed that *The Long Hot Summer* was an adaptation of only the third book of the novel. In fact, the movie took virtually nothing but its title from "The Long Summer," rather drawing material from the novel's other three sections, particularly the first and the last.

Wald's production was to be the first Faulkner film shot in color; except for the 1961 *Sanctuary*, all subsequent films of Faulkner's work would follow suit. *The Long Hot Summer* (1958), which costarred Paul Newman and Academy Award-winner Joanne Woodward (*The Three Faces of Eve*), was made shortly before their marriage, the first of several films that they would make together in the years to come. The screenplay for the picture, by the husband-wife team of Irving Ravetch and Harriet Frank, Jr., was the first of three film adaptations of Faulkner's fiction accomplished by the team.

Oddly enough, it was probably the novel's episodic narrative structure, which literary critics had decried when it came out, that made *The Hamlet* easily adapted for film. Several incidents in the novel, some of which had been published separately as short stories before their inclusion in *The Hamlet*, constitute self-contained units. The screenwriters therefore were able simply to pick the episodes they judged screenworthy and drop the rest; in this way they could develop to their fullest dramatic potential those incidents they did retain.

The principal episodes from the novel that found their way into the script were the barn-burning episode and the incidents dealing with the spotted horses and the hidden treasure. Ravetch and Frank placed these items and the others they lifted from the novel within an overall narrative framework of their own devising. Some of the material supplied by the screenwriters to fill out the movie's scenario departed considerably from the plot of the novel. Nonetheless they combined their own story material with the material from the novel so adroitly that the movie remains essentially what Cleanth Brooks called *The Hamlet*: "a sort of sardonic Horatio Alger story, a tale of commercial success in which the poor but diligent young man marries the boss's daughter and becomes a financial power."[7]

In the film the central character is renamed Ben Quick, a name borrowed from a minor figure in the Snopes saga, because the surname aptly describes the speed with which the opportunistic Ben Quick intends to get ahead in this world. The movie, whose setting has been updated to the 1950s, begins with a pre-credit sequence in which we watch a barn burst into flames; shortly thereafter we see Ben Quick (Paul Newman) being ordered to leave town by the local authorities, who are convinced that he started the blaze. During the opening credits we see Ben traveling; by the end of the credits, he has hitchhiked to the outskirts of Frenchman's Bend. He is given a lift into the village hamlet by Clara Varner (Joanne Woodward) and Eula Varner (Lee Remick, the star of *Sanctuary*). In *The Long Hot Summer*, Eula is not the daughter of Will Varner but his daughter-in-

Ben Quick (Paul Newman) and Will Varner (Orson Welles), playing for keeps in *The Long Hot Summer*. (Movie Star News)

law, the wife of his son Jody (Eula's unmarried brother in the novel). It is Clara who is Will's daughter in the film instead of Eula; therefore, it is for Clara that Ben sets his cap. In *The Long Hot Summer*, Will's daughter does not have to rush into marriage because she is already pregnant by a previous suitor, so Ben must court Clara if he intends to wed her. And woo her he does, for in the movie Ben genuinely loves her and does not merely want to arrange a marriage with her in order to improve his social and financial position in the hamlet.

Why the filmmakers thought it propitious to alter the relationship of Jody and Eula from brother and sister to husband and wife, no-one, including the screenwriting team, has ever explained. One can only surmise that the writers wanted to portray a pair of contrasting couples, one which already has a lasting love relationship (Jody and Eula) and one which must struggle to establish one (Ben and Clara).

At any rate, Ben uses his chance meeting with Eula and Clara to wangle an introduction to Jody (Anthony Franciosa), who hires him as a tenant farmer on the Varner estate. Will Varner (Orson Welles in a bravura performance) is upset to hear that Ben is sharecropping on the Varner land, because he knows of the Quick family's reputation for arson. He accordingly offers Ben a job in his general store if he promises to leave the Varner barns alone, and further challenges Ben to prove himself a worthy employee by having him auction off a batch of horses he owns. One can see how deftly the screenwriters have drawn on both the barn burning and the spotted horses incident in the novel to move the film's plot forward.

In the film, Ben personally disposes of the whole horde of unbroken horses, without the aid of a veteran auctioneer, by displaying slick showmanship that simply bowls over the villagers. When Mrs. Armstid comes to Varner's store and desperately begs Ben to return the hardearned money her husband spent for one of the wild animals, he obliges her by taking the cash from the till and handing it over without further ado. To Jody, who witnesses the transaction, Ben explains that he is trying to foster good will among the store's regular customers. On the surface Ben shows himself more generous in dealing with Mrs. Armstid in this scene than Flem does in the novel; nevertheless, Ben's motive for acting as he does is still selfish. He wants to ingratiate himself with the store's clientele, in order to boost sales and impress Will Varner with his business acumen.

As a matter of fact, the manner in which Ben earlier handled the horse auction and now manages the general store has impressed Will very favorably—so much so that Will repeatedly reminds Clara that the aggressive, attractive young man is her best bet for a husband. Clara reacts negatively to Will's insistent urging, but her overbearing father continues to press her to accept Ben's suit just the same. For his part, Ben welcomes the old man's active support of his campaign to win Clara.

Meanwhile Jody is growing deeply jealous of the way that his father is allowing an outsider to replace his own son as his right-hand man in the running of his business affairs. Finally Jody frantically confronts Ben and threatens to kill him. As an apparent peace offering between himself and Jody, Ben sells Jody the Old Frenchman's place, which Will had turned over to Ben earlier, so that Jody can search for the bags of silver rumored to be buried there; thus the salted mine episode is neatly integrated into the film. Jody is determined to unearth the treasure and show his father how resourceful he can be; but Will scoffingly informs his son that he has simply permitted Ben to dupe him with the venerable old stratagem of the salted treasure.

To Jody this humiliating experience is the last straw. In a fit of rage he decides to revenge himself on both the father he believes has rejected him and the rival he feels is responsible for his father's alienation. He locks Will in one of the barns and puts the torch to it, reasoning that Ben will be blamed for setting the blaze. But Jody cannot bring himself to carry through his plot and rescues his father from the smoke-filled barn before the fire gets out of hand. Will manifests his forgiveness of his son's hysterical behavior by taking the blame for the blaze; he says he inadvertently ignited the fire by carelessly dropping a lit cigar on the barn floor.

This episode, one of the very few dramatic highlights of the movie that is nowhere even suggested in the novel, in the film occasions Ben's admission to Clara that it was not himself, but his father—until now not mentioned in the picture—who was the arsonist in the Quick family. Inevitably, because of the stigma attached to the name he bears, Ben at times has been unfairly blamed for acts of arson committed by others. "Last time I saw my old man," says Ben, "I was a boy of ten, choking on my own tears," watching a fire that his father had started to settle some grudge. It was at that moment that Ben decided to run away from home. "I never saw him again; maybe he died in one of his own fires." By making Ben Quick the one who takes no part in his father's acts of arson, the film has assigned to Quick the role played by Sarty Snopes in the short story "Barn Burning" and in the episode in the novel based on it. Flem Snopes, the character in *The Hamlet* that Ben is mostly modeled on, certainly does participate in his father's arson.

Having shared with Clara the truth about his background, he addresses Will. He admits that, with Will's connivance, he has done his share of doubledealing since he arrived in Frenchman's Bend, most notably in selling off the untamed horses to the gullible populace. But he adds that he now regrets having gone along with Will's plans to push Clara into accepting his marriage proposal, because he has come to realize that she must be allowed to reach her own decision about whom she is going to marry. "We have been associated for one hot summer," Ben says to Will. "We started out playing a horseflesh game, and now we've left horses and gotten around to people; and that's something different. You're old enough to know that, and I'm young enough to learn it." With that, Clara comes forward to speak for herself; she chooses Ben on her own initiative and not because her father has sought to bully her into accepting him. Will is simply glad that everything has worked out for the best, observing that "It's a good summer night to be alive!" On this pleasant note the picture concludes.

Obviously the movie's Ben Quick turns out to be a much better human being than the novel's Flem Snopes. Still, even though Ben may not be as mean-spirited as Flem, like Flem he is quite prepared to foist a string of untamable horses on his neighbors at Will Varner's behest, as well as to employ the ruse of the salted treasure against Jody and so further to discredit him in his father's eyes. Unlike Flem, however, Ben is also capable of seeing the error of his ways. Although Lew Harper, the Paul Newman character in *Harper*, flatly states that only cream and bastards rise to the top, Ben falls somewhere between those two categories. He may not be pure cream, but neither is he the unmitigated bastard Flem was. The upshot of the movie is that Ben Quick deserves to be rewarded for what Bruce Kawin calls "his under-it-all goodness," which finally asserts itself unmistakably at the close of the picture. "In the best Victorian tradition, the hero gets money and a good name along with the girl." The way the movie's plot works out may have little to do with Faulkner, Kawin concludes, "but taken on its own merits the story is coherent, the acting is glamorous but convincing, and the direction is fairly efficient."

In turning to Martin Ritt's direction of the film, which has been deservedly praised as uncluttered and unpretentious, one is pleased to record that he insisted that the bulk of the movie be shot on location in the South. "I prefer to do as much of my pictures on location as I can," Ritt explained to a journalist while the movie was being shot in Clinton, Louisiana. "The sense of atmosphere, the feeling of contact with the real thing, helps the actors in their roles – and helps me too."[8] Clinton was chosen as the location site for the movie because it was similar and less pretentious than the larger southern towns that had been considered.

Paul Newman, who was born in Ohio, showed up in Clinton before shooting began, registered at a local hotel as Ben Snopes (!), and spent three days drifting unrecognized around town, visiting taverns, pool halls, and restaurants, so that he could authentically reproduce in his performance the speech patterns and mannerisms characteristic of the inhabitants of the Deep South. There was no need for Joanne Woodward to utilize similar methods to prepare for her role as a southern belle in the picture, as she is from Georgia.

In one of the strongest dramatic confrontations between the Newman and Woodward characters in the movie, Clara tells Ben in no uncertain terms that she is not a commodity to be bought and sold, and that she resents the concerted effort he and her father have made to induce her to

Joanne Woodward and Paul Newman, as Clara Varner and Ben Quick, struck cinematic sparks in *The Long Hot Summer*. (Movie Star News)

marry him. She adds that Will likes him because "one wolf recognizes another."

"Well, I can see that you don't like me," Ben responds with equal self-assurance, "but you're going to have me. They're going to say, 'There goes that poor old Clara Varner, whose father married her off to a dirt-scratching, shiftless, no-good farmer who just happened by.' Well, let them talk." What people say will not matter to her, he says, because "you're going to wake up in the morning smiling."

Despite the fact that the Newman-Woodward team struck cinematic sparks in scenes like that one, the picture really belongs to Newman. Describing Newman's performance in his book on the actor, Michael Kerber writes, "Behind Quick's hard blue eyes, barely hidden sneer, and devilish grin," Newman projects "enough intelligence, humor, charm, and downright attractiveness to force our involvement in his quest for power." Newman thus manages to make the viewer begin to like Ben long before he is presented in a sympathetic light in the movie's closing scenes. Indeed, Pauline Kael goes so far as to say that "with closeups of his blue, blue eyes and his hurt, sensitive mouth, Newman's Ben Quick could have burned the barns all right," and audiences would have gladly forgiven him for it.[9]

Looking back on the film, Newman told *Time* in 1982 that he thought his performance was pretty good, but that he still remembered how hard he was trying all during shooting to do his best. He evidently succeeded, since Newman's portrayal of Ben Quick won him the Best Actor award at the 1958 Cannes Film Festival, the only prize granted to an American at that year's festival. This very entertaining movie went on to become a box office bonanza; the popular appeal of the movie was such the first time around that nearly two decades later NBC-TV decided to remake the picture as a four-hour television miniseries.

The Long Hot Summer: The Television Movie

The television project got going when Brandon Tartikoff, head of NBC-TV's entertainment division, began looking around for a subject for a two-part miniseries that could be classed as a "literary event" as well as an entertaining telefilm. Independent producer Leonard Hill came up with the idea of an extended television version of the theatrical movie of *The Long Hot Summer,* and NBC agreed that the Faulkner adaptation would fill the bill, so long as two prominent superstars familiar to television viewers were to head the cast. Two veterans of successful television series, Don Johnson (*Miami Vice*) and Cybill Shepherd (*Moonlighting*), were signed to play Ben Quick and Eula Varner. The telefilm was shot on location, mostly in and around Marshall, Texas, in late spring and early summer 1985, with British television director Stuart Cooper at the helm.

"In comparison to feature films, television movies are made on the double and on the cheap," television journalist Kathleen Fury writes in her article on the telefilm of *The Long Hot Summer.* This particular four-hour television production "took two months of filming and more than $6.6 million to make," Fury goes on; "had it been made as a feature film to be shown in movie theaters, the money spent and the time allowed might have been doubled at the least."

Try as he might to stay on schedule and within the budget allotted for the miniseries, Cooper finished shooting six days behind schedule and a half-million dollars over budget. "There's a lot you can do in the miniseries format," the English director commented during the final days of production. "But I've learned there's a television mentality here which finally, under pressure, will simply shoot anything to get it done." Filming a four-hour screenplay in two months, Cooper stated, "creates a kind of pressure I'd wish never to experience again."[10] Granted that different logistics obtain for the shooting of a theatrical feature and a television miniseries, the question remains as to whether or not Cooper's product qualifies as an improvement on the earlier motion picture directed by Martin Ritt.

One can say that the telefilm covers much of the same ground as the original film adaptation of *The Hamlet;* indeed, nearly all of the scenes from the feature film described above turn up in the television movie. The television scenarists, Rita Mae Brown and Dennis Turner, elaborated the plot of the original motion picture to make it fit the more ample dimensions of a miniseries by returning to Faulkner's novel to pick up a few characters who did not appear in the 1958 movie. One of these is mentally retarded Isaac (William Forsythe), who is a relative of Flem Snopes in the novel; but there is no family connection of any kind between Isaac and Ben Quick (the Flem Snopes character) in the telefilm. Isaac, however, is emotionally attached to Eula, who has always been kind to him. In the miniseries, Isaac is made the perpetrator of a murder, something he is not guilty of in the novel. One of Flem Snopes's clan does commit a homicide in *The Hamlet,* but it has nothing to do with Isaac's crime in the teleplay. In sum, the new material developed for the expanded version of *The Long Hot Summer* was largely invented by Brown and Turner, and not derived from the novel; as a consequence, the television film departs from Faulkner to a much greater degree than the previous movie did.

The expansion of the feature picture's scenario to miniseries proportions centered on the creation of an adulterous love affair between Eula Varner and Wilson Mahood (Wings Hauser), a local entrepreneur who figures in neither *The Hamlet* nor the theatrical feature. Early in the telefilm Wilson insists on more than one occasion that Eula leave Jody (William Russ) and marry him, but she consistently refuses to do so. One night Ben and Isaac both happen to come across the place in the woods where Eula and Wilson customarily meet, and find the pair violently quarreling about the viability of their relationship. When Wilson brutally strikes Eula, Ben intervenes and tells her he will take her home; Isaac, however, unnoticed by anyone, remains behind, lurking in the shadows. Following this incident, Wilson Mahood is not seen or heard of again until his corpse is discovered some time later in a swamp. The viewer suspects that Isaac is the murderer; but it is Ben—an outsider still viewed suspiciously by the locals—who is arrested for the slaying of Eula's lover. When gossip spreads throughout Frenchman's Bend about these lurid events, one of the villagers observes, "It's not even high summer, and things are heating up in all directions."

Jody Varner is the first one to accuse Ben of Wilson's murder and to agitate for his arrest. In the motion picture version of *The Long Hot Summer*, we remember, Jody sets fire to the barn in which he has locked his father, with the intention of blaming Ben for the deed; in the telemovie Jody instead wants to see Ben convicted of killing Mahood. But Jody's motive in trying to implicate Ben in a crime he did not commit is the same in both cases: he wants to get even with the interloper Ben for usurping his rightful place as the closest confidant of his father (Jason Robards, Jr.) in handling the family's business affairs. In any case, in the telemovie Eula gets Ben freed of the charge of homicide by revealing publicly that Isaac, who has always been devoted to her, has confessed to her privately that he killed Wilson Mahood for hurting her.

And so we are brought to a positive ending in the television movie similar to the one in the previous film adaptation of *The Hamlet*, with Ben and the Clara character, called Noel (Judith Ivey) in the telemovie, making plans to marry. Noel, who has steadfastly stood by Ben throughout the ordeal of his arrest for Wilson's murder, is now fully vindicated for maintaining her faith in him.

The Brown-Turner script for the television version of *The Long Hot Summer*, is simply not in the same class with the screenplay for the theatrical movie. The new plot material concocted for the two-part miniseries wanders farther and farther from Faulkner as the movie goes on, to the point where the connection between his novel and the miniseries becomes difficult to perceive at times. Furthermore, the writing team concentrated too much of its creative energies on piling up multiple plot complications of their own invention, and not enough on supplying incidents calculated to reveal character, to examine motivation more deeply, and consequently to make it easier for the viewer to identify with the principal characters. Thus, if the cowriters chose to invent an adulterous affair for Eula, they could have made more of an effort to help the audience understand if not

Jason Robards, Jr., played Will Varner in the television remake of *The Long Hot Summer* (1985), which wandered fairly far from the Faulkner novel. (Author's collection)

condone her behavior. As it is, the closest we get to an explanation of Eula's infidelity to Jody in the telefilm is her casual remark, "I do believe in Jesus, I really do; but do you really think He meant life to be dull?"

The miniseries met with mixed response from television critics across the nation when it premiered on 5 and 6 October 1985, although it did draw a large audience. *New York Times* critic John J. O'Connor wrote, "When commercial television executives start talking about a 'literary event,' duck." The telemovie, as he saw it, was simply an excuse for employing the work of a major American novelist "for still another slab of prime-time soap opera"; hence it did not qualify as a "literary event." In recalling Paul Newman's first-rate performance in the 1958 movie, Daniel Ruth of the *Chicago Sun-Times* was obliged to say that Don Johnson's uninspired portrayal of Ben Quick was not in the same league with Newman's.

It is true that Johnson was given solid support by Jason Robards as the gruff and imposing patriarch Will Varner, by Judith Ivey as his tough-minded daughter, and by Cybill Shepherd as the alluring Eula. But all three actors failed to match the definitive performances turned in by Orson Welles, Joanne Woodward, and Lee Remick in the same roles in Martin Ritt's movie. Nor did Cooper's lackluster direction of the miniseries probe the complex relationships of the various characters as capably as Ritt had done in his sensitive handling of the feature motion picture. "Like most television remakes of theatrical films," said Ruth, "NBC takes four hours to tell the same story the 1958 film only took two hours to cover—with no discernable increase in the quality of the tale."[11] To put it more strongly still, the miniseries version of *The Long Hot Summer* is roughly twice as long and about half as good as the theatrical feature.

Producer Jerry Wald reunited the talents of director Martin Ritt, screenwriters Irving Ravetch and Harriet Frank, Jr., and actress Joanne Woodward, all of whom participated in the theatrical film of *The Long Hot Summer*, for the motion picture version of *The Sound and the Fury*, released the following year. Whether or not their second collaboration on a Faulkner film would turn out as well as their first remained to be seen.

CHAPTER 7

Change and Decay:
The Sound and the Fury (1959)

> Change and decay in all around I see.
> *"Abide with Me" (Traditional Hymn)*

> So I, who had never had a sister and
> was fated to lose [a] daughter in infancy,
> set out to make myself a beautiful
> and tragic little girl.
> *William Faulkner*

In early spring 1928, Faulkner sat down to compose a short story he tentatively entitled "Twilight." "It was a story without a plot, of some children being sent away from the house during the grandmother's funeral," he later recalled. "They were too young to be told what was going on, and they saw things only incidentally to the childish games they were playing, which was the lugubrious matter of removing the corpse from the house, etc."[1] The funeral in the short story was based on Faulkner's memory of the events surrounding the funeral of his maternal grandmother, Lelia Swift Butler, who died in 1907 when he and his brothers were still youngsters.

The story involves the relationship of a little girl named Caddy Compson with each of her three brothers, Jason, Quentin, and Benjy. Faulkner put three boys into the story because at the time of his grandmother's funeral there were only three Faulkner brothers, not four—Dean was not born until two months afterward. Faulkner gave the three brothers a sister and elected to make her the focal point of the story, because, as he later realized, he was subconsciously trying to create in one and the same character both a sister and a daughter for himself. He never had a sister, and at the time the short story was conceived he did not yet have a daughter. (His first daughter, Alabama, was born in 1931 and lived only nine days; his second, Jill, his only surviving child, was born two years after that.) It was particularly obvious to him, in retrospect, that he had made up Caddy to take the place of the sister he never had because he recalled that "Caddy had three brothers almost before I wrote her name on paper."

The Sound and the Fury: The Novel

Life's but a walking shadow, a poor player
That struts and frets his hour upon the stage
And then is heard no more; it is a tale
Told by an idiot, full of sound and fury,
Signifying nothing.

Shakespeare, *Macbeth*

When Faulkner began to write "Twilight," he could not have known that it would develop well beyond the limits of a short story to become one of his greatest novels, *The Sound and the Fury.* But the more he worked on the short story, the more he became aware that he had the makings of a novel. He began the story by picturing Caddy and her brothers playing in a pasture near their home while the funeral services are going on. Caddy and Quentin, one of her brothers, are spashing about in a brook, while her other two brothers look on. When Caddy falls in the stream and gets her clothes wet and muddy, Benjy, her baby brother, perhaps fearing that his beloved sister has been hurt, begins to cry. Caddy gets out of the water and comes over to him in her dripping garments to comfort him. At that moment, said Faulkner, the plot of the entire novel "seemed to explode on the paper before me." He saw in a flash how the story of Caddy's involvement with Benjy and her other brothers could be extended beyond childhood to encompass their later lives as well. In the plot as he now conceived it, the day would come when Caddy would no longer be available to comfort her youngest brother Benjy, because the disreputable life she would later lead would carry her far beyond the reach of her family. Faulkner had further decided that Benjy would be mentally retarded, and so would never understand his sister's absence. Thus little Ben would never grow beyond this moment at the brookside; "for him," said Faulkner, "all knowing must begin and end with that fierce, panting, paused and stooping wet figure" offering him reassurance and comfort.

Later that afternoon, toward twilight, the children return home and find that the funeral ceremonies are not quite over. Caddy climbs a pear tree in order to peek in the parlor window and report what she sees to her brothers on the ground below. The image of Caddy's three brothers looking up at the muddy seat of her drawers, while she in turn stares through the window at her grandmother's last rites, constituted for Faulkner the central image of the whole novel. The symbolic significance of Caddy's muddy underpants is crucial to the novel; he therefore brought this symbolism into relief in a scene in which Dilsey Gibson, the Compson's black housekeeper, is "scrubbing the naked backside of that doomed little girl" whose later shameful life the mudstained drawers "symbolized and prophesied."[2]

Faulkner wrote the first of the novel's four parts from Benjy's point of view; that makes the book's first section literally "a tale / Told by an idiot, full of sound and fury, / Signifying nothing," because what Benjy observes has no meaningful significance for him. As a result, the title of the published novel applies principally to the Benjy segment.

Benjy Compson was based on Edwin Chandler, a mentally retarded fellow who lived with his sisters only three blocks away from the house where the Faulkner brothers grew up. The Chandler place was built by William Thompson, whose surname most probably suggested the last name of the Compson family to Faulkner. "It was a big old place . . . with an enormous front yard enclosed by an iron picket fence," John Faulkner remembered. The Faulkner boys frequently passed by the front yard where Edwin Chandler spent much of his time, and they would often stop to play with him. "When we would leave," John continued, "he would follow us along the fence on the inside until he came to its far limits. He would wave us goodbye until next time."

One day some children maliciously taunted Edwin until he became hysterical and left the yard to chase them down the street. The youngsters told their parents how Edwin had scared them; their parents reported the matter to the police, who in turn insisted that Edwin no longer be accorded the freedom of the Chandlers' front yard. So Edwin was prohibited from playing with the Faulkner boys or with any other children ever again. "Of all of us," John Faulkner concluded, "Bill was the most upset" when he heard what had happened.[3] The compassionate portrait of Benjy Compson

Jason Compson (Yul Brynner) and Caddy Compson (Margaret Leighton), in *The Sound and the Fury* (1959). Director Martin Ritt felt that this film was not as successful artistically as his previous Faulkner venture, *The Long Hot Summer*. (Museum of Modern Art/Film Stills Archive)

in *The Sound and The Fury*, then, is rooted in Faulkner's recollections of the pitiable figure of Edwin Chandler.

The events in the novel that take place in the present, as opposed to those which are depicted in flashback, are set on Easter weekend 1928, when Ben Compson is thirty-three years old. Because of his mental handicap, he cannot distinguish between past and present; as a consequence, a vivid memory of some past event is just as real to him as anything that he might experience in the here and now. For instance, at the beginning of the novel, when the grownup Ben's clothing gets snagged on a fence nail and Luster, the black lad who takes care of him, disengages him, this present happening is immediately replaced in his consciousness by his memory of Caddy helping him in the same way many years before. In order to offer the reader some assistance in following the shifts back and forth in time that occur throughout the Benjy segment of the novel, Faulkner frequently introduces them with italics, as here:

> "Wait a minute." Luster said. "You snagged on that nail again. Can't you never crawl through here without snagging on that nail."
> *Caddy uncaught me and we crawled through.*[4]

In the course of the Benjy section, Faulkner covers a thirty-year period in the Compsons' lives: from the funeral of the children's grandmother in 1898 – which was really all that he had intended the short story "Twilight" to deal with – down to 1928, the time of the events that take place in the present. But he does so by constantly switching back and forth in time. Hence, although the whole history of the Compson family is implicitly contained in embryo in Benjy's section, it is presented by way of a complicated shuttling between past and present that makes the Benjy segment hard for the bewildered reader to comprehend. Eventually Faulkner found that he needed to compose no less than "three more sections, all longer than Benjy's, to try to clarify it."

Faulkner elected to have Ben's oldest brother, Quentin Compson, give his version of the facts next; and that became the second part of the book. Then Faulkner decided to let Jason tell his side of the story in what became the novel's third section. Even then he knew the book was not finished; and so he wrote a fourth and final segment, this time from the point of view of an outsider, that is, the writer himself: "I tried to gather the pieces together and fill in the gaps by making myself the spokesman," said Faulkner. And that is how *The Sound and the Fury* grew from a short story into a four-part novel.[5]

The fourth part of the novel, narrated by the authorial voice, presents an inspiring portrait of Dilsey, the Compson's dedicated servant, and therefore is often referred to as the Dilsey section. In the novel her loyal devotion to the family goes largely unappreciated, but William Faulkner personally displayed his abiding esteem for her real-life counterpart, Caroline "Mammy Callie" Barr, who helped raise the Faulkner brothers, by supporting her in her declining years until her death in 1940. In speaking at her funeral, Faulkner said that in Caroline Barr he saw "fidelity to a family which was not hers, devotion and love for people she had not borne."[6] Those words could have been uttered with equal appropriateness about Dilsey Gibson, as will shortly become apparent.

In 1945, sixteen years after *The Sound and the Fury* first appeared, Faulkner wrote an appendix to the novel for an anthology of his work, *The Portable Faulkner*, edited by Malcolm Cowley and published in 1946. In this appendix Faulkner describes, among other things, what happens to the leading characters after 1928. By his own admission, *The Sound and the Fury* remained Faulkner's personal favorite among all of his works to the end of his life, and he just could not let go of these characters. So he was still thinking about them and adding to the story of their lives nearly two decades after he finished the novel.

In essence, the book represents the differing relationships of three brothers with their wayward sister. After Caddy leaves home, Ben goes on loving and remembering her fondly, without ever grasping what has become of her. Since Benjy remains a child all his life, his most enduring memories of his sister, depicted in the opening section of the book, center on the period when she too was a child.

In contrast, Quentin, in his segment of the novel, tends to dwell on the experiences that he and Caddy shared when they were growing from childhood into young adulthood. Quentin's recollections of his sister are, of course, much easier to comprehend than Benjy's; it is abundantly clear, for instance, that Quentin is obsessed with the way that his sister's dissolute life has brought shame upon herself and the whole Compson family. Quentin's reveries about Caddy also indicate that his deep and lasting attachment to his sister is tinged with decidedly incestuous yearnings—as suggested by his fierce jealous resentment of her involvement with her first known lover, Dalton Ames. Indeed, as portrayed in the second part of the novel, Quentin's brooding about his sister is so morbid and morose that, by the end of his first year at Harvard, the emotionally disturbed young man has resolved to commit suicide. He carries out his resolution, drowning himself in the Charles River near the campus on 2 June 1910.

In the third part of the novel, Jason Compson sets forth a far more straightforward account of his dealings with his sister than either his retarded brother Ben or his neurotic brother Quentin was capable of giving. A self-centered, mean-spirited man, Jason despises Caddy and succinctly spells out the reasons why. For one thing, Herbert Head, the man to whom Caddy briefly was married, to bolster the Compson's sagging finances promised to start Jason off in a career in banking. But when, after only a few short months of marriage, Caddy gave birth to a child which Herbert knew positively was not his, Herbert walked out on her and the baby; with him went Jason's hopes of becoming a prosperous banker. Caddy then added insult to injury, as far as Jason was concerned, by returning home long enough to leave her illegitimate daughter, whom she named Quentin after her dead brother, in the permanent care of the Compsons, and then taking off for parts unknown. In the intervening years Jason has cruelly transferred his contempt and hostility for his sister to the motherless and fatherless girl Caddy abandoned.

In contrast with the first two parts of the books, which are heavily freighted with Benjy's and Quentin's remembrances of things past, the Jason and Dilsey segments are firmly anchored in the present, although there are some references to past events in Jason's section. The action of the third and fourth parts, taken together, is largely concerned with the events of Easter weekend 1928. At that time Jason is occupied with attempting to keep his niece, now in her teens, from eloping with a pitchman from the carnival that is currently playing in Jefferson. The girl (whom we shall call Miss Quentin, to distinguish her from her deceased uncle) finally circumvents her uncle on Saturday night by stealthily climbing down the pear tree outside the window of her room and running away with the carnival man who, according to the appendix to the novel, is a convicted bigamist. When Jason discovers on Easter morning, 9 April 1928, that Miss Quentin is gone, he likewise learns that she has made off with the contents of his strongbox; ironically enough, some of the cash she has taken actually belongs to her, since it represents money that Jason had maliciously appropriated for himself from funds Caddy had sent him for Miss Quentin's support.

Thus the novel begins with Caddy as a child shinnying up a pear tree to gaze in a window at a funeral; and it concludes with her daughter climbing down the same pear tree to elope with a virtual stranger. Miss Quentin is escaping, said Faulkner, "from the only home she had, where she had never been offered love or affection or understanding"; and to make matters worse, he concludes, the hapless girl is already well on her way to following the same downward path to perdition as her doomed mother.[7] Needless to say, Jason has no sympathy to spare for either one of them. "Once a bitch always a bitch" is his ultimate judgment on them both.

In his appendix to the novel, Faulkner notes that Caddy, when last heard of, had "vanished in Paris with the German occupation in 1940" and had become the mistress of a German staff general. This fact is attested to by a photo published in a slick news magazine, showing the two of them standing together next to a European sportscar. Concerning Miss Quentin, Faulkner adds ruefully, "whatever occupation overtook her" would not involve a sportscar driven by a "general of staff." Little wonder that Faulkner described *The Sound and the Fury* as "the tragedy of two lost women: Caddy and her daughter."[8]

It is significant that the novel proper, exclusive of the appendix, ends on Easter Sunday, since Dilsey takes Benjy to the Negro church on that day. That means that Benjy is the only member of the Compson family to attend services on Easter, and it is only because Dilsey takes the matter in hand that he is able to do so. In fact, the God-fearing Dilsey is the sole stabilizing factor in the crumbling Compson household, presided over since his father's death by Jason Compson, a heartless, childless bachelor. The rest of the miserable clan includes Jason's nagging, self-pitying mother, Caroline Compson; his mother's alcoholic brother Maury; Ben; and – until her sudden departure – his defiant, self-destructive niece, Miss Quentin. No doubt the message of Christian resignation and hope which Dilsey brings home from the Easter services sustains her in her ongoing efforts to hold together the disintegrating Compson clan.

Dilsey also finds spiritual solace in singing hymns while she does her housework. Although the novel does not indicate which ones she favors, the religious sentiments expressed in the traditional hymn "Abide with Me" seem to have a special application to her and her life with the Compsons: "Change and decay in all around I see. / O Thou, who changest not, abide with me."

Living in the midst of the decadent Compson clan, Dilsey's own spirit remains indomitable because, as the hymn suggests, she looks heavenward for strength. As Faulkner critic Bernhard Radloff maintains, the Dilsey section of *The Sound and the Fury* "shows us that the most powerful influence in Dilsey's life is the Christian religion."

Dilsey Gibson is one of the most admirable characters in all of Faulkner. He once said of her, "She's much more brave and honest and generous than me."[9] On one occasion in particular Dilsey exhibits all three of the qualities Faulkner attributed to her. Just as Jason is about to strike Miss Quentin sadistically with his belt for disobeying him, Dilsey interposes herself between Jason and the girl in order to sustain the blow in Miss Quentin's stead. When Jason backs off, one is reminded that Faulkner describes Jason in the novel's appendix as "thinking nothing whatever of God" but "fearing and respecting only the Negro woman," Dilsey, who is simply above being intimidated by anything he does. If Faulkner had a high regard for Dilsey, he viewed Jason Compson, conversely, as "the most vicious character, in my opinion, I ever thought of."[10] This is because Jason is totally devoid of the kinds of qualities that shine in Dilsey, such as endurance, unselfishness, and compassion. Dilsey herself aptly characterizes Jason at one point when she says to him, "You's a cold man, Jason, if man you is." Asked a quarter of a century after he published *The Sound and the Fury* to name the one character, among all those he had created, that he most disliked, he could still respond without hesitation that it was Jason Compson.

The novel's final scene depicts Jason true to form. Luster, Benjy's attendant, is taking Benjy for a ride in the Compsons' surrey; he decides to vary their usual routine for a change by going clockwise, rather than counterclockwise, around the town square. Ben, who is accustomed to circling round the square in the opposite direction, begins to bellow in anguish when the familiar objects he is accustomed to seeing en route appear in an order that is the reverse of what he expects. Jason comes running out of the farmer's supply store on the square where he works to take charge of the situation. Obsessed with the notion that the Compsons, despite their reduced circumstances, must continue to maintain a respectable image in the community, Jason is chagrined that Luster is letting his retarded brother embarrass the family by throwing a fit in public on the town square. Jason furiously slaps Benjy and orders him to shut up; he likewise smacks Luster and commands him to go round the square the other way. "Ben hushed," Faulkner writes; he watched serenely as the carriage began to move; "cornice and facade flowed smoothly once more from left to right, post and tree, window and doorway and signboard each in its ordered place." Benjy is content with a superficial restoration of order; and surface order is all that Jason is ever capable of supplying in the lives of those around him, for all the highhanded methods he employs to control them.

The Sound and the Fury ends with the clear implication that the Compson family is doomed to extinction. Jason, a confirmed bachelor who maintains a mistress in Memphis, will certainly never marry and raise a family. Nor will his brother Ben, who, according to the novel's appendix, is destined to wind up in an insane asylum. In addition, by the end of the book, both Caddy and her daughter have left home for good, fated to be swallowed up in the dark world of promiscuity. When Miss Quentin's disappearance is discovered on Easter Sunday morning, Dilsey weeps for the ruined Compson clan and mutters to herself, "I've seed de first en de last. . . . I seed de beginnin, en now I sees de endin." Dilsey's words presage the end of the Compson family, whose offspring she has helped to raise – from Quentin, the oldest of the Compson children, down to Miss Quentin, the sole member of the last generation of Compson offspring. Nonetheless, Dilsey "is obviously moved by considerations far deeper than the mere vanishing of a family name," writes Cleanth Brooks. "She is moved by the spectacle of human waste, of promise that has come to nothing, of love and human concern that has been spilled on the ground, of potential goodness that did not fulfill itself."[11] In short, people of compassion and humanity like Dilsey endure, while the decadent Compsons are condemned to die out.

Looking back on the composition of *The Sound and the Fury*, Faulkner said, "I had . . . written my guts into *The Sound and the Fury*, through I was not aware until the book was published that I had done so, because I had done it for pleasure."[12] Trying to get the book published, however, was another matter. Lenore Marshall, who was at the time a reader at the small, short-lived publishing firm that eventually brought out the first edition of the novel, remembered that when *The Sound and the Fury* came across her desk, she could easily tell by looking at the typescript that it had made the rounds of a dozen other publishing houses before it reached her. Even while fighting her way through some of the murkier passages of the novel's opening section, however, she became convinced that she was reading a work of genius; and when the book was published on 7 October 1929, there were many critics who agreed with her. Nevertheless, the novel did not catch on with the reading public when it first appeared; and the publisher's initial printings, totaling three thousand copies, were not exhausted until 1946. It was not until the Faulkner renaissance gathered momentum among academics in the late 1940s that *The Sound and the Fury* began to be more widely read and appreciated.

In 1955, Jerry Wald opened negotiations for the purchase of the screen rights to *The Hamlet* and *The Sound and the Fury* and eventually arranged to produce both pictures for Fox. Having released in 1958 a hugely successful theatrical feature based on *The Hamlet* under the title of *The Long Hot Summer*, Wald set out to try and match this achievement by marshalling for his production of *The Sound and the Fury* many of the key personnel who had contributed their talents to *The Long Hot Summer*. The same screenwriting team, director, and at least one of the stars, Joanne Woodward, would be back on board to collaborate on the film version of *The Sound and the Fury*.

There was a television adaptation of the Dilsey section of *The Sound and the Fury* telecast in late 1955; but the production is not available for viewing. When Harold Ober asked him for his reaction to it, Faulkner telegraphed a noncommittal reply on 30 November 1955: "Story changed from one to another medium bound to lose some meaning, though may gain completely new significance. Which you like depends [on] where you stand. This makes TV version more interesting to me."[13] As for the motion picture version of the novel, Faulkner declined even to read the screenplay for the film. As far as he was concerned, his days of working in motion pictures in any capacity were over for good. He had not taken any part in preparing the screenplay for a feature film adapted from one of his works since he had vetted Ben Maddow's script of *Intruder in the Dust* a decade before.

The Sound and the Fury: The Film

Wald opted to film the majority of the movie on the Fox studio lot, rather than to take the film unit south for an extended period of location shooting as he had done on *The Long Hot Summer*. The reason was that the film crew had lost a total of thirteen days while filming *The Long Hot Summer* in Louisiana, because of the frequently overcast skies. "Studio shooting is really much easier on everybody," Ritt concedes. "You just walk on the set, and everything is ready to go."[14] Still, making the movie mostly in the insulated atmosphere of the studio meant that the authentic atmosphere that location filming can add to a motion picture—which Ritt had so prized while working on *The Long Hot Summer*—would to some degree be missing from the film version of *The Sound and the Fury*.

Other things are missing from the movie as well. For example, the screenplay by Irving Ravetch and Harriet Frank, Jr., which is set in the 1950s, all but eliminates the material of the Benjy and Quentin segments of the novel. Instead the script deals almost exclusively with material gleaned from the Jason and Dilsey sections, both of which primarily concern themselves with events in the book that take place in the present. In this way, Wald has explained, the film could concentrate on the present plight of the Compson family "and gradually reveal the weight of the past through this." Elsewhere he has added, "To make the past function in the present, as we watch, required some changes. For example, instead of killing himself at Harvard in his youth, Quentin Compson lives on—but as a man self-destroyed, making his painful way as an alcoholic." As a consequence, the Quentin character, who is renamed Howard in the film (presumably to avoid confusion with Caddy's daughter Quentin), is still very much alive when Caddy comes home for a visit. And that "precipitates a situation that dredges up the conflicts that existed between them in the past."[15]

The personality of Howard (John Beal) is to some extent also derived from another character in the novel, Mrs. Compson's brother Maury, in that, like Maury, Howard is a middle-aged alcoholic bachelor. But, as Wald suggests, Howard's jealous recriminations of Caddy (Margaret Leighton) about her lovers, especially Dalton Ames, obviously have their basis in the incestuous feelings that Quentin nurtures for his sister in the novel. The scene in the film in which Howard argues with Caddy about her amorous adventures takes place near the stream where they had played as children. Caddy recalls getting her underpants all muddy in the brook, and how miffed Dilsey was about it; this reminiscence in turn triggers Howard's memory of how upset he was over her affair with Dalton Ames. He then recalls the angry confrontation he had with Ames over Caddy and asks her pointedly, "How many were there? Did you love them all?"

This sequence, as well as any in the movie, suggests how much dramatic power is sacrificed in the film by trying to conjure up key scenes from the novel about the Compsons' troubled past by mere verbal references to them in the dialogue. To infer that Caddy's mud-stained drawers were a symbolic forecast of her subsequent soiled reputation as a fallen woman, the filmgoer would have had to witness this childhood incident dramatized directly as a flashback, as it is in the book. And in order to grasp fully the inference in this scene of the film that it was really incestuous jealousy, and not just fraternal solicitude for his sister's welfare, that drove Howard to quarrel bitterly with Dalton Ames over Caddy, the viewer would have had to see the confrontation itself. Instead, allusions to these and other important experiences from the characters' past lives are tossed off in snatches of expository dialogue in the picture, before the moviegoer has a chance to grasp their full import. As a result, the filmmakers' attempts to portray the characters as the embodiments of their collective past simply do not work. Similarly, as we have seen, the deep significance of the shared childhood experiences of the leading characters in *Today We Live* was to a large degree lost when the flashbacks in Faulkner's script for the film were replaced in a later version of the screenplay by mere verbal references to these events.

A second major departure from the novel made in bringing *The Sound and the Fury* to the screen, besides eliminating the use of flashbacks, was opting to have Jason (Yul Brynner) and Miss Quentin fall in love by the end of the movie. This outcome of the film's action required that Jason could not be a blood relative of Miss Quentin in the film. So, in the movie's scenario he becomes a Compson by adoption—namely, the son of the elder Mr. Compson's second wife, by a previous marriage of hers. That makes Jason the stepson of Mr. Compson, Sr., who, it seems, granted Jason the Compson family name after he married Jason's mother. In addition, Jason is portrayed in the film "as having finer motivations behind his actions than in the book," said Wald. "In the process of dramatization this positive note seemed essential" in order to transform Jason from the vile creature Faulkner delineated in the novel into a suitable candidate for his stepniece's hand in marriage at film's end.[16] (By contrast, Ben Quick's behavior was not nearly so positively motivated throughout *The Long Hot Summer.*) Thus, in the movie Jason is often given valid reasons for behaving as he does, in place of the decidedly ignoble motives Faulkner shows him to have in the book.

In the novel, for example, Jason relates how, during a brief return visit Caddy made to Jefferson, he sought to deprive her of the opportunity to see her daughter, who was still a baby at the time. His action was patently vindictive, because he wanted to punish his sister for, among other things, unloading the child on the Compsons in the first place. Jason therefore honored Caddy's request to see Miss Quentin only to the extent that he let her

Benjy Compson (Jack Warden), Dilsey Gibson (Ethel Waters), and Quentin Compson (Joanne Woodward) in *The Sound and the Fury*. (Museum of Modern Art/Film Stills Archive)

have a fleeting glimpse of her little girl while he and the baby rode by her in a carriage at breakneck speed.

In the movie's corresponding sequence, Jason, along with Miss Quentin, who is grown up at this point in the film, speeds by Caddy in his car. But his decision to allow Caddy only a glimpse of her daughter is sincerely well-intentioned: he wishes to discourage Caddy from having any contact with Miss Quentin, because he is concerned that Caddy may be a bad influence on the girl. Later on he relents, however, and yields to Caddy's entreaties to permit her not only to see Miss Quentin, but to stay on indefinitely with her daughter and the rest of the family in the old homestead— something Faulkner's Jason never would have had the decency to do.

In another episode in the book, Jason exhibits his propensity for gratuitous meanness by gleefully burning two carnival passes in front of Luster, who cannot afford to buy a ticket to the show, just because Jason enjoys hurting and teasing the youngster. The movie's Jason does the same thing, but his motive is to teach the lad a lesson by penalizing him for disobeying him. And so it goes. Given the manner in which Jason's character has been sanitized in the picture, it is not at all surprising that at the fadeout Miss Quentin is quite prepared to renounce her plans to elope with the carnival roustabout (Stuart Whitman), in favor of settling down in Jefferson with Jason.

The movie consequently negates the powerful denouement of the novel whereby the Compson clan is irrevocably doomed to die out. In the course of the film Dilsey (the peerless Ethel Waters) utters the same words, quoted above, about having endured long enough to witness the departure of the last of the Compsons; but she does so at the point when Ben is about to be committed to the state asylum. Applied to him, her statement means that Ben, who is the youngest Compson of his generation, is being taken away from the family. But he is not the last of the Compsons: Miss Quentin is; and the import of the ending of the movie is that she and Jason will marry and continue to perpetuate the Compson family. The conclusion of the novel, on the other hand, is a grimly pessimistic one, epitomized by Dilsey's mournful lament, not just for Benjy, but for the decline and fall of the entire Compson line. Though some film reviewers found the positive outcome of the film touching, it is no match for the Faulkner original.

So much for the debit side of the ledger. One good thing that can be said about the picture is that Martin Ritt evoked uncommonly good performances from some of his players, including Margaret Leighton as Caddy and Jack Warden as Ben. Warden elicits the viewer's sympathy for the mute idiot Ben throughout the movie, from the moment when two nasty little boys throw stones at him while he is riding Luster piggyback, to the scene in which the carnival boss coaxes Luster into driving Ben around the square in an open buggy, while Ben is wearing a sandwich board advertising the freak show. The latter sequence recalls the final scene of the novel, in that Jason rushes onto the square to put a stop to a situation in which his brother is making a public spectacle of himself. The film's more benign Jason, however, does not rain blows on Ben and Luster to drive home his displeasure.

Margaret Leighton's portrayal of Caddy was largely underrated when the movie came out; indeed, she was depicted by one reviewer as looking as if she were playing Blanche DuBois in a stranded road company production of *A Streetcar Named Desire*. But in fact she has some fine moments in the film. In one scene the family has assembled in the living room to welcome Caddy back, and she poignantly recounts for them some of the details of the wretched life she has led since leaving home. Ritt keeps her in closeup during this painful speech, and as critic Prudence Ashton comments, "her facial movements are flawless. When she puts her arms around her two brothers—one a drunk and the other a mute imbecile—and says, 'Home is a safe harbor at last,' she makes what could have been lurid melodrama a moment of pathos that is real artistry."

Ritt likewise handles with great finesse the scene which follows this homecoming sequence. It is a delicate encounter between Caddy and Miss Quentin, in which they made their first tentative efforts to get to know one another after years of separation. By placing them on opposite sides of one of the bedposts of the four-poster bed that stands prominently in the center of Caddy's room, the director symbolizes visually that it will not be easy for them to relate to each other. The post is a visual metaphor for the barrier that the years have placed between them, an obstruction that mother and daughter will not easily get around.

While Martin Ritt still thinks that *The Long Hot Summer* is "a good, entertaining commercial film," he remains disappointed in the way that *The Sound and the Fury* turned out. "I made some mistakes on that," he says laconically, probably referring to his willingness to go along with some questionable artistic decisions such as banishing flashbacks from the film. "The one Faulkner film I have liked was *Intruder in the Dust*," he adds. "It was much better than either of mine."[17]

Finally, let us consider briefly Jerry Wald's opinion of the two Faulkner films that he produced. Wald was responsible for some first-rate film adaptations of literature, including his productions of James M. Cain's *Mildred Pierce* (1945) and of D.H. Lawrence's *Sons and Lovers* (1960). Wald was associated with Faulkner during the novelist's screenwriting days at Warner and produced two Faulkner film adaptations. And he was always an articulate spokesman for the film industry. Therefore it seemed appropriate to begin this book with his essay on the business of picture-making; in this way he could have "equal time" at the outset. The opinions offered here may respectfully differ with his in some ways.

The point that Wald reiterates, in the foreword to this book and in his two articles on filming Faulkner which are quoted here, is that the movie version of a work of literature should endeavor to capture in visual and dramatic terms the essence and the spirit of the source work. What's more, in his two Faulkner essays he states his conviction, regarding the movie adaptations of *The Hamlet* and *The Sound and the Fury*, that the spirit of each of the books has been kept intact in its transfer to the screen. His opinion, however, can be justified more readily in the case of the first film than of the second.

Some of the best individual episodes in *The Hamlet* were incorporated into *The Long Hot Summer*, and were adeptly sewn together by the screenwriting team into an interesting movie that is certainly superior to the television remake. After all, as Kawin reminds us, the Ravetch-Frank screenplay for *The Long Hot Summer* departs no more from the substance of *The Hamlet* than Faulkner's script for *To Have and Have Not* does from Hemingway's novel; yet each of the movies succeeds in rendering on film the tone and quality of its literary source.

This is not equally true of the film *The Sound and the Fury*. Faulkner saw his novel as encompassing the tragedy of two women who are irrevocably damned to a life of vice, whereas in the movie the older woman is redeemed from a disreputable existence by returning to the bosom of her family and her daughter is saved from a sinful life by never leaving home at all. For Faulkner, what one thinks of the screen adaptation of a work of fiction depends on where you stand; and from where he stood, as author of *The Sound and the Fury*, he must have judged the picture to be a dilution of one of his darkest, most uncompromising works.

The Hamlet, as noted before, is a serio-comic novel, containing elements of farce as well as melodrama; and the movie version could therefore sustain the happy ending that was provided for it. But *The Sound and the Fury* is an unmitigated tragedy; a happy ending could not be grafted on to the film version of the novel and still be faithful to Faulkner. Hence, it is safe to say that Jerry Wald's expressed hope that Faulkner, when he saw the picture, would "recognize the good faith in our effort" went unfulfilled.[18]

Wald and Ritt may have had their last encounter with filming Faulkner when *The Sound and the Fury* was in the can; but Ravetch and Frank were destined to write a third Faulkner screenplay. And their last effort, possibly because practice makes perfect, would be the best of the three.

CHAPTER 8

Growing Pains:
The Reivers (1969)
and *Barn Burning* (1980)

> You learned too much in these days before you came
> of age. . . . This savage knowledge . . . ought to come
> slowly, the gradual fruit of experience.
>
> *Graham Greene*

> You should be prepared for experience, knowledge,
> knowing: not bludgeoned unaware in the dark as by a
> highwayman or footpad.
>
> *William Faulkner*

Faulkner wrote to his publishers in spring 1940 that he had two novels in mind, a mystery story and a sort of Huck Finn tale. The detective story evolved into *Intruder in the Dust*, published in 1948. But Faulkner did not get around to developing the other idea into a full-length novel until the end of his career, when he wrote *The Reivers*, which appeared in summer 1962, only a month before his death. The latter book, as Faulkner synopsized its plot for his publisher in 1940, was not appreciably different from the plot of the novel that was finally published more than two decades afterward. At the center of the story is Lucius Priest, a youngster who takes a trip to Memphis with Boon Hogganbeck, a white handyman employed by his father, and Ned McCaslin, a black domestic servant in the Priest home. In the course of their stay in Memphis, the trio, along with Boon's girlfriend, a harlot named Corrie, get into trouble over a stolen racehorse.

"During that time the boy grows up, and becomes a man" as the result of his adventures, Faulkner explained in his 1940 letter. "He goes through in miniature all the experiences of youth which mold the man's character."[1] To that extent the book would be a novel about a young boy's initiation into manhood, like Twain's *Huckleberry Finn* and like Faulkner's own *Intruder in the Dust*, which dramatized Chick Mallison's development toward emotional maturity.

Faulkner began writing the book in earnest, under the working title of *The Horse Stealers*, in summer 1961. The novel's original subtitle, *A Reminiscence*, was never altered, since it perfectly fit a story set in 1905, when Faulkner himself was young. In fact, some of the book's fictional characters clearly resemble people from Faulkner's own remembered past. To begin with, Lucius's three younger brothers recall William Faulkner's own three male siblings. "Boss" Priest, the grandfather of young Lucius, is a banker, as was Faulkner's paternal grandfather, Col. J.W.T. Falkner. In addition, Lucius' father, Maury, owns a livery stable, just as Faulkner's own father, Murry, once did. Moreover, Murry Falkner employed in the livery stable a big, strong man with the mentality of a child, named Buster Callicoat; he was the model for Boon Hogganbeck, who likewise possesses more brawn than brains. Ned McCaslin in turn was inspired by "Uncle Ned" Barnett, who served Faulkner's family for two generations.

Reba Rivers, who presides over the Memphis brothel where Corrie plies her trade in the novel, was modeled on an actual Memphis madam Faulkner had met. Miss Reba is, of course, the very same individual who is in charge of the same bordello in *Sanctuary*. That novel, though written before *The Reivers*, recounts events taking place a quarter of a century after the action of *The Reivers*. In both books Miss Reba exhibits a fondness for gin similar to that of her real-life counterpart. One evening in 1934 Faulkner took his wife Estelle, at her insistence, to meet the real Miss Reba. When the lady in question greeted them at the door of her establishment, though it was still early, she was already tipsy. She was a woman of fifty, wearing a gown, Blotner wryly remarks, "that might have been elegant had it not been stretched to tent size."[2] In sum, as Millgate notes, *The Reivers* reflects not only Faulkner's nostalgia for his early life, a fact suggested by the number of characters in it who are based on people he had known; but also his nostalgia for his early work, since Miss Reba and some other characters in his last novel had appeared before in his fiction. Boon Hogganbeck, for example, figured prominently in "The Bear."

Boss McCaslin (Will Geer) and his grandson Lucius (Mitch Vogel) in *The Reivers* (1969). This is the best of the three Faulkner films coauthored by Irving Ravetch and Harriet Frank, Jr., who also scripted *The Long Hot Summer* and *The Sound and the Fury*. (Museum of Modern Art/Film Stills Archive)

The Reivers (an archaic term for plunderers) is narrated from beginning to end by Lucius Priest, who is, at the time he relates the tale, an aging southern gentleman recalling a picaresque escapade that took place fifty years before. He graphically narrates a misadventure of his youth, giving his reflections on this boyhood experience as he goes along. Millgate comments that the novel thus "offers an always eventful and sometimes moving narrative of the boy's precocious initiation into the facts of life." And it does so, moreover, by means of a narrator who is able not only to recount the events first-hand, but simultaneously to interpret them sagely from the vantage point of his mature years and thereby to "give coherence, shape, and meaning to the whole experience."[3]

The story begins when eleven-year-old Lucius' parents and grandparents temporarily go out of town. Lucius then accepts Boon's invitation to join him in commandeering Boss Priest's brand new Winton flyer for an unauthorized excursion to Memphis, where Lucius will have the opportunity to see the big city and Boon will have the chance to visit Corrie at Miss Reba's "boardinghouse."

When Ned learns of their expedition, he stows away in the back of the car because, as he insists when he is discovered, "I wants a trip too."[4] Ned, like Lucas Beauchamp, is part white, belonging to a branch of the Priest family. Hence he feels he has a right to join Lucius, who is one of his kin, on the journey to the big city; and he goes along.

Once in Memphis, Ned conceives a scheme all his own. Without the knowledge or consent of his companions, Ned swaps Boss Priest's automobile for a stolen racehorse he christens Lightning. He makes this deal on the assumption that a live racehorse is far more valuable than a mere piece of machinery. Besides, Ned is confident that he can retrieve Boss's motor car by the simple expedient of getting the current possessor of the auto to go along with his plan to stage a race between Lightning and another horse, with the Winton Flyer going to the owner of the winning horse.

Ned succeeds in arranging for the race to be held in the nearby town of Parsham, with Lucius as Lightning's jockey; and Boon and Corrie go along to see the contest. But the local deputy sheriff, a swaggering bully named Butch Lovemaiden, finds out that Lightning is stolen property and impounds the animal. Corrie, who has resisted Butch's sweaty advances up to this point, gets him to release Lightning in the only way she can think of. Because Corrie had earlier confided to Lucius her determination to renounce her sordid profession, the boy is crushed when he realizes that, in order to get him and his pals out of their predicament, she has allowed a revolting swine like Butch to force himself on her. More and more the youngster becomes aware that he has learned more about the dark under-side of adult life in the course of this journey than he is capable of absorb-ing or coping with at his tender age. As old Lucius Priest, the novel's nar-rator, reflects about his younger self at this point, "I knew too much, had seen too much. I was a child no longer; innocence and childhood were for-ever lost, forever gone from me."

Lightning turns out to be a sure bet to win the race, because Ned has discovered that the horse has a passion for sardines and is guaranteed to run its heart out once it knows that its favorite delicacy awaits it at the end of the race. During the race, therefore, Ned stands at the finish line holding up Lightning's personal prize for winning; and the horse responds as ex-pected. So Lucius duly wins the race and regains Boss's car. But the guilt he feels for taking the auto and for making the trip without the sanction of his elders, plus his painful knowledge of the grim role Corrie played in arranging the race, undercuts to a great extent the joy that attends his triumph. He returns home from the journey a sadder but wiser young man.

When *The Reivers* came out on 4 June 1962, there were a few reviewers who saw the book merely as bargain basement Mark Twain; but critical response was mostly enthusiastic. Many critics characterized it as a funda-mentally amusing tale about a young man's initiation into adult life. As much as anything Faulkner had published in the decade or so following his receipt of the Nobel Prize in 1950, *The Reivers* certainly gave the lie to a flippant remark that Ernest Hemingway once made, that "no son of a bitch that ever won the Nobel Prize ever wrote anything worth reading afterwards." Furthermore, selection of the novel by the Book-of-the-Month Club made it an assured bestseller. National General Pictures purchased the novel for filming and in due time recruited Irving Ravetch and Harriet Frank to essay the third and last of their Faulkner scenarios.

The Reivers: **The Film**

Even before the production of the picture was announced, Faulkner critic Edmond Volpe stated that the novel was "a natural for Hollywood. Faulk-ner probably never turned out so tailor-made a script when he was actually writing for the movies."[5] Volpe added that the book could be transferred to the screen as easily as Clarence Day's play *Life with Father* (1947) had been. What a novel that has a Memphis sporting house as one of its principal settings might have in common with Day's sentimental comedy about a stuffy family of elite New Yorkers is unclear. But Volpe is correct in maintaining that the novel's straightforward plot, climaxed by a dandy horse-race, made it easily adaptable to the screen.

Lucius's family name is changed to McCaslin in the film version of *The Reivers* (1969), possibly to underline the blood relationship that exists between Ned McCaslin and the Priest family. Since the novel was narrated by Lucius as an old man, the screenplay attempts to approximate the book's narrative point of view by having the elderly Lucius McCaslin (voice by Burgess Meredith) give a running commentary on the action, voice-over on the sound track, as the plot unfolds on the screen. Most of the aging narrator's remarks are taken verbatim from the novel. Take, for instance, the sequence in which young Lucius (Mitch Vogel) is forced to fabricate several lies about where he is going to be during the time he actually plans to be in Memphis with Boon. He tells these fibs to the people who are supposed to be looking after him while his family is away, and they take what he says as true. Lucius's older self comments, voice-over, in words lifted right from the book, "I had already told more lies than I believed myself capable of inventing, and had had them believed or at least accepted with a consistency which had left me spellbound, if not already appalled." Looking back, the old Lucius remembers feeling that his facility in practicing deception made the road to perdition smooth and easily traversed.

But Lucius and the others encounter some obstacles on the road to Memphis that make him realize that the path to sin can be bumpy after all. The chief problem is Hell Creek bottom, a muddy mess where their car bogs down in the muck. Faulkner drew this incident from a trip he took to Memphis as a child in his grandfather's Buick, during which the automobile was caught in a quagmire very much like the Hell Creek of the book and film. The vehicle had to be hauled out of the mud for a price, by a couple of men who kept some mules handy for just such eventualities.

The episode is dramatized in the movie exactly as Faulkner handled it in the novel. After a farmer employs his two mules to free the Winton Flyer from the mud hole, he cooly informs Boon (Steve McQueen) that for this service he charges two dollars for each occupant of the car. Boon objects to the heavy tariff, pointing out that the farmer should not exact payment for Ned (Rupert Crosse) because "he ain't even white." Unruffled, the enterprising farmer responds, "Son, both these mules is color-blind." Ned chuckles with satisfaction, delighted that Boon has been forced to pay up on his behalf. Even though this scene is mainly comic, the serious point still comes through: racial equality can be recognized even by a southern redneck like the mule owner, when it suits his purposes.

Of Boon's treatment of Ned in this sequence, Pauline Kael writes that, when one views a scene like this one early in the film, one at first wonders if the movie is going to take a patronizing stance toward its black characters, as so many older Hollywood movies did. But as the film goes on, one is reassured: "We remember that we are in William Faulkner country and that we need not have worried." Faulkner's ability to depict the complex relationships of southern whites and blacks in a nuanced fashion is clearly displayed in his last novel and in the picture adapted from it. What's more, Kael goes on, Rupert Crosse's Ned is very likely the finest portrayal of a Negro character in an American movie since Juano Hernandez's Lucas Beauchamp in *Intruder in the Dust* twenty years before. (It is a pity that Crosse, who received an Oscar nomination for his role, died an untimely death only a few years later, in his mid-forties.) "Not that there haven't been marvellous performances by black actors," she explains, "but there haven't been *characters* one remembers, like Lucas and Ned—multidimensional, with individual sensibilities and temperaments." As Crosse plays him, Ned is an immensely likeable fellow, "a man of sudden impulses who takes sublime satisfaction in carrying them out."[6] He is quite capable of whimsically trading Boss's car for a racehorse and then engineering a horserace to win the auto back.

Juano Hernandez also turns up in *The Reivers* in a small but meaty role, as Uncle Possum, the dignified old black man with whom Lucius is invited to stay while he and his friends are in Parsham for the big race. When Butch Lovemaiden, the deputy sheriff (Clifton James), balks at allowing a white boy to spend even one night with a black family, Ned intervenes with a thought-provoking comment that is verbatim from the novel: "There's somewhere the Law stops and just people starts." Ned is suggesting that the deputy has no business interfering in a private matter of this kind. He wins his point, and Lucius stays overnight with the gracious old patriarch Uncle Possum, who reminds him very much of his grandfather, Boss McCaslin.

Lucius' grandfather is played by Will Geer (*Intruder in the Dust*), who, like Juano Hernandez, makes the most of the few scenes in which he appears. Early on, when Boss and the rest of the family are making ready

Boon Hogganbeck (Steve McQueen) and Uncle Possum (Juano Hernandez) in *The Reivers*. Hernandez did the best work of his career in this movie and in his other Faulkner film, *Intruder in the Dust*. (Museum of Modern Art/Film Stills Archive)

for their trip, he reassures Lucius that he shouldn't lose any sleep over the fact that his family as gone away and left him behind. "Trust in the Lord," Boss says with serene conviction; "He's up all night." The next time Lucius sees Boss is at the conclusion of the race. After returning to Jefferson and learning what has transpired in his absence, Lucius' grandfather has followed the three Reivers to Memphis and on to Parsham, to ascertain what has become of them and his Winton Flyer. While everyone is crowding around Lucius to congratulate him on winning the breathtaking race, Boss says to him in measured tones, "We'll talk about this later; I can see you're busy now."

Lucius does not have an audience with his grandfather until they all get back to Jefferson. Boss stops his son Maury, Lucius' father, from giving Lucius the whipping Maury feels the boy deserves. "This is what you would have done to me twenty years ago," Maury protests to Boss, his own father.

"Maybe I have more sense now," Boss answers, aware that the lad is getting too old for disciplinary measures of that sort. Then the old man takes Lucius onto his lap, and the boy, deeply ashamed of his behavior, begins to sob. In an interchange that closely follows the novel's dialogue, Boss advises his grandson that he can redeem himself in the eyes of his family for his recent delinquency if he is willing to profit by the mistakes he has made. Lucius responds that he just wants to try to forget everything that has happened in the last few days, but Boss counters, "Nothing is ever forgotten. Nothing is ever lost. It's too valuable." He further explains, "A gentleman accepts the responsibility of his actions and bears the burden of their consequences, even when he did not himself instigate them, didn't say no though he knew he should." On the sound track we then hear the voice of Lucius, now an old man himself, remembering how his grandfather pressed his face against his starched collar as the venerable old gentleman held him close while he cried. The collar, like its wearer, is stiff but not inflexible. "Now go wash your face," Boss concludes. "A gentleman cries too, but he always washes his face." On this note of symbolic cleansing, an emblem of his grandfather's forgiveness, the sequence ends.

In the following sequence Boon proudly announces to Lucius that he and Corrie are engaged, and he promises Lucius that their first boy will be named after him. After all, it is because Lucius, since meeting her, has consistently treated Corrie like a lady that her self-respect has been rekindled and she has been inspired to reform her life by taking on the respectable role of wife and mother. In consequence, both Corrie and Boon feel that Lucius deserves this token of their gratitude. The happy ending with which the movie concludes is the same one arranged by the author in the novel; it was not superimposed by the filmmakers—as were the upbeat endings of some of the other movies treated in this book, such as *The Sound and the Fury*.

Among the creative contributions to this delightful film is the excellent musical score by composer John Williams, who received an Oscar nomination for it. Most of Williams' background music for *The Reivers* constitutes a cross-section of Americana—harmonicas, banjos, and honky-tonk pianos. Admittedly, occasionally the underscore can sound too thick and lush, as in the case of the rather fulsome main theme during the opening credits, where the composer seems to be scoring a large-scale epic rather than the relatively simple tale of a small-town boy's junket to the big city. But that is the exception, not the rule; on the whole, Williams' music is quite suited to the dramatic needs of the movie, and is pleasing to listen to.

The Reivers was only the second feature film directed by Mark Rydell (*On Golden Pond*); prior to filming *The Reivers*, his experience had been gained mainly in directing one-hour television dramas. "*The Reivers* came to me by default," says Rydell. Veteran filmmaker William Wyler (*Ben Hur*) was initially slated to direct, but he was close to retirement and in failing health. When he learned that the production schedule called for a substantial amount of filming in Carrollton and Greenwood, Mississippi, he decided that living and working on location for several weeks would be beyond his strength. Hence Rydell, whose film adaptation of D.H. Lawrence's *The Fox* just then was receiving plaudits, was ultimately called upon to take the helm. Meta Carpenter went along on location as the film's script supervisor, the same position she had held on *Road to Glory* when Faulkner first met her.

Despite the fact that Rydell evoked uniformly splendid performances from Rupert Crosse, Will Geer, Juano Hernandez, and the other principal players, he still attributes the high quality of the picture, not primarily to his directorial efforts but to the Ravetch-Frank screenplay. "You know, it's very, very difficult to turn a novel into a movie," he explains. "Sometimes I think it's impossible, because, in effect," the screenwriters are "taking something that's 400 or 500 pages and somehow reducing it to a 110-page screenplay. . . . It's almost a herculean job to distill the essence of a novel and still capture it. I think *The Reivers* is an example that it can be done by people who do love the book." And in his view, the Ravetch and Frank's fondness for Faulkner's novel was the main reason that their script was so "very well articulated."[7]

Ravetch and Frank described their approach to adapting Faulkner for film in a joint statement they prepared for the studio on the occasion of the release of *The Long Hot Summer*; their remarks can easily be applied to any of their three Faulkner screenplays. Their brief essay begins by reminding us that "it is clearly impossible to bring Faulkner to the screen by just writing camera angles into the body of his scenes and then going out to shoot them." His work is far too complex for that. What screenwriters instead must strive to do, in order to create a worthy screen version of a Faulkner novel, as Wald suggested above, is to present a faithful portrayal of "Faulkner's conception of things. When one looks at the whole shelf of his fiction, when his entire lifetime as an artist is considered, his devotion to men, his pity and compassion for them, his respect for their worth, can clearly be seen."[8] Since Ravetch and Frank believe that they have tried as a matter of policy to translate Faulkner's attitudes and intentions into filmic terms when dramatizing his fiction, they contend that, in the final analysis, they have kept faith with the novelist.

Their aim of being true to Faulkner in adapting his work to the screen is not equally realized in the three Faulkner films on which they collaborated. As we have seen, *The Long Hot Summer* was more faithful to the novel from which it was derived than was the movie of *The Sound and the Fury*, and the screen adaptation of *The Reivers* adheres more closely to the tone and spirit of its source material than either of the other two films.

The movie version of *The Reivers*, like the novel itself, portrays Lucius' odyssey to Memphis as a genuine parable of the journey of a youngster toward maturity, a theme which is crystallized in the movie in Boon's observation to Lucius, "If you're going to reach your manhood, you have to say goodbye to the things you are and hello to the things you're not." The movie's fidelity to the novel is furthered by generous use throughout the film of Faulkner's dialogue, judiciously abridged for screen purposes. The film's use of dialogue from the book is exemplified most particularly in the voice-over narration on the sound track and in the "confessional scene" between Lucius and his grandfather. In fact, *The Reivers* includes more substantial passages of dialogue brought over from its literary source virtually intact than any other Faulkner movie except *Intruder in the Dust*.

"*The Reivers* did enjoy some real success," says Rydell; "it made a lot of money and was critically reviewed well." The director himself was among those singled out for critical praise in reviews of the film; "Mark Rydell directs his cast," one reviewer wrote, "with a sure feel for Faulkner's humor and earthy characterizations." The film was applauded for having caught the rich flavor of the period, and *Time* noted that the picture is climaxed by what its reviewer styled the damnedest, most exciting horserace anyone every saw. The movie, adds Rydell, "has become a kind of cult film. Colleges ask for it, film festivals ask for it, all the time."[9] And so they should; for Rydell's film has earned a place with *Intruder in the Dust* and *Tomorrow* as one of the best theatrical films made from Faulkner's work so far.

"Barn Burning": The Short Story

In the condensed version of "Barn Burning" that appears in *The Hamlet*, the episode mostly focuses on Ab Snopes. The short story in its complete form, as published in *Harper's Magazine* a year before the novel's appearance, brings to the fore Ab's ten-year-old son, Colonel Sartoris "Sarty" Snopes. And it is from Sarty's point of view that the events are narrated in "Barn Burning." In its original form, "Barn Burning," like *The Reivers*, is a tale about a youngster's achieving some degree of maturity and self-mastery by struggling with a serious emotional crisis.

Sarty is aware that his vengeful, volatile father punishes anyone who dares to cross him by putting a torch to that person's barn. Young as he is, Sarty knows that it is not fair for his father to destroy someone's barn, and with it the individual's harvest or livestock, because of some petty grievance. The lad is consequently confronted with a severe moral dilemma when he is summoned to testify against his father at the time that Ab is sued by his most recent victim. Sarty cannot approve of his father's behavior; yet he cannot bring himself to betray his own flesh and blood, especially the father he has been taught to honor and obey. The plaintiff apparently senses the boy's emotional conflict when he is forced to come forward at the trial to give testimony, and the man therefore directs the presiding judge to excuse the witness from testifying. When the suit against Ab is accordingly dismissed for lack of evidence, the judge pointedly advises the defendant to leave the county and not to come back.

Ab and his itinerant family pull up stakes once more and move on, this time to Frenchman's Bend, where Ab rents some farm land from Major de Spain, in order to continue supporting his family by sharecropping. The first time Ab goes to see his new employer at his mansion, he deliberately tracks horse manure across an imported rug in the entrance hall, as his way of exhibiting his hostility toward those of a higher social class. Later that day, the angry major personally delivers the carpet to the dilapidated cabin the Snopses inhabit on his property, and orders them to clean the rug. Spiteful as always, Ab scrubs the rug ferociously with harsh homemade lye and returns the ruined carpet to de Spain. The major in turn informs Ab that he intends to assess twenty bushels of corn from Ab's first crop to pay for the expensive article, and Ab counters de Spain's demand for restitution by defiantly suing his own boss in order to avoid paying the corn. The judge upholds de Spain's right to be reimbursed for his loss, but he reduces by half the number of bushels of corn Ab owes the major. Needless to say, the court's decision does not satisfy Ab, so the compulsive arsonist determines to mete out his own brand of justice by setting fire to de Spain's barn.

This is the last straw, as far as Sarty is concerned. On the night that

Ab sets out to wreak vengeance on de Spain for winning the case against him, Sarty runs all the way to the major's house and warns him what his father plans to do. De Spain jumps on a horse and races off to intervene; but the glowing sky, already ablaze with the conflagration that Ab has ignited, confirms Sarty's fears that the major has reached the barn too late to save it. Shots ring out, and Sarty is sure that his father has been killed by de Spain while making his escape. He is horrified that he has been the cause of his own father's death and is convinced that, under the circumstances, he can never return to his family. As a consequence, he runs away from home, determined to start a new life on his own. There the short story ends.

We know from a related scene in *The Hamlet*, however, that Ab is still very much alive; the day after the de Spain fire, he and his family, minus Sarty, are pictured once more setting out for nowhere in particular. But in the short story, Sarty is not aware that his father has survived; hence "Barn Burning" ends with the lad deciding that he must strike out on his own and disappearing into the night. Soon, however, the dawning of a new day will signal a fresh start in life for Sarty.

Barn Burning: The Television Movie

"Barn Burning" was recognized as a superb short story almost immediately after its publication in 1939, when it won the very first O. Henry Award for the best American short story of the year. Considering the story's critical stature and strong plotline, it seemed apt for dramatization. As a matter of fact, Faulkner and Albert Bezzerides had sketched out a scenario for a motion picture adaptation of the story in summer 1945, but nothing came of it. "Barn Burning" was, however, produced in a half-hour television version in 1954 on the live series *Suspense*, under the direction of Robert Mulligan, who later directed the teleplay of "Tomorrow." The more recent television production of "Barn Burning," first broadcast on 17 March 1980, was adapted for television by Horton Foote, who wrote both the television and motion picture adaptations of "Tomorrow." This forty-one-minute adaptation of "Barn Burning" was part of the *American Short Story* series on PBS. ("Spotted Horses" was initially considered as the Faulkner entry, but it was felt that the stampede of wild horses that climaxes the tale would be too complicated and expensive to stage, given the tight shooting schedule and modest budget allotted for each show.)

Since "Barn Burning" is largely told from Sarty's point of view, Foote's script has Sarty's voice on the sound track from time to time, giving his subjective reaction to what is happening, much as the elderly Lucius McCaslin did in the film of *The Reivers*. Sarty's voice-over comments are generally extracted right from Faulkner's prose. There is, for example, the scene in which Ab (Tommy Lee Jones) and Sarty (Shawn Whittington) first visit the major. When Sarty catches sight of de Spain's imposing mansion, which to this backwoods boy looks like a courthouse, we hear Sarty say to himself, voice-over on the sound track, that anyone who lives in a house as big as this one is simply beyond the reach of his father's nasty machinations. These remarks are taken directly from Faulkner, as is much of the rest of the dialogue in the telefilm.

Given the surge of optimism the lad feels at this point, he is absolutely crestfallen when shortly afterward Ab antagonizes de Spain by wantonly soiling his costly rug, and willfully precipitates a feud with his employer that quickly escalates into a legal battle. After the judge renders his verdict in the case, Ab insists that he and Sarty hang around town for the rest of the day. The boy listens to his father boasting to some other men about serving in the Civil War under Colonel Sartoris, after whom he named Sarty. The boy overhears one of the group informing a friend that Ab spent most of the war stealing horses and selling them indiscriminately to the cavalry of both armies. Indeed, the man goes on, Ab sustained the injury in his foot, which still causes him to limp, not in the line of duty, but when he was shot while making his getaway with some horses he had filched.

Significantly enough, in the short story Sarty never learns about his father's disgraceful war record, though Faulkner contrives to inform the reader of the exact nature of Ab's activities during the war. In fact, at the conclusion of the short story, when Sarty thinks Ab is dead, he even consoles himself by thinking how brave his father had been in battle, so that he will have some positive memories of his father to hold on to. When in the telefilm Sarty learns the awful truth about Ab's spurious war service, his last illusion about his father is shattered. This additional information about his father's disreputable character provides further motivation in the television film for Sarty's final renunciation of the filial loyalty he hitherto felt he owned his father, and his consequent decision to betray Ab to Major de Spain.

Sensing that his son may want to let de Spain know of his plans to burn his boss's barn, Ab binds the boy with cord to make sure that Sarty will be confined to the cabin while the father is away on his hateful mission.

In the short story, Ab commands his wife to keep Sarty home while he is gone, but he does not tie the lad up. In the telefilm the physical effort the boy must exert to extricate himself from his bonds becomes a visual metaphor for the inner struggle he has been undergoing all along as to whether or not he is duty-bound to remain faithful to a father like his. When Sarty finally succeeds in throwing off the rope with which Ab had attempted to hold him fast, he no longer feels bound to his father by ties of family fidelity and goes off to sound the alarm about the impending fire.

Another notable difference between Faulkner's story and the television drama is that in the telefilm Sarty is fully aware that Ab has not been shot and killed by de Spain. The final scene of the teleplay shows Sarty secretly watching his father and the remaining family members leaving their temporary home to travel on once again. Sarty's motivation in the television movie for not returning to his family, therefore, is not that he thinks he is responsible for his father's death; it is rather that he realizes that he can never again face his father, since he is well aware that, in Ab's mind, he has committed the unforgivable sin of betraying his own blood kin.

The final stark shots of Sarty, as he observes his family rumbling down the desolate road aboard a creaky wagon loaded with all its earthly possessions, brings to mind the similar shots which occur at the beginning of the telefilm, when Sarty was traveling with them. As the *Film News* reviewer points out, the marked resemblance between the austere images with which director Peter Werner opens the television movie and the ones with which he concludes it "indicates the never-ending, hopeless cycle from which Sarty has broken free." In addition, Ab Snopes is pictured at both the beginning and the end of the telemovie sitting imperiously in the driver's seat of the wagon, with a tight grip on the reins; and this implies the tyrannical hold he has on the members of his family, who will never prosper while they remain under his despotic domination.

Many elements contribute to the overall excellence of Werner's telefilm. Shawn Whittington gives a moving performance as the harried son who at last makes up his mind to get off the frustrating treadmill of the migrant existence imposed upon the family by his tyrannical father. Ab Snopes is equally well played by Tommy Lee Jones. The location photography deserves honorable mention, particularly the scenes shot in and round Faulkner's antebellum home, Rowan Oak, Major de Spain's mansion in the film. (Faulkner's own nephew Jim, who lives in the Oxford area, played Major de Spain.) *Film News* said that the "bird's-eye" view of de Spain's estate, shown at the point when Ab and Sarty go to visit him, beautifully suggests the kind of happy home life the Snopses have never experienced, for de Spain's home represents the stable existence that Ab Snopes's itinerant family seems destined never to achieve.[10]

Finally, producer Robert Geller deserves no little credit for opting to make from Faulkner's short story a mini-movie of less than an hour's running time, so that the filmmakers could develop Faulkner's compact tale to its full dramatic potential without having to concoct additional plot material to turn the story into a full-length telefeature. In short, the television production of "Barn Burning," in the main, is as true to its literary source as the other Faulkner scripts authored by Horton Foote; to that extent Faulkner himself may have liked the television version of "Barn Burning." What he thought about the concept of a television documentary designed to present his personal life to the viewing public, however, was a different matter; we shall examine the television documentaries made about him in the epilogue.

Epilogue

I said what I wanted to say in my books. The film
can never in any way alter what I have said.

William Faulkner

Some good pictures come from Hollywood. God knows
how, but they do.

William Faulkner

The growing interest in Faulkner and his fiction that followed World War
II was climaxed by his winning the Nobel Prize for literature on 10 December
1950. Prior to this event, the appearance in 1946 of *The Portable Faulkner,*
Malcolm Cowley's anthology of some of his best fiction, and the publication of *Intruder in the Dust,* his first bestseller in more than fifteen years,
had helped to bring him increased recognition in his native land. And with
the Nobel Prize in 1950, his fame spread worldwide.

Because of his inveterate shyness, Faulkner did not want to attend the
award ceremonies in Stockholm, but he was cajoled into doing so by his
family and friends, along with the State Department. For some days before
his scheduled departure, he drank heavily, as he usually did when he felt
trapped by circumstances beyond his control. To make certain that he would
be in condition to travel, his family surreptitiously moved the calendar forward three days. When Faulkner asked the whereabouts of his stepson Malcolm one evening, someone told him that Malcolm had gone to the high
school football game. "You've been lying to me," he barked. "They don't
play football games on Monday. I have three more days to drink."[1] As the
third day came round, he did stop drinking and began to prepare for the
journey to Sweden, where he did himself and his country proud.

That same year, 1950, Faulkner received the William Dean Howells Medal for American fiction from the American Academy of Arts and Letters. The following year the French government decorated him with the emblem of the French Legion of Honor, and he won the National Book Award for his *Collected Stories*. (Both the Pulitzer Prize and the National Book Award were later bestowed on his 1954 novel, *A Fable,* and in 1962 the National Institute of Arts and Letters honored him with its Gold Medal for fiction.)

The Biographical TV Films

Since he was being showered with prestigious awards, Faulkner seemed a logical subject for a short television documentary on "The Writer in America," to be produced for the weekly CBS-TV series *Omnibus.* As might be expected of someone who cherished privacy as much as he did, Faulkner balked at the idea of getting involved in project of this kind. But he finally consented to participate in the making of the short documentary when he learned that its director, Howard Magwood, was more than willing to come to Oxford to photograph him there. Under those circumstances, the movie would afford the public the opportunity to observe him in his own milieu, and in the company of old cronies like Phil Stone, Mac Reed, and Ike Roberts and his other hunting companions.

Magwood and a crew of ten came to Oxford to shoot the film in November 1952. As the *Eagle* observed on 13 November 1952, the town of Oxford, which three years earlier had been the site of the filming of *Intruder in the Dust,* was once again serving as a movie set, this time for a documentary about Oxford's first citizen.

The principal scriptwriter for the film was Harry Behn, who coincidentally had coauthored the 1933 film adaptation of Faulkner's short story "Honor," never produced. At Faulkner's suggestion, Behn was assisted with the television script by the novelist's longtime friend Phil Mullen, who was for several years associate editor of the *Oxford Eagle.*

The screenplay called for Faulkner to recreate for the camera the historic day, 10 November 1950, on which he was officially notified that he had won the Nobel Prize. Two years after the actual event, Faulkner and Mullen reenacted the journalist's visit to Rowan Oak to interview Faulkner about the award. "I was darned respectful that first morning," Mullen remembered afterward, "and in the film I was trying to play it that way." Between takes, Faulkner said to him, "Phil, you sound too worshipful. We're old friends. You should have told me that morning, 'You sap, you got the fame and you got to take the publicity.'" It goes without saying that Mullen did not use those precise words in the scene; but, as he has since said, on the second take "the scene got a whole lot better."

Faulkner also agreed to restage his delivery of the commencement address at his daughter Jill's high school graduation in May 1951. His brief speech, which proved to be one of the highlights of the film, exhorted graduates everywhere never to be afraid "to raise your voice for honesty and truth and compassion, against injustice and lying and greed. If you . . . will do this," he assured them, "you will change the earth."[2]

The seventeen-minute film was televised on *Omnibus* on 28 December 1952. Much of this first-rate documentary's key footage, including the two scenes just described, would be incorporated into a two-hour television documentary about Faulkner's life and work, entitled *William Faulkner: A Life on Paper,* produced more than a quarter of a century later. This feature-length documentary, first televised on PBS on 17 December 1979, was scripted by Albert Bezzerides, a Hollywood screenwriter with whom Faulkner had become friends when they were both at Warner Brothers in the 1940s. Bezzerides did not see much of Faulkner in his post-Hollywood years; hence, he says, "I actually learned more about Faulkner's activities during the last fifteen years of his life by doing research for the documentary script commissioned by the Public Broadcasting System on Bill's life than from anything else."[3]

This superbly crafted, thoughtful documentary, directed by Robert Squier and narrated by Raymond Burr, features interviews with a wide variety of people who knew Faulkner – from relatives such as his daughter Jill and his sister-in-law Louise, to friends and colleagues such as Howard Hawks, Ruth Ford, and Malcolm Cowley. While studiously emphasizing his achievements, the telefilm pulls no punches about the darker side of Faulkner's life, including his chronic drinking problem. Toward the end of the picture, mention is even made of the electroshock therapy which Faulkner underwent in a private New York hospital in late November 1952. Faulkner had gone east on business, and during his stay he went on a binge which precipitated an emotional and physical collapse. He was hospitalized in West Hills Sanitarium in the Bronx, where the shock treatments were administered on the advice of a trained psychiatrist, who supervised the procedure. (Faulkner, it seems, never made any reference to this experience once he returned home, very likely in order to spare his family distress over the matter.)

A Life on Paper concludes by documenting the circumstances surrounding Faulkner's final illness and death. Throughout his life Faulkner had been a devotee of horseback riding, and over the years he had suffered some serious injuries in riding accidents. The narrator of the documentary concisely explains on the sound track: "Hardly the best of riders, thrown with regularity, reckless, Faulkner broke ribs, collarbone, cracked his spine." On 17 June 1962, Faulkner was thrown by his horse Stonewall, who had thrown him before; and he took the brunt of the fall on his back. Neither sedatives nor whiskey could ease the severe pain he endured for the next two weeks and more. On 5 July he was admitted to the private sanitarium at Byhalia, Mississippi, where he died of a heart condition exacerbated by alcoholism, in the early hours of Friday, 6 July 1962. He was sixty-four years of age. The narrator reminds us in his closing remarks that Faulkner died on the birthday of his redoubtable great-grandfather, Col. William Falkner, whom he had idolized all his life. On this elegiac note the documentary concludes.

The Faulkner Legacy

William Faulkner was buried on the afternoon of 7 July in St. Peter's Cemetery, Oxford. Bennett Cerf, Faulkner's publisher, remembered the funeral vividly:

> Some people have the impression that William Faulkner's townsfolk in Oxford, Mississippi, didn't appreciate their famous neighbor. They should have been in the Court House Square of Oxford—made famous in Mr. Faulkner's writings—when his funeral cortège passed slowly by Saturday afternoon. Every store in town was closed, although Saturday is market day in those parts. The entire population of the town was grouped in the square—hats off, solemn and immobilized—as the cars wound their way slowly up to the old churchyard three blocks from the square. There wasn't a sound to be heard or a movement. We knew then that, although many of the people of Oxford might not understand or approve of or even know William Faulkner's writings, they did know him as a man and they respected him deeply.[4]

The tributes and memorials that poured in from all parts of the globe in the days immediately following Faulkner's demise frequently pointed to his Nobel Prize acceptance speech as synthesizing his personal vision of the human condition. A writer, Faulkner had said on that occasion, must see to it that his works reflect the old universal truths of the heart, "lacking which any story is ephemeral and doomed—love and honor and pity and pride and compassion and sacrifice. Until he does so, . . . he writes not of love but of lust, of defeats in which nobody loses anything of value, of victories without hope. . . . He writes not of the heart but of the glands." Faulkner stated, in conclusion, that he could not bring himself to envisage mankind as ultimately doomed: "I believe that man will not merely endure: he will prevail. He is immortal, . . . because he has a soul, a spirit capable of sacrifice and endurance." In the graduation address already quoted, Faulkner had added that he was convinced that man will "be able to save himself" precisely because he is "created in the image of God," and so is "worth saving."[5]

Although Faulkner made no attempt to expound a coherent religious philosophy in his work, his personal vision, nevertheless, was a deeply religious one. He once said that "no writing will be too successful without some conception of God, you can call Him by whatever name you want." When he was asked specifically about the role of Christian doctrine in his work, Faulkner answered that Christianity, as it is reflected in his fiction, leads one to "evolve for himself a moral code and standard within his capacities and aspirations, by giving him a matchless example of suffering and sacrifice and the promise of hope," all of which are enshrined in the Passion and Death of Christ.[6]

Again and again Faulkner implies in his fiction that one gains salvation through sacrifice and suffering; and the concept of redemption through sacrificial suffering is, as he himself suggests, one of the central tenets of the Christian faith.

In surveying the screen versions of Faulkner's fiction discussed in this book, one finds that the impact of this same theme of redemptive suffering resonates in many of the films as well. To consider only the very best of them, in the movie of *Intruder in the Dust,* one sees how Chick Mallison atones through self-sacrifice for his racist behavior toward Lucas Beauchamp. It is only at great personal risk that Chick spearheads the effort to uncover the evidence needed to save Lucas from the lynch mob; and he becomes a better person for having weathered this crisis. Therefore the film, like the novel, implicitly vindicates Faulkner's own evaluation of Chick as compared to his Uncle Gavin. Gavin Stevens, Faulkner told an interviewer, "was a good man but . . . his nephew, the boy, I think he may grow up to be a better man than his uncle. I think he may succeed as a human being . . . better than his uncle did."[7]

The film of *The Reivers* too remains faithful to Faulkner's thematic vision in portraying the way in which young Lucius redeems himself by facing up to the painful ordeal of confessing his transgressions to his grandfather in a spirit of sincere contrition.

The film adaptations of "Tomorrow" and "Barn Burning," like the short stories from which they were derived, are both stunning tributes to the remarkable capacity of human beings to survive dreadful tribulations and trials. Despite Jackson Fentry's tragic loss of his surrogate son and Sarty Snopes's agonizing renunciation of his family, both of these self-sacrificing individuals endure. They thereby exhibit the astonishing resilience of which the human spirit is capable in the face of appalling personal experiences—a quality Faulkner frequently celebrated in his fiction.

Most of the other screen versions of Faulkner's work retain enough of the spirit of the author's originals to be regarded as fundamentally faithful to their respective literary sources. All of the Faulkner films, whatever their individual shortcomings, invariably contain at least a few memorable moments which do Faulkner justice; such scenes have been cited throughout this book.

One hopes that Faulkner will continue to challenge those who would adapt his work to a visual medium. It might seem at first that the television miniseries format might be better suited than the theatrical feature for presenting a screen adaptation of a novel. After all, a miniseries has more screen time to devote to the plot of a novel than does a feature-length film. But not even a miniseries can capture the full scope of a novel. Television producer Stan Margulies (*The Thorn Birds*) admits frankly that one of the problems inherent in working in television is that "you are locked into an inexorable time frame." If any of the installments of a miniseries exceeds the stipulated running time determined in advance by network executives, it will simply have to be shortened to the required playing time. "The scenes that have to come out are inevitably the scenes devoted to character rather than plot," explains Margulies, "and I hate to lose those scenes." In the miniseries version of *The Long Hot Summer*, for example, scenes devoted to character development were sorely lacking.

In addition, feature motion pictures are made with more polish than telefilms of whatever length. The makers of a theatrical feature have the luxury of reshooting a scene until it is satisfactory; that is not the case with a television movie. Richard Chamberlain, star of *The Thorn Birds, Shogun,* and other television miniseries, concedes that "you want to do things over again, and you don't have the time."[8] One recalls in this context television journalist Kathleen Fury's observation, cited earlier, that telefilms, in contrast to theatrical films, are made on the double and on the cheap. Consequently, a finely crafted theatrical feature drawn from a novel will not automatically be overshadowed by a television miniseries derived from the same work. Martin Ritt's original film of *The Long Hot Summer*, which remains superior to the subsequent television remake, is definitely a case in point.

Perhaps television is best suited to dramatizing short fiction, which can be presented comfortably in a one-hour time slot, as "Barn Burning" was. This approach eliminates the need to extend the plotline of the original story to the degree that is called for by a feature-length film, as Faulkner himself had to do when he adapted *Today We Live* from his short story "Turn About." The television version of "Barn Burning" proved beyond a doubt that the little screen can be just as felicitous a medium for Faulkner adaptations as the big screen. Faulkner's fiction continues to be eminently adaptable to visual media because his fictional works generally have rather melodramatic plots and high emotional central characters—two elements which together help to engage and hold the viewer's attention. At the same time, the episodic nature of his plots makes it easy to adjust them to the needs of both motion pictures and television.

Even as we come to the end of this study of the movies based on Faulkner's fiction, the Center for the Study of Southern Culture at the University of Mississippi is promoting a film adaptation of Faulkner's 1930 novel, *As I Lay Dying*. The National Endowment for the Humanities has made grant money available to develop a script for the movie, and additional funds to finance the production are being sought from several sources, according to William Ferris and Ann Abadie, directors of the center. The script was composed by independent filmmaker Robert Clem. If the project is funded, the movie will be shot on location in and around Oxford and will be released theatrically. That the film will be a faithful rendition of the novel is augured by the fact that several Faulkner scholars are serving as advisers on the production. So Faulkner's association with the cinema is by no means at an end.

Faulkner always said that he did not care if he personally were forgotten, so long as his work was remembered. "It is my ambition to be, as a private individual, abolished and voided from history, leaving it markless, no refuse save the printed books," he wrote to Malcolm Cowley. "It is my aim, and every effort bent, that the sum and history of my life, which is the same sentence is my obit and epitaph too, shall be them both: He made the books and he died." Faulkner expressed these same sentiments on another occasion, when he ran his finger along a shelf of his fiction and remarked, "Not a bad monument for a man to leave behind him." The best of the Faulkner films — with *Intruder in the Dust* leading the list — are likewise a monument to him.

Since the Faulkner films remain accessible for viewing as reruns on television and in revival houses, and through the 16mm and videocassette channels of distribution, they continue to be seen, just as his books continue to be read. This is no mean achievement for a writer who once declared that all he ever hoped to do through his work was "to lift up or maybe comfort or anyway at least entertain, in its turn, man's heart." Elsewhere Faulkner added that a writer usually has only a short span of time in which to accomplish this goal: "You're given only sixty years to do it. Saving a few exceptions that's all anybody has; a short time."⁹

For William Faulkner that was long enough.

Notes

PROLOGUE

1. Regina K. Fadiman, *Faulkner's Intruder in the Dust: Novel into Film* (Knox-ville: Univ. of Tennessee Press, 1978), 9; Gene D. Phillips, *Fiction, Film, and F. Scott Fitzgerald* (Chicago: Loyola University Press, 1986).

2. Edward Murray, *The Cinematic Imagination: Writers and the Motion Pictures* (New York: Ungar, 1972), 158.

3. Joseph Blotner, *Faulkner: A Biography*, rev. ed. (New York: Random House, 1984), 651. Although I shall usually cite this updated, revised, one-volume edition of the Blotner biography in these notes, I have also constantly consulted the original two-volume edition (New York: Random House, 1974), since it remains the more amply detailed account of Faulkner's life and work. Page references in these notes to the earlier edition will be easily identifiable by the presence of a volume number.

4. William Faulkner, *Requiem for a Nun* (New York: Vintage, 1975), 238.

5. Cleanth Brooks, "Faulkner's Vision of Good and Evil," in *Religious Perspectives in Faulkner's Fiction*, ed. J. Robert Barth, S.J. (Notre Dame: Univ. of Notre Dame Press, 1972), 57.

6. Tom Dardis, *Some Time in the Sun* (New York: Scribner's, 1976), 90.

CHAPTER I

1. Blotner, *Faulkner: A Biography*, 342.

2. Bruce Kawin, "Introduction" to *Faulkner's MGM Screenplays*, ed. Kawin (Knoxville: Univ. of Tennessee Press, 1982), p. xxii.

3. Ibid., xxiv; A.I. Bezzerides, *William Faulkner: A Life on Paper*, (Jackson: Univ. Press of Mississippi, 1980), 31, 91. See Louis Daniel Brodsky, "Reflections on William Faulkner: An Interview with Albert I. Bezzerides," *Southern Review* 21, no. 2 (Apr. 1985), 383–85.

4. Murry C. Falkner, *The Falkners of Mississippi: A Memoir* (Baton Rouge: Louisiana State Univ. Press, 1968), 52. (It was William Faulkner who restored the

"u" to the family name after it had been dropped by his great-grandfather; not all of the family followed suit, Murry Falkner among them.) For a detailed treatment of Faulkner's youthful moviegoing, see Jeffrey J. Folks, "William Faulkner and the Silent Film," in *The South and Film*, ed. Warren French (Jackson: Univ. Press of Mississippi, 1981), 171–82.

5. Blotner, *Faulkner*, II, 1357; Kawin, "Introduction" to William Faulkner, *Today We Live*, in *MGM Screenplays*, ed. Kawin, 114.

6. Robert Coughlan, *The Private World of William Faulkner* (New York: Cooper Square, 1972), 106.

7. Kawin, "Introduction" to William Faulkner, *Absolution*, in *MGM Screenplays*, ed. Kawin, 55.

8. Bezzerides, *Faulkner: A Life on Paper*, 74–75; Blotner, "Faulkner in Hollywood," in *Man and the Movies*, ed. W. R. Robinson (Baltimore: Penguin, 1967), 268.

9. Kawin, "Introduction" to Faulkner, *Today We Live*, in *MGM Screenplays*, ed. Kawin, 111.

10. Because no publisher would accept the full-length version of Faulkner's vast, complex novel *Flags in the Dust*, Faulkner agreed to allow the book to be published in an abridged version as *Sartoris* in 1929. In 1973, however, the complete novel was brought out with its original title, and it is to that definitive edition that I refer.

11. Cleanth Brooks, *William Faulkner: Toward Yoknapatawpha and Beyond* (New Haven: Yale Univ. Press, 1979), 404. Brooks erroneously says that John Sartoris is one of the drunken flyers in "Ad Astra," but that story is set several months after John's death.

12. William Faulkner, *War Birds*, in *MGM Screenplays*, ed. Kawin, 416–17.

13. Todd McCarthy, "Phantom Hawks," *Film Comment* 18, no. 5 (Sept.–Oct. 1982), 65.

14. Kawin, "Introduction" to Faulkner, *Mythical Latin-American Kingdom Story*, in *MGM Screenplays*, ed. Kawin, 433.

15. Blotner, "Faulkner in Hollywood," 271.

16. Dardis, *Time in the Sun*, 96–97.

17. Kawin, "Introduction" to *MGM Screenplays*, ed. Kawin, xxvi.

18. William K. Everson, "Rediscovery: Raymond Bernard and *Les Croix de Bois*," *Films in Review* 36 (March 1985), 174; Meta Carpenter Wilde with Orin Borsten, *A Loving Gentleman: The Love Story of William Faulkner and Meta Carpenter* (New York: Simon and Schuster, 1976), 109. Meta Carpenter was Faulkner's constant companion during his Hollywood days; hence her book concentrates mainly on their personal relationship rather than on his screen work.

19. George Garrett, "Afterword" to William Faulkner and Joel Sayre, *The Road to Glory: A Screenplay*, ed. Matthew J. Bruccoli (Carbondale: Southern Illinois Univ. Press, 1981), 174.

20. George R. Sidney, "Faulkner in Hollywood: A Study of His Career as a Scenarist" (Ph.D. diss., Univ. of New Mexico, 1959), 86.

21. Graham Greene, *Graham Greene on Film: Collected Film Criticism, 1935–40* (New York: Simon and Schuster, 1972), 162.

22. Sidney, *Faulkner in Hollywood*, 151; Pauline Kael, *Reeling* (New York: Warner Books, 1977), 630–31.

23. James B. Meriwether and Michael Millgate, eds., *Lion in the Garden: Interviews with William Faulkner, 1926–62* (New York: Random House, 1968), 240; Coughlan, *Private World*, 109.

CHAPTER 2

1. Joel Sayre, "Real Writers Who Wrote Movies," *New York Times Book Review*, 8 Aug. 1976, 3.

2. Bezzerides, *Faulkner: A Life on Paper*, 88–89.

3. Jerry Wald, "Faulkner and Hollywood," *Films in Review* 10, no. 3 (March 1959), 130.

4. Blotner, "Faulkner in Hollywood," 292.

5. Jerry Wald to Steve Trilling, 11 July 1944, in William Faulkner, *The Letters*, ed. Louis Daniel Brodsky and Robert W. Hamblin (Jackson: Univ. Press of Mississippi, 1984), 29. Subsequently referred to as *Letters*, to distinguish it from *Selected Letters*, the other volume of Faulkner's correspondence.

6. F. Scott Fitzgerald, "The Curious Case of Benjamin Button," in Fitzgerald, *Tales of the Jazz Age* (New York: Scribner's, 1922), ix.

7. Joseph Blotner, "Speaking of Books: Faulkner's *A Fable*," *New York Times Book Review*, 25 May 1969, 34.

8. Frederick L. Gwynn and Joseph Blotner, eds., *Faulkner in the University: Class Conferences at the University of Virginia, 1957–58* (New York: Vintage, 1959), 27, 86.

9. Blotner, "Faulkner's *A Fable*," 39.

10. William Faulkner, *The De Gaulle Story: A Screenplay*, ed. Brodsky and Hamblin (Jackson: Univ. Press of Mississippi, 1984), 335.

11. Henri Diamant-Berger, "Critique of *The De Gaulle Story*," in Faulkner, *De Gaulle*, 376, 378.

12. Faulkner to William Buckner, 19 Nov. 1942, in Faulkner, *De Gaulle*, 396; Brodsky and Hamblin, "Introduction" to Faulkner, *De Gaulle*, pp. xxix–xxx.

13. Faulker, *De Gaulle*, 312.

14. Faulkner to William F. Fielden, 27 Apr. 1943, in William Faulkner, *Selected Letters*, ed. Blotner (New York: Random House, 1977), 173. Subsequently referred to as *Selected Letters*, to distinguish it from *Letters*, the other volume of Faulkner's correspondence, already cited. Dardis, *Time in the Sun*, 125; see the scenario for

Life and Death of a Bomber, contained with two other rejected scenarios in William Faulkner, *Country Lawyer and Other Stories for the Screen,* ed. Brodsky and Hamblin (Jackson: Univ. Press of Mississippi, 1987).

15. William Faulkner, *Battle Cry: A Screenplay,* ed. Brodsky and Hamblin (Jackson: Univ. Press of Mississippi, 1985), 185; 302.

16. McCarthy, "Phantom Hawks," 73.

17. Ernest Hemingway, *To Have and Have Not* (New York: Scribner's, 1962), 225.

18. Faulkner to Harold Ober, 22 Apr. 1944, in *Selected Letters,* 180.

19. Meriwether and Millgate, *Lion in the Garden,* 241.

20. Blotner, "Faulkner in Hollywood," 289.

21. Robin Wood, *Howard Hawks* (Garden City, N.Y.: Doubleday, 1968), 26.

22. Blotner, "Faulkner in Hollywood," 292.

23. Gene D. Phillips, *The Movie Makers: Artists in an Industry* (Chicago: Nelson-Hall, 1973), 54.

24. George P. Garrett, O.B. Hardison, Jr., and Jane R. Gelfman, "Introduction" to William Faulkner, Leigh Brackett [and Jules Furthman], *The Big Sleep,* in *Film Scripts One,* ed. Garrett et al. (New York: Appleton, Century, Crofts, 1971), 137. The draft of the screenplay included in this volume was composed solely by Faulkner and Brackett, and does not include Furthman's subsequent revisions.

25. Faulkner to James J. Geller, mid-Dec. 1944, in *Selected Letters,* 187.

26. Frank MacShane, "Raymond Chandler on Hollywood," *American Film* 7, no. 11 (Nov. 1981), 77; Gene D. Phillips, *Alfred Hitchcock* (Boston: Twayne, 1984), 38.

27. McCarthy, "Phantom Hawks," 75; Hart Wegner, "A Chronicle of Soil, Seasons, and Weather: Jean Renoir's *The Southerner,*" in *The South and Film,* ed. French, 67.

28. Harry Castleman and Walter J. Podrazik, *Watching TV: Four Decades of American TV* (New York: McGraw-Hill, 1982), 78; Jack Gould, "*The Brooch,*" *New York Times,* 12 Apr. 1953.

29. Faulkner to Saxe Commins, 24 Dec. 1952, in *Letters,* 104; Gene D. Phillips, *Graham Greene: The Films of His Fiction* (New York: Columbia Teachers College Press, 1974), 14.

30. Phillips, *Movie Makers,* 54; Blotner, "Faulkner in Hollywood," 299.

31. Joseph McBride, *Hawks on Hawks* (Berkeley: Univ. of California Press, 1982), 59–60; Arthur Knight, "Faulkner in Pharaoh-Land," *Saturday Review,* 25 June 1955, 24.

32. David Niven, *Bring on the Empty Horses* (New York: Dell, 1976), 104.

33. Blotner, "Faulkner and Hollywood," 302.

34. Faulkner to Harold Ober, 20 Aug. 1945, in *Selected Letters,* 200.

35. Dardis, *Time in the Sun,* 149.

36. Gene D. Phillips, *Fiction, Film, and F. Scott Fitzgerald* (Chicago: Loyola Univ. Press, 1986), 145.

37. Kawin, "The Montage Element in Faulkner's Fiction," in *Faulkner, Modernism, and Film,* ed. Evans Harrington and Ann J. Abadie (Jackson: Univ. Press of Mississippi, 1979), 109.

CHAPTER 3

1. Murry Falkner, *The Falkners of Mississippi,* xviii.

2. Coughlan, *Private World,* 43.

3. Blotner, *Faulkner,* 53.

4. Ibid., 48.

5. Bezzerides, *Faulkner: A Life on Paper,* 48.

6. Jack Cofield, *William Faulkner: The Cofield Collection* (Oxford, Miss.: Yoknapatawpha Press, 1978), 68. This book, filled with photographs of Faulkner and his family, is virtually a Faulkner family album.

7. Coughlan, *Private World,* 60.

8. Ibid., 63.

9. Robert A. Jelliffe, ed., *Faulkner at Nagano* (Tokyo: Kenkyusha, 1956), 80; Meriwether and Millgate, *Lion in the Garden,* 255. Concerning the alternate title of *Flags in the Dust,* see ch. 1, n. 10, of this book.

10. William Faulkner, "Introduction" to *Sanctuary,* corr. ed. (New York; Vintage, 1987), 388. This introduction contains some factual errors. For example, Faulkner says he wrote the first version of *Sanctuary* in three weeks, whereas Noel Polk and other Faulkner scholars have established that he composed it in four months, January to May 1929.

11. Cofield, *Faulkner: The Cofield Collection,* 89.

12. Noel Polk, "Afterword" to William Faulkner, *Sanctuary: The Original Text* (New York: Random House, 1981), 298.

13. Faulkner, "Introduction" to *Sanctuary,* 339.

14. Jelliffe, ed., *Faulkner at Nagano,* 65, 66, 143.

15. John Faulkner, *My Brother Bill: An Affectionate Reminiscence* (New York: Pocket Books, 1964), 153.

16. William K. Everson, unpublished program notes for *The Story of Temple Drake,* New School of Social Research, New York, 26 March 1971.

17. Frederick J. Hoffman, *William Faulkner,* rev. ed. (New York: Twayne, 1966), 133.

18. Charles Higham and Joel Greenberg, "Jean Negulesco," in *The Celluloid Muse: Hollywood Directors Speak* (New York: New American Library, 1972), 210.

19. Richard Griffith and Arthur Mayer, *The Movies,* rev. ed. (New York: Simon and Schuster, 1970), 293.

20. Gwynn and Blotner, *Faulkner in the University,* 79, 96, 122.

21. Faulkner to Robert K. Haas, 22 May 1950, in *Selected Letters,* 305; see Hugh

M. Ruppersburg, *Voice and Eye in Faulkner's Fiction* (Athens: Univ. of Georgia Press, 1983), 133.

22. Gwynn and Blotner, *Faulkner in the University*, 196.

23. Faulkner, *Requiem for a Nun* (1975), 140.

24. Faulkner, *Requiem for a Nun*, adapted to the stage by Ruth Ford (New York: Random House, 1959), p. i.

25. Murray Schumach, *The Face on the Cutting Room Floor*: The Story of Movie and TV Censorship (New York: Morrow, 1964), 145.

26. E. Pauline Degenfelder, "The Four Faces of Temple Drake: Faulkner's *Sanctuary*, *Requiem for a Nun*, and the Two Film Adaptations," *American Quarterly* 28 (Winter 1976), 555.

CHAPTER 4

1. Patrick H. Samway, S.J., *Faulkner's Intruder in the Dust: A Critical Study of the Typescripts* (Troy, N.Y.: Whitston, 1980), 12.

2. Faulkner to Robert K. Haas, 3 May 1940; Faulkner to Robert K. Haas, 20 Apr. 1948, in *Selected Letters*, 122, 266.

3. Blotner, *Faulkner*, 493.

4. Phil Mullen, "William Faulkner, Great Novelist, also Great, Gentle Man," *Oxford (Miss.) Eagle*, 6 Aug. 1976 (special Faulkner edition).

5. Fadiman, in *Intruder in the Dust: Novel into Film*, 27, places this event in 1916; but 1906 is consistently given as the date by other sources, e.g., Dorothy B. Jones, "William Faulkner: Novel into Film," *Quarterly of Film, Radio and TV* (later *Film Quarterly*) 18, no. 1 (Fall 1953), 52.

6. Blotner, *Faulkner*, 502.

7. Samway, *Intruder in the Dust: Typescripts*, 38.

8. Blotner, *Faulkner*, 502; see Samway, *Intruder in the Dust: Typescripts*, 63–65.

9. Fadiman, *Intruder in the Dust: Novel into Film*, 60 (see 170), 61 (see 217).

10. Degenfelder, "The Film Adaptation of Faulkner's *Intruder in the Dust*," *Literature/Film Quarterly* 1, no. 2 (Spring 1973), 147. An abridged version of this article appears in Gerald Peary and Roger Shatzkin, eds., *The Modern American Novel and the Movies* (New York: Ungar, 1978), 178–86. In both versions the author confuses the first names of Nub Gowrie, the father of the Gowrie family, and his son Crawford.

11. Pauline Kael, *Kiss Kiss Bang Bang* (New York: Bantam Books, 1969), 356.

12. Alan Estrin, *The Hollywood Professionals*, vol. 6 (New York: Barnes, 1980), 175.

13. Kael, *Kiss Kiss Bang Bang*, 356.

14. Fadiman, *Intruder in the Dust: Novel into Film*, 32.

15. Faulkner to Samuel Marx, 12 Oct. 1949, in *Selected Letters*, 293.

16. Richard Koszarski, ed., *Hollywood Directors: 1941–76* (New York: Oxford Univ. Press, 1977), 165.

17. Brodsky, "Reflections on William Faulkner: Interview with Bezzarides," 387.

18. William Faulkner, "An Error in Chemistry," in *Knight's Gambit* (New York: Vintage Books, 1978), 111; "Tomorrow," in *Knight's Gambit*, 101.

19. Jack Barbera, "Tomorrow and Tomorrow and *Tomorrow*," in *The South and Film*, ed. French, 189; Faulkner, *The Mansion* (New York: Vintage, 1959), 230.

20. Horton Foote, "*Tomorrow*: The Genesis of a Screenplay," in *Faulkner, Modernism, and Film*, ed. Harrington and Abadie, 150.

21. Ibid., 159.

22. Ibid., 161.

23. David G. Yellin and Marie Connors, eds., *Tomorrow and Tomorrow and Tomorrow* (Jackson: Univ. Press of Mississippi, 1985), 167.

24. Yellin and Connors, *Tomorrow and Tomorrow and Tomorrow*, 179.

25. Barbera, "Tomorrow and Tomorrow and *Tomorrow*," 195; Yellin and Connors, *Tomorrow and Tomorrow and Tomorrow*, 164.

26. Yellin and Connors, 171.

27. Ibid., 174–75, 183.

28. Ibid., 180; Samuel G. Freedman, "From the Heart of Texas," *New York Times Magazine*, 2 Feb. 1986, 50; Louise Tanner, "An Interview with Horton Foote," *Films in Review* 37, no. 11 (Nov. 1986), 531.

29. Horton Foote, "On First Dramatizing Faulkner," in *Faulkner, Modernism, and Film*, ed. French, 65.

CHAPTER 5

1. Cofield, *Faulkner: The Cofield Collection*, 97; Thomas (Tennessee) Williams to Josephine Johnson, 17 May 1935 (unpublished letter) preserved at Washington University, St. Louis, Missouri.

2. John Faulkner, *My Brother Bill*, 246; McBride, *Hawks on Hawks*, 57.

3. Brooks, *Faulkner: Toward Yoknapatawpha*, 201, 399; McBride, *Hawks on Hawks*, 57.

4. Michael Millgate, *The Achievement of William Faulkner* (New York: Random House, 1966), 142.

5. Joseph Blotner and Noel Polk, "Note on the Texts," in William Faulkner, *Novels: 1930–35*, corr. ed. (New York: Library of America, 1985), 1026.

6. William Faulkner, *Pylon*, in corr. ed. (New York: Vintage, 1987), 16–17.

7. Karl F. Zender, "Money and Matter in *Pylon* and *The Wild Palms*," *Faulkner Journal* 1 (Spring 1986), 21–22.

8. Olga W. Vickery, *The Novels of William Faulkner: A Critical Interpretation*, rev. ed. (Baton Rouge: Louisiana State Univ. Press, 1973), 154.

9. Brooks, *Faulkner: Towards Yoknapatawpha*, 396.

10. Ernest Hemingway, "On Being Shot Again," in *By-Line: Ernest Hemingway*, ed. William White (New York: Bantam Books, 1968), 174.

11. John Faulkner, *My Brother Bill*, 151.

12. William Faulkner to Harold Ober, 18 Jan. 1956, in *Selected Letters*, 391; Michael Stern, "From the Folklore of Speed to *Dance Macabre*," in *The Modern American Novel and the Movies*, ed. Gerald Peary and Roger Shatzkin (New York: Ungar, 1978), 44.

13. Jon Halliday, *Sirk on Sirk* (New York: Viking, 1972), 170.

14. E. Pauline Degenfelder, "Sirk's *Tarnished Angels*: *Pylon* Recreated," *Literature/Film Quarterly* 5, no. 3 (Summer 1977), 243; Stern, "Folklore of Speed," 44.

15. Halliday, *Sirk on Sirk*, 120–21.

16. Degenfelder, "Sirk's *Tarnished Angels*," 245.

17. Ibid., 243; Stern, "Folklore of Speed," 47.

18. Halliday, *Sirk on Sirk*, 170; Kael, *5001 Nights at the Movies*, 580.

CHAPTER 6

1. Gwynn and Blotner, *Faulkner in the University*, 90; John Faulkner, *My Brother Bill*, 242.

2. Malcolm Cowley, *The Faulkner-Cowley File: Letters and Memories, 1944–62* (New York: Viking, 1966), 25–26.

3. John Faulkner, *My Brother Bill*, 142.

4. Millgate, *The Achievement of Faulkner*, 188.

5. Gwynn and Blotner, *Faulkner in the University*, 66.

6. Arthur Knight, "Filming Faulknerland," *Saturday Review*, 7 Dec. 1957, 52.

7. Brooks, *William Faulkner: The Yoknapatawpha Country* (New Haven: Yale Univ. Press, 1966), 174.

8. Kawin, *Faulkner and Film*, 57–58; Knight, "Faulknerland," 52.

9. Michael Kerbel, *Paul Newman* (New York: Pyramid Books, 1974), 43; Pauline Kael, *I Lost It at the Movies* (New York: Bantam, 1966), 80.

10. Kathleen Fury, "*The Long Hot Summer* of Don, Cybill, and Company," *TV Guide*, 5 Oct. 1985, 38, 40.

11. John J. O'Connor, "Dipping a Toe in Faulkner Country," *New York Times*, 6 Oct. 1985; Daniel Ruth, "The Heat is on in *Summer*," *Chicago Sun-Times*, 4 Oct. 1985.

CHAPTER 7

1. Jelliffe, ed., *Faulkner at Nagano*, 103.

2. William Faulkner, "An Introduction to *The Sound and the Fury*," *Mississippi Quarterly* 26, no. 3 (Summer 1973), 413–14. This introduction was composed in 1933 for a projected special edition of the novel that never materialized. Another shorter version of this introduction was published in *New York Times Book Review*, 5 Nov. 1972, 7. It is probably an earlier draft of the longer, more detailed version quoted here.

3. John Faulkner, *My Brother Bill*, 244–45.

4. William Faulkner, *The Sound and the Fury*, corr. ed. (New York: Vintage, 1987), 4.

5. Faulkner, "An Introduction to *The Sound and the Fury*," 414; Meriwether and Millgate, *Lion in the Garden*, 245.

6. Faulkner to Robert K. Haas, 7 Feb. 1940, in *Selected Letters*.

7. Meriwether and Millgate, *Lion in the Garden*, 245. In this interview and in his appendix to *The Sound and the Fury*, published in *The Portable Faulkner*, Faulkner mistakenly states that Miss Quentin climbed down a rain pipe; but the text of the novel makes it clear that it is a pear tree and not a rain pipe that is involved; see William Faulkner, "Appendix: The Compsons," in *The Portable Faulkner*, ed. Malcolm Cowley, rev. ed (New York: Penguin Books, 1984), 74, 282, 286. This inconsistency on Faulkner's part resulted from trusting his memory at a time when it was not feasible to check the text. In the case of the appendix, Faulkner specifically notes in a letter to Cowley dated 18 Oct. 1945 that he did not have a copy of the book ready to hand when he composed the piece.

8. Faulkner, "Appendix: The Compsons," 711, 721; Meriwether and Millgate, *Lion in the Garden*, 245.

9. Bernhard Radloff, "The Unity of Time in *The Sound and the Fury*," *Faulkner Journal* 1, no. 2 (Spring 1986), 61; Meriwether and Millgate, *Lion in the Garden*, 245.

10. Faulkner, "Appendix: The Compsons," 716; Jelliffe, *Faulkner at Nangano*, 104.

11. Cleanth Brooks, *William Faulkner: First Encounters* (New Haven: Yale Univ. Press, 1983), 74.

12. Faulkner, "Introduction" to *Sanctuary*, 338.

13. Blotner, *Faulkner: A Biography*, II, 1586.

14. Knight, "Filming Faulknerland," 53.

15. Jerry Wald, "From Faulkner to Film," 42, 7 March 1959, 16, 42; and "Faulkner and Hollywood," *Films in Review* 10, no. 3 (Mar. 1959), 132.

16. Wald, "From Faulkner to Film," 42.

17. Sidney, "Faulkner in Hollywood," 335; Pat McGilligan, "Ritt Large: An Interview with Martin Ritt," *Film Comment* 22, no. 1 (Jan.–Feb. 1986), 45.

18. Wald, "From Faulkner to Film," 42.

CHAPTER 8

1. Faulkner to Robert K. Haas, 3 May 1940, in *Selected Letters,* 123–24.
2. Blotner, *Faulkner: A Biography,* 330.
3. Millgate, *The Achievement of Faulkner,* 256–57.
4. William Faulkner, *The Reivers: A Reminiscence* (New York: Vintage, 1962), 70.
5. Carlos Baker, *Ernest Hemingway: A Life Story* (New York: Bantam, 1970), 666; Murray, *The Cinematic Imagination,* 163–64.
6. Pauline Kael, *Deeper into Movies* (New York: Bantam, 1974), 94.
7. Judith Crist, *Take 22: Moviemakers on Moviemaking* (New York: Viking, 1984), 181.
8. Sidney, *Faulkner in Hollywood,* 242, 244.
9. "Cinecapsules," *Catholic Film Newsletter,* 15 Jan. 1970, p. 3; Crist, *Take 22,* 183.
10. *"American Short Story* Reviews," *Film News* 37, no. 3 (Fall 1980), 29.

EPILOGUE

1. Mullen, "Faulkner, Great Novelist," in *Oxford Eagle.*
2. Ibid.; William Faulkner, "Address to the Graduating Class," in *Essays, Speeches, and Public Letters,* ed. James B. Meriwether (New York: Random House, 1965), 123–24.
3. Brodsky, "Reflections on Faulkner," 396.
4. Bezzerides, *Faulkner: A Life on Paper,* 120; Bennett Cerf, "From William Faulkner's Publisher," *Saturday Review* (special Faulkner issue), 28 July 1962, 12.
5. William Faulkner, "Address Upon Receiving the Nobel Prize for Literature," in *Essays, Speeches, and Public Letters,* ed. Meriwether, 120; Faulkner, "Address to the Graduating Class," 123.
6. Gwynn and Blotner, *Faulkner in the University,* 161; Meriwether and Millgate, *Lion in the Garden,* 247.
7. Meriwether and Millgate, *Lion in the Garden,* p. 225.
8. Stephen Farber, "Making Book on TV," *Film Comment* 18, no. 6 (Nov.–Dec. 1982), 45, 47.
9. Cowley, *The Faulkner-Cowley File,* 126; Blotner, *Faulkner: A Biography,* 576; Faulkner to Sven Åhman, 16 Nov. 1950, in *Selected Letters,* 309; "He Will Prevail," *Time* 13 July 1962, p. 85.

Bibliography

I. PRIMARY SOURCES*

Faulkner, William. *Battle Cry: A Screenplay*. Edited by Louis Daniel Brodsky and Robert W. Hamlin. Jackson: University Press of Mississippi, 1985. From the Brodsky Collection.

——. *The Big Sleep: A Screenplay*. With Leigh Brackett [and Jules Furthman]. In *Film Scripts One*, edited by George P. Garrett, O. B. Hardison, Jr., and Jane R. Gelfman, pp. 139–329. New York: Appleton, Century, Crofts, 1971. Furthman's subsequent revisions of the screenplay are not included in this version of the script.

——. *Collected Stories*. New York: Random House, 1950.

——. *Country Lawyer and Other Stories for the Screen*. Edited by Louis Daniel Brodsky and Robert W. Hamblin. Jackson: University Press of Mississippi, 1987. From the Brodsky Collection.

——. *The De Gaulle Story: A Screenplay*. Edited by Louis Daniel Brodsky and Robert W. Hamblin. Jackson: University Press of Mississippi, 1984. From the Brodsky Collection.

——. *Essay, Speeches, and Public Letters*. Edited by James B. Meriwether. New York: Random House, 1965.

——. *Faulkner's MGM Screenplays*. Edited by Bruce Kawin. Knoxville: University of Tennessee Press, 1982.

——. *Flags in the Dust* (1929). Edited by Douglas Day. New York: Vintage, 1974.

——. *The Hamlet* (1940). New York: Vintage, 1964.

——. "An Introduction to *The Sound and the Fury*" (1933). *Mississippi Quarterly* 26, no. 3 (Summer 1973), 410–15.

——. "An Introduction to *The Sound and the Fury*" (1933). *New York Times Book Review*, 5 Nov. 1972, p. 7.

——. *Intruder in the Dust* (1948). New York: Vintage, 1967.

*Note: original date of publication appears after the title when the edition consulted is of a later date.

————. *Knight's Gambit* (1949). New York: Vintage, 1978.

————. *The Letters*. Edited by Louis Daniel Brodsky and Robert W. Hamblin. Jackson: University Press of Mississippi, 1984. From the Brodsky Collection.

————. *The Mansion*. New York: Vintage, 1959.

————. *The Novels: 1930–35*. With Notes by Joseph Blotner and Neil Polk. Corr. eds. New York: Library of America, 1985.

————. *The Portable Faulkner*. Edited by Malcolm Cowley. Rev. ed. New York: Penguin, 1984

————. *Pylon* (1935). Corr. ed. New York: Vintage, 1987.

————. *The Reivers: A Reminiscence*. New York: Vintage, 1962.

————. *Requiem for a Nun* (1951). New York: Vintage, 1975.

————. *Requiem for a Nun*. Adapted to the stage by Ruth Ford. New York: Random House, 1959.

————. *The Road to Glory: A Screenplay*. By William Faulkner and Joel Sayre. Edited by Matthew J. Bruccoli. Carbondale: Southern Illinois University Press, 1981.

————. *Sanctuary* (1931). Corr. ed. New York: Vintage, 1987.

————. *Sanctuary: The Original Text* (1931). Edited by Noel Polk. New York: Random House, 1981.

————. *Selected Letters*. Edited by Joseph Blotner. New York: Random House, 1977.

————. *The Sound and the Fury* (1929). Corr. ed. New York: Vintage, 1987.

————. *To Have and Have Not: A Screenplay*. By William Faulkner and Jules Furthman. Edited by Bruce Kawin. Madison: University of Wisconsin Press, 1980.

Gwynn, Fredrick L., and Joseph Blotner, eds. *Faulkner in the University: Class Conferences at the University of Virginia, 1957–58*. New York: Vintage, 1959.

Jelliffe, Robert A., ed. *Faulkner at Nagano*. Tokyo: Kenkyusha Ltd., 1957.

Meriwether, James B., and Michael Millgate, eds. *Lion in the Garden: Interviews with William Faulkner*. New York: Random House, 1968.

II. SECONDARY SOURCES*

A. Books

Barth, S.J., J. Robert, ed. *Religious Perspective in Faulkner's Fiction*. Notre Dame: University of Notre Dame Press, 1972.

Beck, Warren. *Faulkner: Essays*. Madison: University of Wisconsin Press, 1976.

Bezzerides, A.I. *William Faulkner: A Life on Paper*. Jackson: University Press of Mississippi, 1980. A television script.

*Only the more significant and substantial research materials are included here; other books and articles alluded to in the text are not listed.

Blotner, Joseph. *Faulkner: A Biography.* 2 vols. New York: Random House, 1974.
―――. *Faulkner: A Biography.* Rev. ed. New York: Random House, 1984.
Brooks, Cleanth. *William Faulkner: First Encounters.* New Haven: Yale University Press, 1983.
―――. *William Faulkner: Toward Yoknapatawpha and Beyond.* New Haven: Yale University Press, 1979.
―――. *William Faulkner: The Yoknapatawpha Country.* New Haven: Yale University Press, 1966.
Campbell, Jr., Edward D.C. *The Celluloid South: Hollywood and the Southern Myth.* Knoxville: University of Tennessee Press, 1981.
Cofield, Jack. *William Faulkner: The Cofield Collection.* Oxford, Miss.: Yoknapatawpha Press, 1978.
Coughlan, Robert. *The Private World of William Faulkner.* New York: Cooper Square, 1972.
Cowley, Malcolm. *The Faulkner-Cowley File: Letters and Memories, 1944–62.* New York: Viking, 1966.
Crist, Judith. *Take 22: Moviemakers on Moviemaking.* New York: Viking, 1984.
Dardis, Tom. *Some Time in the Sun.* New York: Scribner's, 1976.
Estrin, Allen. *The Hollywood Professionals,* vol. 6. New York: A. S. Barnes, 1980.
Fadiman, Regina. *Faulkner's Intruder in the Dust: Novel into Film.* Knoxville: University of Tennessee Press, 1978.
Falkner, Murry C. *The Falkners of Mississippi: A Memoir.* Baton Rouge: Louisiana State University Press, 1967.
Faulkner, Jim. *Across the Creek: Faulkner Family Stories.* Jackson: University Press of Mississippi, 1986.
Faulkner John. *My Brother Bill: An Affectionate Reminiscence.* New York: Pocket Books, 1964.
French, Warren, ed. *The South and Film.* Jackson: University Press of Mississippi, 1981.
Halliday, Jon. *Sirk on Sirk.* New York: Viking, 1972.
Harrington, Evans, and Ann J. Abadie, eds. *Faulkner, Modernism, and Film.* Jackson: University Press of Mississippi, 1979.
Hoffman, Frederick J. *William Faulkner.* Rev. ed. New York: Twayne, 1966.
Howe, Irving. *William Faulkner: A Critical Study.* Rev. ed. Chicago: University of Chicago Press, 1975.
Kawin, Bruce. *Faulkner and Film.* New York: Ungar, 1977.
McBride, Joseph. *Hawks on Hawks.* Berkeley: University of California Press, 1982.
Millgate, Michael. *The Achievement of William Faulkner.* New York: Random House, 1966.
Minter, David. *William Faulkner: His Life and Work.* Baltimore: Johns Hopkins University Press, 1981.

Murray, Edward. *The Cinematic Imagination: Writers and the Motion Pictures.* New York: Ungar, 1972.

Peary, George, and Roger Shatzkin, eds. *The Classic American Novel and the Movies.* New York; Ungar, 1977.

———. *The Modern American Novel and the Movies.* New York: Ungar, 1978.

Robinson, W. R., ed. *Men and the Movies.* Baltimore: Penguin, 1969.

Ruppersburg, Hugh M. *Voice and Eye in Faulkner's Fiction.* Athens: University of Georgia Press, 1983.

Samway, Patrick H., S.J. *Faulkner's Intruder in the Dust: A Critical Study of the Typescripts.* Troy, N.Y.: Whitston, 1980.

Skaggs, Calvin, ed. *The American Short Story,* vol. 2. New York: Dell, 1982.

Tuck, Dorothy. *Crowell's Handbook of Faulkner.* New York: Crowell, 1964.

Vickery, Olga W. *The Novels of William Faulkner: A Critical Interpretation.* Rev. ed. Baton Rouge: Louisiana State University Press, 1973.

Wagner, Linda Welshimer, ed. *William Faulkner: Four Decades of Criticism.* East Lansing: Michigan State University Press, 1973.

Warren, Robert Penn, ed. *Faulkner: A Collection of Critical Essays.* Englewood Cliffs, N.J.: Prentice-Hall, 1966.

Webb, James W., and A. Wigfall Green, eds. *William Faulkner of Oxford.* Baton Rouge: Louisiana State University Press, 1965.

Wilde, Meta Carpenter, with Orin Borsten. *A Loving Gentleman: The Love Story of William Faulkner and Meta Carpenter.* New York: Simon and Schuster, 1976.

Yellin, David G., and Marie Connors, eds. *Tomorrow and Tomorrow and Tomorrow.* Jackson: University Press of Mississippi, 1985.

B. Articles

Blotner, Joseph. "Speaking of Books: Faulkner's *A Fable*," *New York Times Book Review* 118 (25 May 1969), 2, 34.

Brodsky, Louis Daniel. "Reflections on William Faulkner: An Interview with Albert I. Bezzerides." *Southern Review* 21, no. 2 (Apr. 1985), 376–403.

E. Pauline Degenfelder. "The Film Adaptation of Faulkner's *Intruder in the Dust.*" *Literature/Film Quarterly* 1, no. 2 (Spring 1973), 138–48.

———. "The Four Faces of Temple Drake: Faulkner's *Sanctuary, Requiem for a Nun,* and the Two Film Adaptations." *American Quarterly* 28, no. 1 (Winter 1976), 544–60.

———. "Sirk's *The Tarnished Angels*: *Pylon* Recreated." *Literature/Film Quarterly* 5, no. 3 (Summer 1977), 242–51.

Everson, William K. "Rediscovery: Raymond Bernard and *Les Croix de Bois. Films in Review* 36, no. 3 (March 1985), 171–75.

Faulkner Journal. 1 (1985) through 3 (1988).

Faulkner Newsletter and Yoknapatawpha Review. 1 (1981) through 7 (1988).

Fury, Kathleen. "*The Long Hot Summer* of Don, Cybill, and Company." *TV Guide* 5 Oct. 1985, 36–41.

Hogue, Peter. "Hawks and Faulkner: *Today We Live*." *Literature/Film Quarterly* 9 no. 1 (Jan. 1981), 51–58.

Jones, Dorothy B. "William Faulkner: Novel into Film." *The Quarterly of Film, Radio, and TV* 18 (Fall 1953), 51–71.

Knight, Arthur. "Faulkner in Pharaoh-Land." *Saturday Review* (25 June 1955,) p. 24.

——. "Filming Faulknerland." *Saturday Review*, 7 Dec. 1957, pp. 52–53.

McCarthy, Todd. "Phantom Hawks." *Film Comment* 18, no. 5 (Sept.–Oct. 1982), 63–76.

MacShane, Frank. "Raymond Chandler on Hollywood." *American Film* 7, no. 11 (Nov. 1981), 75–80.

Oxford (Miss.) Eagle. Special Faulkner edition, 6 Aug. 1976.

Radloff, Bernhard, "The Unity of Time in *The Sound and the Fury*," *Faulkner Journal* 1, no. 2 (Spring 1986), 56–68.

Saturday Review. Special Faulkner issue, 28 July 1962.

Tanner, Louise. "An Interview with Horton Foote." *Films in Review* 37, no. 11 (Nov. 1986), 530–31.

Wald, Jerry. "Faulkner and Hollywood." *Films in Review* 10, no. 3 (Mar. 1959), 129–33.

——. "From Faulkner to Film." *Saturday Review*, 7 Mar. 1959, pp. 16, 42.

III. UNPUBLISHED MATERIAL

Sidney, George R. "Faulkner in Hollywood: A Study of His Career as a Scenarist." Ph.D. dissertation, University of New Mexico, 1959.

Singleton, Carl. "Gavin Stevens: Faulkner's Good Man." Ph.D. dissertation, Loyola University, Chicago, 1982.

Williams, Thomas (Tennessee). Letter to Josephine Johnson. 17 May 1935. Washington University Library, St. Louis, Missouri.

Filmography

Note: Described below are the motion pictures for which William Faulkner received an official screen credit as coauthor of the script, and which are highlighted in the text accordingly.

Today We Live (MGM, 1933), 113 minutes
Director: Howard Hawks
Producer: Howard Hawks
Screenplay: Edith Fitzgerald, Dwight Taylor, and William Faulkner (based on the Faulkner story "Turn About")
Cinematography: Oliver T. Marsh
Cast: Joan Crawford (Diana), Gary Cooper (Bogard), Robert Young (Claude), Franchot Tone (Ronnie), Roscoe Karns (McGinnis)

The Road to Glory (Twentieth Century–Fox, 1936), 95 minutes
Director: Howard Hawks
Producers: Darryl F. Zanuck, Nunnally Johnson
Screenplay: Joel Sayre and William Faulkner (based on Raymond Bernard's film *Les Croix de Bois*)
Cinematography: Gregg Toland
Music: Louis Silvers
Cast: Fredric March (Lt. Michel Denet), Warner Baxter (Capt. Paul Laroche), Lionel Barrymore (Papa Laroche), June Lang (Monique), Gregory Ratoff (Bouffiou)

Slave Ship (Twentieth Century–Fox, 1937), 92 minutes
Director: Tay Garnett
Producers: Darryl F. Zanuck, Nunnally Johnson
Screenplay: Sam Hellman, Lamar Trotti, Gladys Lehman, and William Faulkner (based on the novel *The Last Slaver* by George S. King)
Music: Alfred Newman

Cinematographer: Ernest Palmer
Cast: Warner Baxter (Jim Lovett), Wallace Beery (Jack Thompson), Elizabeth Allan
    (Nancy Marlowe), Mickey Rooney (Swifty), George Sanders (Lefty)

To Have and Have Not (Warner Brothers, 1944), 100 minutes
Director: Howard Hawks
Producer: Howard Hawks
Screenplay: Jules Furthman and William Faulkner (based on the novel by Ernest
    Hemingway)
Cinematography: Sidney Hickox
Music: Leo Forbstein
Cast: Humphrey Bogart (Harry Morgan), Walter Brennan (Eddie), Lauren Bacall
    (Marie Brown), Hoagy Carmichael (Crickett), Marcel Dalio (Frenchy Gerard)

The Big Sleep (Warner Brothers, 1946), 114 minutes
Director: Howard Hawks
Producer: Howard Hawks
Screenplay: William Faulkner, Leigh Brackett, and Jules Furthman (based on the
    novel by Raymond Chandler)
Cinematography: Sidney Hickox
Music: Max Steiner
Cast: Humphrey Bogart (Philip Marlowe), Lauren Bacall (Vivian), John Ridgely
    (Eddie Mars), Elisha Cook, Jr. (Jones), Martha Vickers (Carmen), Bob Steele
    (Canino), Dorothy Malone (Bookshop Girl)

Land of the Pharaohs (Warner Brothers, 1955), 101 minutes
Director: Howard Hawks
Producers: Howard Hawks, Arthur Siteman
Screenplay: William Faulkner, Harry Kurnitz, and Harold Jack Bloom
Cinematography: Lee Garmes and Russell Harlan (color/CinemaScope)
Music: Dimitri Tiomkin
Cast: Jack Hawkins (Cheops the Pharaoh), Joan Collins (Princess Nellifer), Dewey
    Martin (Senta), Sydney Chaplin (Treneh)

II. FILM ADAPTATIONS OF FAULKNER'S FICTION

Today We Live (above)

The Story of Temple Drake (Paramount, 1933), 71 minutes
Director: Stephen Roberts
Screenplay: Oliver H.P. Garrett (based on *Sanctuary*)

Cinematography: Karl Struss
Cast: Miriam Hopkins (Temple Drake), Jack La Rue (Trigger), William Gargan
  (Stephen Benbow), Sir Guy Standing (Judge Drake), Florence Eldridge (Ruby),
  Irving Pichel (Lee Goodwin), Elizabeth Patterson (Aunt Jenny)

Intruder in the Dust (MGM, 1949), 87 minutes
Director: Clarence Brown
Producer: Clarence Brown
Screenplay: Ben Maddow (based on the novel)
Cinematography: Robert Surtees
Music: Adolph Deutsch
Cast: David Brian (John Stevens), Claude Jarman, Jr. (Chick Mallison), Juano Her-
  nandez (Lucas Beauchamp), Porter Hall (Nub Gowrie), Elizabeth Patterson
  (Miss Habersham), Will Geer (Sheriff Hampton)

The Tarnished Angels (Universal-International, 1957), 91 minutes
Director: Douglas Sirk
Producer: Albert Zugsmith
Screenplay: George Zuckerman (based on *Pylon*)
Cinematography: Irving Glassberg (CinemaScope)
Music: Frank Skinner
Cast: Rock Hudson (Burke Devlin), Robert Stack (Roger Shumann), Dorothy Ma-
  lone (Laverne Shumann), Jack Carson (Jiggs), Chris Olsen (Jack Shumann)

The Long Hot Summer (Twentieth Century–Fox, 1958), 115 minutes
Director: Martin Ritt
Producer: Jerry Wald
Screenplay: Irving Ravetch and Harriet Frank, Jr. (based on *The Hamlet*)
Cinematography: Joseph La Shelle (color/CinemaScope)
Music: Alex North
Cast: Paul Newman (Ben Quick), Joanne Woodward (Clara Varner), Anthony Fran-
  ciosa, (Jody Varner), Lee Remick (Eula Varner), Orson Welles (Will Varner), An-
  gela Lansbury (Minnie, Will's Mistress).

The Sound and the Fury (Twentieth Century–Fox, 1959), 115 minutes
Director: Martin Ritt
Producer: Jerry Wald
Screenplay: Irving Ravetch and Harriet Frank, Jr. (based on the novel)
Cinematography: Charles G. Clarke (color/CinemaScope)
Music: Alex North
Cast: Yul Brynner (Jason Compson), Joanne Woodward (Quentin Compson), Mar-

garet Leighton (Caddy Compson), Jack Warden (Benjy Compson), Ethel Waters (Dilsey)

Sanctuary (Twentieth Century–Fox, 1961), 100 minutes
Director: Tony Richardson
Producer: Richard D. Zanuck
Screenplay: James Poe (based on *Sanctuary* and *Requiem for a Nun*)
Cinematography: Ellsworth Fredericks
Music: Alex North
Cast: Lee Remick (Temple Drake Stevens), Yves Montand (Candy Man), Harry Townes (Ira Stevens), Bradford Dillman (Gowan Stevens), Odetta (Nancy)

The Reivers (National General, 1969), 111 minutes
Director: Mark Rydell
Producers: Irving Ravetch and Robert E. Relyea
Screenplay: Irving Ravetch and Harriet Frank, Jr. (based on the novel)
Cinematography: Richard Moore (color)
Music: John Williams
Cast: Steve McQueen (Boon Hogganbeck), Rupert Crosse (Ned McCaslin), Mitch Vogel (Lucius McCaslin), Will Geer (Boss McCaslin), Juano Hernandez (Uncle Possum)

Tomorrow (Filmgroup, 1972), 103 minutes
Director: Joseph Anthony
Producers: Gilbert Pearlman and Paul Roebling
Screenplay: Horton Foote (based on the short story)
Cinematography: Alan Green
Music: Irwin Stahl
Cast: Robert Duvall (Jackson Fentry), Olga Bellin (Sarah Eubanks), Sudie Bond (Mrs. Hulie), Peter Masterson (Thornton Douglas), Johnny Mask (Jackson and Longstreet Fentry)

III. TELEVISION ADAPTATIONS OF FAULKNER'S FICTION

Note: The major television productions of Faulkner's works, principally those dealt with in the text, are listed below.

Tomorrow (CBS-TV, first telecast 7 March 1960), 90 minutes
Director: Robert Mulligan
Producer: Herbert Brodkin
Screenplay: Horton Foote (based on the short story)

Cast: Richard Boone (Jackson Fentry), Kim Stanley (Sarah Eubanks), Beulah Bondi
(Mrs. Hulie), Charles Aidman (Thornton Douglas), Peter Oliphant, (Jackson
and Longstreet Fentry) Elizabeth Patterson (Mrs. Pruitt)

Barn Burning (PBS-TV, first telecast 17 March 1980,) 41 minutes
Director: Peter Werner
Producer: Robert Geller
Screenplay: Horton Foote (based on the short story)
Cast: Tommy Lee Jones (Ab Snopes), Shawn Whittington (Sarty Snopes), James
Faulkner (Major de Spain)

The Long Hot Summer (NBC-TV, first telecast 6 and 7 October 1985), 4 hours
Director: Stuart Cooper
Producers: Dori Weiss, Leonard Hill, and John Thomas Lenox
Screenplay: Rita Mae Brown and Dennis Turner (based on *The Hamlet* and a pre-
vious screenplay by Irving Ravetch and Harriet Frank, Jr.)
Cast: Don Johnson (Ben Quick), Judith Ivey (Noel Varner), William Russ (Jody
Varner), Cybill Shepherd (Eula Varner), Jason Robards, Jr. (Will Varner), Ava
Gardner (Minnie, Will's mistress)

Index

Fiction, Film, and Faulkner was designed
by Dariel Mayer, composed by Lithocraft, Inc.,
and printed and bound by Braun-Brumfield, Inc.
The book is set in Plantin and printed on
60-lb. Glatfelter Natural Smooth.